CW01476985

Translation, Text and Theory

Translation, Text and Theory

The Paradigm of India

Edited by

Rukmini Bhaya Nair

SAGE Publications
New Delhi/Thousand Oaks/London

Copyright © Rukmini Bhaya Nair, 2002

All rights reserved. No part of this book may be reproduced or utilized in any form or by any means, electronic or mechanical, including photocopying, recording or by any information storage or retrieval system, without permission in writing from the publisher.

First published in 2002 by

Sage Publications India Pvt Ltd
M-32 Market, Greater Kailash-I
New Delhi 110 048

Sage Publications Inc.
2455 Teller Road
Thousand Oaks, California 91320

Sage Publications Ltd
6 Bonhill Street
London EC2A 4PU

Published by Tejeshwar Singh for Sage Publications India Pvt Ltd, typeset in 10/12 pt Palatino by Line Arts, Pondicherry and printed at Chaman Enterprises, Delhi.

Library of Congress Cataloging-in-Publication Data
Translation: text and theory: the paradigm of India/edited by Rukmini Bhaya Nair.
p. cm.
Includes bibliographical references and index.
1. Translating and interpreting—India. I. Rukmini Bhaya Nair.
P306.8.I5 T736 418'.02'0954—dc21 2002 2001048422

ISBN: 0–7619–9587–0 (US-Hb) ISBN: 81–7829–068–5 (India-Hb)

Sage Production Team: Dipika Nath, Shahnaz Habib, Radha Dev Raj and Santosh Rawat

Contents

Pragmatic Considerations

Linguistic Descriptions

Philosophical Foundations

Introduction

There is a logic to linguistic transfer. When a text moves from one language to another, from one medium to another and from one society to another, it displays in its changed contours the inexorable logic of metamorphosis. All things in nature are subject to change—and so is all cultural material. The excitement of translation, both as everyday practice and as an intellectual project, is that it shatters the comfortable illusion of unity that our primary languages give us. To translate is to live dangerously, to explore the frangible edges of literary universes, where languages exert contrary gravitational pulls on each other.

India is a linguistic galaxy of unparalleled richness. Almost all the contributors to this volume begin by pointing out that few contexts could be better suited than the Indian for a discussion of the processes of translation within a spectacular stellar setting. The flip side of this seemingly obvious intuition is, in my view, the fundamental insight that 'India' itself is a concept that *presupposes* the act of translation. How does a common 'idea of India' make itself available to a Bengali, a Kannadiga or a speaker of Metei? Only through translation. Yet, although translation is the 'only way', it is by no means an innocuous Milky Way, especially on this subcontinent. Rather, this galactic path is fraught with pitfalls, projectiles, dangers. As long ago as 1935, Jawaharlal Nehru expressed these apprehensions in an essay he wrote in Hindi, which he himself later translated into English as 'The Meaning of Words'[1]

> To translate from one language to another language is a very difficult task. The fact is that real translation of even slightly profound thoughts is just impossible. What is the function of language? Language is semi-frozen thought—imagination converted

> into statues...[D]ifficulty can arise between two persons who speak the same language, are literate and civilized and brought up in the same culture.... But these difficulties look small when compared to two persons who speak two different languages and do not know much about the cultures of each other. Their mental ideas differ as heaven and earth... [W]e laymen should not forget that words are dangerous things and the more abstract, the more deceiving. And the most dangerous words, perhaps, are *dharma* and *mazhab*. Everyone in his heart understands them in his own way.... It means that *dharma* or *mazhab* has a dozen facets, each of which should have a different word for it. They say that there were more than two hundred words used for making love in the old American Maya language. How can we translate all those words correctly?

Not only does Nehru uncannily anticipate in this passage Derrida's famous postmodern phrase 'impossibility of translation', he also foreshadows several of the themes that make translation such a potentially dangerous enterprise today. In a striking formulation, Nehru describes language as 'semi-frozen thought'. The task of the translator is, presumably, to unfreeze the shapes that thought has taken in one language and then to refreeze them in another. This is that process of metamorphosis that I mentioned earlier. But what happens when polar ice caps melt, when glaciers are subjected to extraneous greenhouse effects, when icebergs float out into new tossing seas? The danger signalled by such events must, as far as possible, be predicted and reduced.

Nehru identifies two 'dangerous words', *dharma* and *mazhab*, which could wreck the great ship of Indian unity, but there are countless others. Hence, the translator's job does not merely involve light-hearted pleasure. Along with the undoubted delights and seductions of translation—those many faces of what Nehru mythologises as the Mayan vocabulary of love, or desire for union, linguistic as well as emotional—come the divisive pressures of politics and ideology. By now, more than 50 years on, this paradox of which Nehru had warned has become part of the national consciousness. For it seems unarguable that the only way in which the ideology of 'unity' can be explored in a multilingual society such as ours is by accepting both the need for, and the problems of, translation.

That the present volume seeks to present a variety of positions on translation rather than rigidly settle for one 'correct' approach is, in this sense, evidence of the kind of tolerance of mind and spirit that translation studies in India could foster. As Nehru asked with distinct unease long ago, how after all can one ever hope to translate all those Mayan words for 'love' correctly? 'Correctness'—so revealingly called 'faithfulness' in many traditional descriptions of translation—can no longer be regarded as the guiding value in translation. It is just too simplistic a slogan for the complicated set of manoeuvres that constitute an act of translation today. 'Contestation' and 'consensus' would perhaps be a more useful set of terms, the one implying argument and the other, the agreement that might be arrived at, at the end of an argument about how to go about translating a text. Insofar as some approaches to translation deny or contest the validity or scope of others, it now appears that the problem of translation, somewhat like the enigma that constitutes the metaphor 'India' itself, cannot be exhausted, but merely delineated.

What is translation? Wherein lies its complexity? Why does translation necessitate a series of approaches rather than just a set of protocols that can govern its practice? While it is impossible, as Nehru maintained, to even pretend to answer these questions directly, we attempt to make a start here by drawing up an inventory of approaches to translation under five headings: Cultural Attitudes, Historical Perspectives, Pragmatic Considerations, Linguistic Descriptions and Philosophical Foundations. These rubrics trace a movement from the personal and pragmatic to the public and philosophical.

One way of characterising these groupings is to see the first set of contributors as engaged with the **'How?'** of translation. Theirs is a personal as well as professional contract with translation. Sujit Mukherjee, Samantak Das, Lachman M. Khubchandani and Tejaswini Niranjana each provides a documentary yet passionate account of the space, the individual arena, that creates, as it were, a commitment to translation. Such a contextual space could be said to be culturally designed to produce 'translators'. For example, it could be a period in history which makes translators out of the students who pass through the institutions of the time, as demonstrated by Mukherjee's evocative yet forthright recounting, point by point, of the factors that persuade, or even compel him to practice the 'craft' of translation. It could be geographical placement, such as Das's upbringing in the almost legendary surrounds of Shantiniketan, that throws up a translator or a theorist of translation. Or it could involve belonging within a cultural tradition that 'filters' one's responses to both 'source' and 'target' languages, as Lachman M. Khubchandani asserts in his essay.

Tejaswini Niranjana's is the final piece in the first section and it complements and clinches the foregoing intense concentration on the contexts of translation via a sharp critique of colonial practices of translation. Niranjana suggests that the process of disruption is a crucial psychological exercise that the post-colonial subject must undertake. One should also note that my closing piece returns to Niranjana's contribution and contrasts it with Sujit Mukherjee's very different stance on translation in order to complete the circle and demonstrate how genuinely varied the theoretical contributions to translation on the Indian subcontinent are today.

Time, geography, location, intellectual traditions and social institutions—each of these, then, is a variable that can uniquely affect the psychological make-up of an individual committed to translation, because each involves the person in a first-hand brokering of authorial power and the politics of linguistic exchange.

Moving on from the cultural contexts of translation to the section Historical Perspectives, the nature of the question alters and the focus becomes what one might call the **'When?'** of translation. This section begins with a crisp essay by Krishna Rayan that highlights the rewards, problems and, above all, the methodologies which might be adopted in translating critical terms from the intellectual heritage that Sanskrit literary and philosophical treatises from the 11th century on, and earlier, have provided us. In chronological sequence, the next essay, by Aditya Behl, both theorises and exemplifies, with a wealth of original material, the intellectual interchanges that took place in medieval India through the medium of translation. Behl's essay brings out a particularly important aspect of translation in the Indian subcontinent in that it shows how religion was interpreted and new syncretic forms of worship such as Sufism and Sikhism developed through translation. Next, Ayyappa Paniker carries forward the theme of translating religious texts into contemporary times by discussing his own fascinating experience of rendering the Guru Granth Sahib into

Malayalam as a pristine experience, for never before had this text been translated into Malayalam.

Paniker's and Behl's essays, taken in tandem, yet again lend resonance to Nehru's intuition that *dharma* and *mazhab* are two of the most potent words in the vocabulary of the subcontinent. They reflect not only the perils of translation in history but history as the perils of translation.

If the second section succeeds in proving that translation on this subcontinent encodes a shifting pattern of memories and of historical amnesias and adversities that we all, however ignorant, carry about as part of our cultural baggage, the next section moves away from this region of sociological guilt. This section on pragmatic issues is about the '**Where?**' of translation. Jhumpa Lahiri's essay begins by making the case that, for a 'diasporic' bilingual author like herself, translation is that fertile land where her fiction originates. She declares with poignant force:

> Fiction is the foreign land of my choosing, the place where I strive to convey and preserve the meaningful. And whether I write as an American or an Indian...one thing remains constant: I translate, therefore I am.

At other times, an environment as specific as a feminist publishing house might provide that ideal context in which translation successfully takes place. Ritu Menon, co-founder of Kali for Women, provides a lively description of the special nurturing relationship which holds between a publisher and the author whose work is being translated—in this case by the major writer Qurratulain Hyder herself! A 'concise history' of post-Independence publishing initiatives in the field of translation is another very useful aspect of Menon's article. The next essay by Vanamala Viswanatha also focuses on choices of texts for translation, but this time it is pedagogic imperatives that dictate decisions. A classroom, where the onus is on the teacher not only to influence young minds but equally to mould the young academic discipline of Translation Studies, thus constitutes yet another space where translation can flourish as a form of questioning both academic theory and its practice, as Viswanatha's 'possible syllabus' demonstrates.

The last piece in this section, on the hermeneutics of translation, carries forward some of the themes outlined in broad brush strokes by Viswanatha. Which linguistic contexts and sets of reader-expectations lend significance and give 'body' to a translation? C.T. Indra brings out the interpretive dimensions of translation, not only by tracing a brief history of the ancient discipline of textual commentary, but also by applying its insights to a reading of two Tamil short stories.

Language and its infinite possibilities situates the link between Indra's essay in the third section and the next section, Linguistic Descriptions. These contributions invite us to view translation through an astronomer's telescope rather than with the naked eye. The stars look different through this instrument, farther away and yet, more sharply defined. Linguistic tools are deployed, scalpel-like, to reveal the bare bones of grammatical structure that all translators have perforce to deal with. This section is about the **'What?'** of translation. What is translation in its most pared down version but just a skeletal linguistic structure—of phonemes, morphemes, phrases, clauses and syntactic modifiers? Sujit Mukherjee, who has written the first essay in this volume, incorporates a famous line by the poet Dylan Thomas when he entitles his piece 'The Craft, Not Sullen Art, of Translation'. I would now like to quote from yet another poem by Thomas where he refers to an epiphanic moment when

> the bones are picked clean
> and the clean bones gone
> we shall have stars at elbow and foot!

Were we to return to that interstellar metaphor which initiated this Introduction, it could be said that linguistic treatments of translation seek to return to that originary, starry moment when we first break into speech, when we first translate without the burden of all that social angst and politically correct self-consciousness that we later develop. Technical though its descriptions might sometimes seem, linguistics seeks ultimately to simplify the concept of translation.

When R. Narasimhan identifies translation as just another aspect of 'language behaviour', comparable to writing a letter or issuing instructions, and when he characterises translators as 'intentional agents' genetically programmed to be sophisticated 'information processing systems', he is performing the unsparing, reductionist role that linguists and cognitive scientists have assigned themselves in this century. Translation as a socially and historically charged activity is defamiliarised by such terminology—and useful insights emerge as a result.

In this section, translation is regarded from quite a different perspective: what was seen as communitarian activity in the previous essays, now becomes, in Narasimhan's words, 'a cognitive act'. While it is still accepted that translation must involve a set of actors, such as authors, translators and readers, these actors now metamorphose into Narasimhan's 'agents' and the mode of subjectivity is thereby radically altered. This change of vocabulary also involves an important kind of 'translation'. It is my submission in this volume that, in seeking to explore the academic potential of Translation Studies, we should be especially sensitive to such 'interdisciplinary' translation as well.

A similar style of argumentation is to be observed in the profusely illustrated essay by Udaya Narayana Singh, who deals with problems in the area of lexicography. Singh's descriptions of the tools that can be utilised to solve the 'crises of cognition' which arise when translating show that linguistic analysis has common, practical aspects as well as intellectual ones.

Within language studies, translation occupies a public domain where it is subject to technical scrutiny, remote but revealing for just that reason. The last essay in Linguistic Descriptions thus returns to an image used by Khubchandani in the very first section of this volume—the metaphor of 'fine-tuning' a machine-translation, making one think both of cybernetics and of radio-waves in space. Indeed, the subject of this essay is, if not radios, then another global communicating machine—the computer. Here, the Akshar Bharati team, Vineet Chaitanya, Amba P. Kulkarni, Rajeev Sangal and G. Umamaheshwar Rao manage to extend through their powerful telescope the actual boundaries of the vast stellar horizon of translation by demonstrating how machine-translation between the Indian languages is no longer a faraway dream but an imposing, practical, exciting reality actually implemented by the authors of the essay—the Akshar Bharati team.

The essays in the fifth and final section of *Translation* concern the Philosophical Foundations of the enterprise of translation, the **'Why?'** of translation, if you will. The topics dealt with here may seem abstract, but they seemed to me essential in initiating a truly thoughtful conversation about translation within academia. After all, how can translation studies invade the ivory tower if it will have nothing to do with either ivory or towers? Jane Austen once wrote that she carved her novels on 'two inches of ivory'; the initial essay in this section covers a far greater span. Raman Prasad Sinha's is a survey which traces the development of translation as an intellectual discipline across the world, and especially in the modern west. It examines the universalist claims made by translation theorists in the sixties and ends with a look at the post-modern deconstructionist position on translation in the nineties, which now attempts a dissolution of the very concept of translation.

In contrast, Shiva Kumar Srinivasan's piece on the theme of psychoanalysis and translation casts every human subject as intrinsically 'bilingual' because s/he must perforce translate between her various mental functions. Far from being 'impossible', translation in Srinivasan's reading is part of our very being. On occasions when such translation fails, the result is displayed as a symptomatic 'pathological compulsion' on the part of the translator. Why does a translator choose the texts she does, how does she cope with her symptoms? These are some of the basic psychological questions framed by Srinivasan's essay.

Saranindranath Tagore's contribution, entitled 'Just Words', then homes in on some of ethical issues implicit in both Sinha's and Srinivasan's essays by presenting a Hegelian thesis. He argues that certain connections must be drawn between the politics and philosophy of multiculturalism and the act of translation. Translation incorporates not just a linguistic transaction but an ethics—a position which brings us back to the Nehruvian perspective on the grave responsibility that a translator has to shoulder.

My own essay which winds up the volume, dwells on the concept of the speech act, so central in 20th century philosophy. It is by now well known that the speech act is a notion which is meant to be both intentional and conventional, concerned both with the speaker's psychological, including moral, motives and the hearer's interpretive moves. Here, I extend the boundaries of the speech act to include the act of translation, offering an original set of 'felicity conditions' for the speech act of translation, and showing how attention to these conditions might help identify the actual problems that arise when literary and other kinds of translation are being undertaken, especially in the Indian context, so full of 'dangerous words' and 'the more abstract, the more deceiving'.

Deception, abstraction, multifariousness—these concepts force us to consider possible criticisms of the present volume. Despite the individual excellence of the contributions to this volume, there is no denying that there exist two major classes of problems with it. First, there is the sort of 'taxonomic' approach that I have adopted, and second, there is the 'resistance to theory' that any collection of this sort is bound to summon up. Taxonomies, of course, will always have gaps—and gaffes. For instance, I very much wanted to include, when I first conceived of the idea of a such a volume, essays on translation and the media, translation as performance and translation as a genre where gender becomes a crucial issue. Alas, contingent circumstances prevented me from finding contributors who could write on these subjects within the projected time frame.

Another set of problems close to my own heart was connected to the sounds of the Indian languages—the Sanskrit 'schwa' for instance—and how these are to be represented in the Roman script. English, after all, as many contributors remark, has to be admitted as a vast reservoir of translation in contemporary India. It may no longer be a colonial language but it is increasingly a conduit language. This 'filter language', as Khubchandani terms it, has today a certain inescapable presence. Sooner or later, as translations storm academia, where transactions are still mostly in English, we shall have to discuss how specific diacritic marks for nasalisation, aspiration, retroflexes and other sounds and tones typical of many Indian languages may be incorporated into the Roman script without making it too clumsy or cumbersome. But these remain projects for the future.

What gives some cause for optimism is that the ground is so rich; there are so many veins still to be mined, so many palimpsest layers to be uncovered when translations become the subject of research in India. Nehru, in fact, explicitly referred to India as

> ...an ancient palimpsest upon which layer upon layer of thought and reverie has been inscribed and yet no succeeding layer had completely hidden...what had been written previously.[2]

More recently Salman Rushdie—whose controversial opinion on the inadequacy of quality literature and quality translation in the post-Independence Indian languages, with the notable exception of English, has shocked Indian intellectuals—echoes Nehru with a wicked wit when in *The Moor's Last Sigh* he describes India as a 'Palimpsestine'.

Speaking of English, the possible gaffes this book contains may have to do with such features as its underemphasis on both 'post-coloniality' and 'nativism' as the two countervailing force fields that dominate cultural criticism today. It is quite true that the volume does not have individual essays devoted to 'postcolonial translation' or 'nativist trends in translation', but the discerning reader will find throughout the text that the contributors to this volume are well aware of these debates and attend to them even when they are not explicitly hammering home either a post-colonial nail or a nativist one.

This brings us to the second major objection that can be brought against the book. Those who deal in the practice of translation are often bored with theory. They tend to invoke arguments analogous to the one which says that knowing the laws which govern the physics of motion does not in the least help someone who wants to learn to ride a bike! In other words, abstract knowledge of the sort offered in this book is not going to help the practical translator. It is all a waste of time and theory remains dreary. I would like to remind such intellectual Luddites among translators that our subject here is not riding a bike but monitoring the infancy of a new discipline in Indian academia. In this respect, a more apt comparison would be the rise of literary criticism in the 19th century. From being a marginal preoccupation of some scholars two hundred years ago, it has become a dominant, even hegemonic, discipline in intellectual centres the world over. Literary criticism now has alliances with history, cultural studies, politics, philosophy, linguistics, psychology and even with studies of style in the 'hard sciences'.

Translation studies, like gender studies, for example, is undeniably a fledgling academic subject at the moment. However, given the immense range of questions that it spawns, as well as its growing profitability as a world profession—the new European Union requires constant translation between its official languages; the Net constitutes another site of burgeoning translation, and so on—translation could well have a future similar to that of lit crit. Today, few would (dare!) claim that literature in academia can be studied without any recourse to critical insights. In the same way, it is quite likely that tomorrow, a subtler and more sophisticated understanding of what constitutes 'good' translation will result from the fact of its being studied in a disciplined fashion, across marketplaces and communities, rather that just being 'done' willy-nilly.

This is not to deny that wonderful translations can be produced without any academic training whatsoever, but simply to insist that serious and sustained discourse around any intellectual activity is likely, in the long run, to benefit that activity and take it further. Here, it should be admitted right away that few of the contributions to this book are easy to assimilate at one go. The interested reader will have to return to some of them more than once, for they certainly do not offer fast food for the consumerist. These essays unabashedly 'talk up' rather than 'talk down' translation—this indeed is part of their attraction. They are meant for serious students of translation looking for a meta-vocabulary to 'talk about' translation to a virtual community of translators and will therefore not resist re-reading—because they realise that repeated re-readings are an intrinsic part of the labour of translation.

Every discipline, especially in its initial stages, has certain defining moments. Such moments could be characterised, for instance, in terms of a 'critical mass' of seminars, books and other material produced around the discipline suddenly appearing like a phalanx of comets over the horizon. This volume, too, looks forward to being there on the horizon somewhere. It hopes to be able to deliver, through its contributors, reflections on both the practice and the ethics of translation as it has taken shape in a country where the very structure of the educational system seems to decree that a linguistic subject must translate herself into different registers under the aegis of the 'three language formula'—a 'core' self symbolised by her mother tongue, a 'national' self represented by Hindi or some other link language and an 'international' self represented by English or another 'library' language. It is true that such a representation is ideal and that, in real life, the educational situation is both gravely unjust and terribly complicated. Even so, it would be hard to deny the availability of rich linguistic opportunities for 'the presentation of self in every day life' on this particular subcontinent, which means that the matrix of translation is not an arcane academic speciality here but a 'sociological compulsion'.

It is indeed our cooperative attempt to formalise the interplay between such a compulsion and the ways in which it impinges on the study of literature that gives the present work a sense of urgency. I cannot help but believe that it will provide a useful manual for all those interested in translation studies, both because of the range of theoretical approaches that it presents and because of the richness of the linguistic experience which is so intrinsic a part of this unique enterprise. To all our contributors, I owe an immense debt for their patience and their intellectual generosity.

These essays, almost all written originally for the book, often march to very different drummers. Although attempts to introduce some uniformity may be observed in the sectional format of the book and in the fact that each essay has been given internal subheadings and a few substantially recomposed, these are minor changes. While some degree of commonality had to be introduced for the sake of the reader, I have made no attempt to make our contributors march in uniform. For example, the lengths of the articles differ noticeably, just as there are visible variations, say, in height among a population; but as any geneticist would maintain, such variability is all to the good in terms of the human gene pool. I have thus sought hard not to muffle or stifle the play of any of the *dholaks* and *mridangams* and other instruments that I thought I heard throughout my editing of the work. Yet I feel that an impression of harmony comes through. There is a great variety of tone and theme, appropriate for a book on translation produced in India, but listen for it, and you will also hear a grand, and not necessarily narrowly national, polyphony. This work may be meant for a primary audience of Indian readers but its reverberations could be international.

At this point, it may be appropriate to mention the subtitle of this volume. It is by now common knowledge that the word 'paradigm' was made a part of modern, international, academic parlance by Thomas Kuhn in *The Structure of Scientific Revolutions*, but it is perhaps less known that he analyzes the problem of 'cultural translation' at length in the 'Postscript' to this seminal work:

> Briefly put, what the participants in a communication breakdown can do is to recognize each other as members of different

> language communities and *then become translators* [italics mine]. Taking the differences between their own intra- and inter-group discourse as itself a subject for study, they can first attempt to discover the terms and locutions that...are foci of trouble for inter-group discussions... Since translation...allows the participant in a communication break-down to experience vicariously the merits and defects of each other's points of view, it is a potent tool for both *persuasion* and for *conversion* [italics mine]. But even persuasion need not succeed, and, if it does, it need not be accompanied or followed by conversion. The two experiences are not the same, an important distinction that I have only recently fully recognized.[3]

I have myself 'only recently recognized' how crucial is the line Kuhn here draws between 'persuasion' and 'conversion' in relation to 'communication breakdowns'. The *bhasha mela* or carnival of languages that the Indian subcontinent has long hosted has meant that, in practice, we daily negotiate 'foci of trouble' via translation—a theme to which I return in my own essay in this volume. Given this long-standing 'paradigm', it is possible that we have deeply internalized the stance of 'adjusting' to each other's points of view without needing to 'convert' them to our own. Indeed, it is here the singular 'paradigm of India', in its 'resitance' to the mode of homogenizing conversion and its espousal of many-valued 'persuasion', may paradoxically indicate a multiplicity of paradigms.

The self-evident fact of linguistic pluralism, in short, has culturally trained us to concede that no perspective is perfect and to tacitly accept that everyone may be forced to 'become a translator' at any time. A recent incident amusingly illustrates this point. My school-going son happened last week to chance upon the image used by the illustrator for the cover of the present volume—a large, old-fashioned, ungainly typewriter. Why have you chosen a fractional weight box out of our physics lab for your book-cover, he enquired in amazement. And it was only then I realized that, however quickly our technologies change, our propensity for immediate guess-work via the unreliable processes of 'translation' remains the same. My son's interpretation was misguided, but I could only prove partially successful in 'persuading' him that what he saw represented a manual instrument in an environment where computers were the predominant tool for typing. 'Conversion' was certainly impossible: for history ensures that all we ever have at our disposal, in our daily struggle to communicate across generations and geographies, are the 'fractional weights' of difference, which may in turn themselves become, as in this book, a Kuhnian 'subject for study.'

Translation provides, so to speak, a cognitive map of India's linguistic world in all its interrelatedness as well as estrangement. In the end, of course, given this complex backdrop, all sorts of whispered questions remain. For example, the Sanskritised term we currently use for 'translation' in many Indian languages is *anuvada*—a word which does not appear to possess any especial etymological pedigree to recommend it. *Anuvada* literally means 'after speech' so it seems strange in the first place to discuss it in an 'Introduction'. One recognises too, that *anuvada* in Sanskrit stands in contrast to *anukaran*, which would imply mere aping or slavish imitation, but ought not there be more to the word than just the suggestion that it could involve creative licence of a kind? Are perhaps new conceptual translations urgently needed in our globalised world for the word 'translation' itself? After all, as Nehru and Kuhn both noted, the 'dangers' that attach to the business of translation can never be entirely avoided. No translator can get things perfectly right for false etymologies always lurk round the corner as do inappropriate equivalents and uncomfortable questions, which is why involvement in translation always tends to foster in the end that ultimate Gandhian virtue—a spirit of tolerance. In this sense, we could argue that linguistic tolerance and the willingness to cross boundaries underwrites all other forms of social tolerance.

It is a measure of the human spirit, then, that translators keep at it, constantly trying, in Nehru's words, to turn imaginative fluidity into perfect verbal 'statues' just for the love of it. Or, if we recall the metaphor—and the metamorphosis—of the Greek legend, this book can be seen as offering a set of tools to the Pygmalions of translation. I would be amply rewarded if, among those who undertake the 'impossible' task of breathing linguistic life from one language into the 'ivories and ebonies' sculpted in another, there are some who find our volume of assistance.[4]

Rukmini Bhaya Nair Delhi, January 2002

Notes

1. See Jawaharlal Nehru, *Selected Works*, 1.6: 445. See also King 1997: 189, 194, where I first came across the quotation.
2. This reference is taken from the 20th impression (1999) of Nehru 1946, published by the Jawaharlal Nehru Memorial Trust, New Delhi, p. 59.
3. See Thomas Kuhn 1970, p. 202–03.
4. See Brewer 1892:

> Pygmalion, sculptor of Cyprus...became enamoured of his own ivory statue, which Venus endowed with life. Lord Brooke (*Treatise on Human Learning*, 1554–1628) calls the statue 'a carved tree'. There is a vegetable ivory no doubt, one of the palm species, and there is the ebon tree, the wood of which is black as jet. The former could not have been known to Pygmalion, but the latter might, as Virgil speaks of it in his *Georgics*, ii, 117, 'India nigrum fert ebenum'. Probably Lord Brooke blundered from the resemblance between *Eber* (ivory) and *Ebon*, in Latin, *ebenum*.

Lord Brooke's 'blunder' in translating between Latin and English, caught out so many centuries afterwards by Brewer with his serendipitous reference to 'India nigrum' by Virgil, and then quoted another century later in the present volume, illustrates, in my view, not only the Nehruvian point about the dangers of translation but also draws attention to its amazingly long-lasting cultural afterlife.

References

King, Robert D., 1997. 'Nehru's Essays on Language' in *Nehru and the Language Politics of India*. New Delhi: Oxford University Press.

Kuhn, Thomas S., 1970. *The Structure of Scientific Revolutions* (Second edition, enlarged). Chicago, London: University of Chicago Press.

Nehru, Jawaharlal, 1946. *The Discovery of India*. Kolkata: Signet Press.

Brewer, E. Cobham, 1892. *The Reader's Handbook of Allusions, References, Plots and Stories*. London: Chatto and Windus.

Notes

References

1. Cultural Attitudes

One

Personal Commitment: The Craft Not Sullen Art of Translation

SUJIT MUKHERJEE

In this country, we have been practising translation for a long time without giving it such a name or style. Whatever be the language our very early ancestors used—quite possibly these people were not numerous—once our numbers grew and a Bower of Babble began to form, it became necessary for the speakers of one language to communicate with the speakers of another. Such communication continued to be practised without being regarded as anything unusual. You did so because you needed to. Ever since then, the presence of more than one language in one's daily life or the need to learn more than one language in one's lifetime has not, generally, been regarded as a problem throughout India's known history.

In due course, within Jambudvipa—an old name for India that was Bharatvarsha and is now Bharat—the literary compositions of one language began to be recomposed by telling or writing in another language. Most often these were texts from so-called master languages, such as Sanskrit, being retold or rewritten in what are now being called *bhashas* (the modern Indian languages). Even more often, it was not sacred texts such as the Vedas or the Upanishads that got retold or rewritten, but *kavya* works such as the Ramayana, *purana* works such as the *Srimad-Bhagavat*, and *itihasa-purana* works such as the Mahabharata. Down the centuries, every *bhasha* acquired its own Ramayana and its own Mahabharata, and in some cases more than one. This acquisition can only loosely be regarded as 'translation', because, while the basic story remained, some of it was left out and a lot of new writing done to fill it out again. Elsewhere I have called this process 'translation as new writing' and I venture the claim that this has been our tradition.

Translation in India has often been out of step with translation in the rest of the world. Thus, in these post-colonial times, it should have been possible to regard Sanskrit as a 'master' language and ascribe various misdeeds to it. But we find that literary works were translated from Sanskrit into Asamiya, Bangla, Gujarati, Hindi, and so on—and not the other way round, as would happen with a master language. Whatever high regard Sanskrit enjoyed in the past—and continues to enjoy even now—as the language of scriptural texts and of ritual practices, by no means did it ever lord over the bhashas as far as literature was concerned, once these had found their feet (or hands, with which they wrote). Long before that, Sanskrit had been gagged by grammar, its creativity crippled by commentary, effectively silenced though not killed, by sparing and exclusive employment.

The case of Persian in India illustrates another aspect of the role of translation in our subcontinent. During the Mughal period, Persian became the ruler's language but never the ruling language. To satisfy their curiosity, the rulers occasionally got Indian texts translated into Persian, using the language as it were for transmission or dissemination. During the reign of Akbar, Badauni laboured four years over translating the Ramayana into Persian, while Dara Shukoh, Shah Jahan's eldest son, got the *Upanishads*, the *Bhagavad' Gita* and the *Yogavashishtha Ramayana* rendered into Persian by a team of translators. Even after Persian was replaced by English as the official language of administration, it continued to be the language of gracious composition and useful translation.

With the advent of English, the context and role of translation in India changed substantially. A governor like Warren Hastings (in office from 1772 to 1785) believed that Hindus should be governed by Hindu laws. Accordingly, he had the *Dharmashastras* (which he was told were law books) translated from Sanskrit into Persian by

Indians, then from Persian into English by Europeans. By then, however, Charles Wilkins had translated the *Bhagavad' Gita* directly from Sanskrit into English (in 1785), William Jones had similarly translated *Shakuntala* into English (in 1789) and had also proclaimed his discovery (in a paper presented to the Asiatic Society in 1786) that Sanskrit belonged to the Indo-European family of languages, from which were born many European languages. Translation thus became the foundation on which a new discipline such as comparative philology could be established in the 19th century; it also opened up a new area of scholarly enquiry which came to be known as Indology.

We sometimes forget that it was the trading firm called the East India Company—and not the British Government of India, which had not yet taken over—which decided, in 1837, that English would thereafter be the 'official' language, that is, the language in which the Company could transact business with Indians and within India. This meant, on the one hand, that Englishmen—or Europeans, as they were then called—began to learn Indian languages, while Indians began to learn English. Europeans had already been learning Indian languages much earlier, when Christian missionaries came to various parts of India and sought to elevate the natives to the blessed state of those who manned or moneyed such missions. This learning became more organised as Fort William College was set up in Kolkata (then Calcutta) in 1800 for the purpose of teaching East India Company writers, as they were called, Indian languages and culture. The first round of languages to be cultivated included Hindi and Urdu, Bangla and Marathi. Thus was laid the foundation of translating, not from Sanskrit or Pali or Tamil, but from the bhashas, or the modern Indian languages.

As for the complementary process of Indians learning English, even before 1835 when Macaulay made recommendations in his 'Minutes on Education', a small but influential group of Indians in some emerging new cities had already taken to English. Between 1816 and 1833, Raja Rammohan Roy wrote several books in English; Henry Derozio wrote the long poem, *The Fakeer of Jangheera* in 1828; C.V. Ramaswami wrote *Biographical Sketches of the Dekkan Poets* in 1829; Kashiprosad Ghosh wrote *The Shair or Minstrel and Other Poems* in 1830. It was only to be expected that such proficiency in English acquired by Indians would in due course by demonstrated by translating from the *bhashas* into English. The worldwide recognition of such enterprise culminated in Rabindranath Tagore's winning an international award for literature in 1913. A curious situation was created thereby. Whereas, prior to this, Rabindranath's poems and short stories used to be translated by friends and admirers, in the case of *Gitanjali*, the poet himself had done the job. Ever since then, Indian writers have been alleged to have wanted to—sometimes actually done so—themselves translate their works into English. Not that all of them aspired to a Nobel Prize, but the fascination of modern Indian writers with being read and appreciated in English has outlasted the 20th century.

In the late 18th and the 19th century, translations of Indian literature into English were generally undertaken by the British, a few by Americans as well, and the source language was mostly Sanskrit. The latter part of the 19th century onwards, Indians joined the enterprise in growing numbers, with source texts being drawn from many Indian languages, ancient as well as modern. Well past fifty years of India's independence, it now seems obvious that Indians have appropriated the language of their recent rulers so extensively that almost the entire business of translating Indian literature into English has been taken over by Indian translators and, not to forget them, publishers. My friend P. Lal of Kolkata, a friend of translation as well as of publishing, has stated, 'I strongly believe that, all other things being equal, an Indian is better equipped to translate India's sacred works than a foreigner' (*Transcreation*, 1996; p. 29). I would go further and claim that Indians are better equipped to translate their profane texts as well.

What we don't yet have in India is a theory or theories of translation. This may be because, as I said at the outset, we have been practising translation for so many years—so many centuries, in fact—that we forgot to stop and theorise. But odd things did happen in the colonial period which must be affecting our post-colonial outlook on translation without us realising it, and this needs to be studied. For example, my own first experience of translation was at the early stages of learning English. In the usual school timetables of my time, one of the classes for English was allotted to translation. That is, pupils were required to translate passages from their mothertongues into English. Such passages were broadly literary, always informative and generally edifying. Textbooks were available, containing such passages and offering some model translations along with suggested English equivalents in Roman of mothertongue words and occasional Indian language transcription as aids to pronunciation. Question papers in the class-promotion examinations for English included such exercises, and marks were duly awarded. Teachers sometimes lamented that this or that pupil, who seemed to be very competent in translation, could not compose a single sentence in English.

Within the pious precincts of academia, the test was nominated as 're-translation'. The colonial situation had to devise some such solution to the problem of a body of examinees owning more than one mothertongue. This was perfectly normal in any even moderately urbanised centre of education in modern India. For example, in the school I attended in the mid-1930s in Patna, the capital of Hindi-speaking Bihar, at least three mothertongues were recognised—Hindi, Urdu and Bangla. By the time I began teaching in a college there in the early 1950s, two more tongues were acknowledged—Maithili and Nepali (the latter because, at that time, Patna University used to conduct examinations for Nepal). While distributing question papers for this test, therefore, one had to make sure that each student got the passage in the language that his or her mother spoke.

At the time such a test was being formalised, the head examiner was most certainly an Englishman (never, in those colonised and unfairly gendered times, an Englishwoman) who certainly knew at least one Indian language, but couldn't very well be expected to know more than one. To tackle the multilanguage situation, a typically British compromise was worked out. After a passage in English had been selected, Indian teachers were commissioned to translate it into Hindi, Urdu, Bangla, later into Maithili and Nepali as well. These passages were then distributed among the children according to their mothertongues and they were then required to re-translate these passages into English. Approximation achieved to the original passage was eventually evaluated, and it did not matter whether the examiner was English or Irish or Scot—all that he had to do was compare the examinee's effort with the original passage. And the exercise was rightly called re-translation rather than translation.

That is how we learnt English at one time—through translation and re-translation, through transcription in Hindi and annotation in Bangla, through learning grammatical rules by rote and English idioms by heart (the latter process popularly known as 'by-hearting'). As latter-day Calibans we were taught English and our profit on it has been that we learnt how to translate into English. Out of such remembering and recording will come India's theories of translation, especially of translating into English.

Meanwhile, practising translators—that is, from Indian languages into English—sometimes give the impression that they know better than the original authors, hence their efforts are so creative that such translation should be looked upon more as an art than as a craft. I feel uneasy when I hear talk about the 'art' of translation. My unease springs, among other apprehensions, from the fear that by talking about the art of translation, we may be surreptitiously seeking to defend translation against the usual charge, namely, that it is a secondary activity—secondary, that is, in rank to an activity such as creative writing; secondary also in activation, because translation must always follow after. Whereas, in my own perception, underlined by some practice, translating a literary work stands very close and nearly equal to the writing of it.

My other hesitation in accepting the translator as an artist is related to my having been a translator all my life but never regarding myself as an artist. Again, this is not my peculiar achievement. Most Indians who grow up in urban conditions and go to school and college tackle shifts from one language to another so often and so comfortably that translation seems second nature to them. When I began to apply this familiar process to translating a literary work from one language to another, I did not think I was doing anything removed from everyday practice. To regard such a habit as art would be to claim an unwarranted distinction. That habit can be refined into a craft rather than be exalted to an art.

In the course of translating from an Indian language into English, we (that is, we Indians) land ourselves in an unusual position. The usual position in most literary cultures of the world is to translate into one's first language a work from some other language one understands at a literary level. We have, for about one hundred years or more, reversed the process in one area. During this period of time, some of us acquired the English language well enough to communicate with native speakers of English, while a few among us mastered the language even better and earned recognition in English-speaking countries as writers of English. This situation is likely to continue in the foreseeable future, so will the position held by many of us who know English and indulge in translating into English from the Indian language or languages we happen to know. In my own case, Bangla is my first language and I acquired Hindi long before I could read or write it. Then came English, at best a third language for me, yet I translate into that language from Bangla and get invited to conferences.

By aspiring to translate Indian literary works into English, we take on a grave responsibility. Sometimes our English is not good enough and we do irreparable harm to a writer in Bangla or Hindi or Tamil by representing him or her inadequately in English translation. More English translations are being published in India these days than ever before, but our awareness of the need to ensure quality in translation has not heightened to the same extent. Of course, the basic question remains: Who should judge a translation—somebody who can read the original or somebody who cannot? A person who can read the original may find no translation satisfactory, whereas someone who cannot is likely to regard readability in English as the prime requisite. That narrow isthmus lying between these two flows shows no signs of widening.

At the risk of stating the obvious, let me insist that the basic equipment for a translator of literary works is a secure hold upon the two languages involved, supported by a good measure of familiarity with the culture represented by each language. I have the impression that when we translate from an Indian language into English, we err less often over items of British culture and more often in our control of contemporary English. Whereas, when a British or American translator tackles an Indian language text, especially a modern text, he is more likely to make mistakes of cultural understanding though his grasp of the grammar and syntax of the Indian language concerned may be more than adequate.

Between these two alternatives, in my publishing incarnation I used to prefer the former. As any publishers' editor knows, it is much easier to remedy lapses in language than it is to repair flaws of content. That is, since it is easier for an Indian to learn the English language than it is for a Briton or American to comprehend

Indian culture, translations of the kind being discussed here had better be left to Indians and other natives of the subcontinent.

However, I must not prescribe a theory nor labour to formulate one to justify what I have deduced from practice. Once when I had the opportunity I pontificated (actually, wrote), 'I have no theory of translation. I leave such theories to those who do not translate'. But even the mere practice of translation does throw up a variety of issues that a better qualified person than I would surely be able to lodge at theoretical levels. Instead of letting them remain as issues, let me turn some of them into questions for myself which I try to answer when I am engaged in translation.

1. First, why do I translate? It so happens that, except in one instance, I have never undertaken to do so at somebody else's bidding. Which means I generally translate when I enjoy the original work so much that I want to present its joys, however attenuated, to another set of readers in another language. Given the limits of my linguistic abilities, this has meant translating only from Bangla into English. But I have done so only when I have wanted to translate, not when somebody else has wanted me to and has even been prepared to pay for it.

Quite often I have translated without any offer of publication and certainly without any expectation of payment. In case this seems an impractical and unduly idealistic position to take, let me point out that my position enjoys a freedom of action which no professional translator can hope to enjoy.

A.K. Ramanujan once added one more level to such a labour of love when he said, 'one translates not just out of love, but also out of envy of the past masters'. He was a poet himself, thus entitled to envy older poets. I am no poet but can partake of such envy of all writers of all time.

2. For whom do I translate? If I was translating from Hindi (my second language) into Bangla (my first), this question would be easy to answer because each modern Indian language or bhasha is said to command a particular region or 'anchal', and its writers can focus on a known area of readership. No such focus is available to the Indian user of English, and the Indian translator into English can tie himself up into knots trying to decide which part or parts of the English-reading world to address. Given our normal tendency to look westwards for approbation, some of us may translate for the Middle West (i.e., the United Kingdom) while

others aim at the Far West (i.e., the United States). From my own experience, after some trial and much error, I have settled for readers nearest home. That is, if I may repeat something I have stated elsewhere, while converting the language medium (originally Bangla) to English, I seek to replace the target audience (originally the Bengali reader) not so much with the 'English reader' but with the 'reader in English'. Not being certain of where else this reader may live or lurk, I address my translations primarily to other Indians who read English.

3. What do I translate? Like most translators, I began with poetry. Like most Indian translators into English whose first language is Bangla, I began by assaulting the poetry of Rabindranath Tagore. (There are, of course, other reasons why so many Bengalis want to translate Rabindranath's poetry into English—the latest being the anxiety to protect him from British or American translators—but this is not the time or place to go into such reasons.) My early essays in this direction were fired by the desire to render his rhyming poems into rhymed verse. Inevitably, I had to give up this unequal struggle, finding Rabindranath's language far too rich and complex to be contained by my poor and simple English. I have tried to work on some other poets—Samar Sen, Amiya Chakravarty, Sunil Gangopadhyay, Niren Chakrabarti—mainly because I felt translation was one way to understand their poems better. Thereafter I have translated some short fiction (by Moti Nandy), one substantial work of literary criticism (by Buddhadev Bose), three long stories (by Rabindranath), and now one large novel.

What I wish to deduce from this biblio-biography is that a translator ought to try out various literary forms and authors, then stick to one for as long as possible.

4. How much do I translate? The answer to this has at least two parts, one of which concerns the amount or volume of cultural content to be transferred from one text to another. I see no problem here because a language expresses a culture, and any translation must strive to bring this over to the culture represented by the language into which the text is being translated. Therefore, to me, a term such as 'cross-cultural translation' seems quite worthless because it merely names the obvious. How can anybody translate from one language to another without a recognisable transfer of culture? Any attempt to conceal or subvert such transfer would go against the grain of literary translation. All or nothing must be the translator's aim.

The other part of the question relates mainly to the translation of novels or of long prose narratives from our languages into English. Here 'how much' is a truly quantitative factor. I do not know what liberties are taken when a novel by Marquez, Mishima or Mahfouz is rendered into English by a British or American translator. But in India there is a regrettable tendency among translators into English, of both foreign and native species, to interfere with the original text in various ways while translating, out of the earnest desire to improve upon the original.

There is a measure of hegemony involved here. Even after more than half a century of conscious decolonisation, the English language continues to hold such a position of authority in modern India that those who translate literary works into English somehow convince themselves that they are doing a favour to the Indian language writer by presenting him or her through translation to a wider world. In return for such service, some of our translators feel free to chop and change, omit from or rearrange the original to their own satisfaction. And sometimes it is our writers who are guilty of easy compliance, as was pointed out by Adil Jussawalla when he was putting together the Penguin anthology, *New Writing in India* (1974).

5. Finally, when is the translation over and done with? Here is an area in which the translated work enjoys an enormous advantage over the original. A novel or a poem or a play in the original tends to get fixed in form as soon as it becomes widely known. Famous authors have, of course, revised even their published works in subsequent editions. But no revision can ever match the free hand with which a translator can redo his or her own translation or re-translate a text that has been done earlier. Precarious as this may sound, translation bestows an indefinitely long life upon a text whose original career may have terminated much earlier had it not drawn a translator's attention.

In other words, a translation is never complete, or is so only transitionally. Was it not the late Ramanujan who once said that a translation is never finished, only abandoned? In conclusion, let me revert to my earlier submission about there being more craft than art to translation. The truly crafty translator will know why he translates, for whom he translates, what he should translate, how much to translate and, semi-finally, when to stop. Even after such knowledge, he may still be in need of forgiveness.

Two

Multiple Identities: Notes Towards a Sociology of Translation[1]

SAMANTAK DAS

My interest in translation stems from the fact that, like many urban Indians, I grew up within ('with' and 'in') several languages. None of these languages retained their 'purity' in the complex processes of use, misuse, abuse, hybridisation, and mongrelisation we (family, friends, neighbours) subjected them to in our daily usage. Even now, I am most comfortable in a 'language' (parole, really) that is a complicated mixture of Bangla (my mother tongue), English (the medium of instruction at my school and university) and Hindi (thanks to, in that order, Hindi movies, radio and television), with a smattering of Urdu, Gujarati, Punjabi, Oriya and Assamese (thanks to friends who spoke/speak these languages) thrown in for good measure. Despite efforts to prevent 'impurity' (by having the example of Tagore held up to us whenever we lapsed from 'chaste' Bangla or being taught, at school, that 'pindrop silence' was 'wrong English'), I, like most of my friends and acquaintances, have continued to use the diverse resources of the three primary language systems I have access to, and to add the occasional flourish from several others.

This essay is, therefore, not a finished product but rather an attempt to set down thoughts about the ways in which language is used in the multilingual society which has created and shaped me and which, in turn, will be shaped and further modified by myself and others like me. It is only in this sense that this piece may be said to deal with the sociology of translation in the Indian context.

Ghostly Presences, Multiple Selves

I mention these bits of personal linguistic history not (merely) in order to grab the limelight whilst I can, but also to make the rather more germane point that any kind of theorising about language *in our context* must take into account (a) the multilingual character of our society/nation; and (b) the ways in which this multilinguality directly impinges on our existence.

So far, it seems to me that theorists of translation have, for the most part, been products of (a) monolingual cultures (though they may well be competent in several languages themselves); and (b) (Western) metropolitan academies where there is one dominant, monolingual discourse to which they must submit. By this, I do not mean that there is a single language used in the Western metropolitan academies. Rather, it seems to me that each of these metropolitan languages (English, French, German, Italian, Spanish, and so on) possesses its own dominant academic discourse.

If a new body of theory and praxis is to emerge from India, it must take into account our own multilingual selves which are constantly negotiating—with varied degrees of competence and success—between different languages and language systems. This negotiation is far more complex than the usual case studies and analyses which appear in books and articles dealing with translation and its attendant discontents from the Western metropolitan academies. Although there is, undeniably, a considerable amount of cross-influence among these languages, an assessment of which is beyond the scope of this essay, most Western discussions around translation appear to concentrate on two principal languages, the source language text and the target language into which the text is being translated.

When a target language is the dominant/more politically powerful one, the source language text is forced into submission to the dominant discourse, with the translator playing ringmaster. Such was the case with translations from the languages of the colonised peoples to those of the colonisers in the heyday of imperialism. Edward Fitzgerald's observation, while translating Attar's *Bird Parliament* from Persian, is the paradigmatic expression of this kind of attitude. Although Fitzgerald was writing about a Persian text, belonging to a people who had not been colonised, it is the attitude I wish to draw attention to here. Fitzgerald wrote to the Reverend E.B. Cowell in 1851:

> *It is an amusement to me to take what liberties I like with these Persians who (as I think) are not Poets enough to frighten one from such excursions, and who really do need a little Art to shape them.*[2]

Conversely, a text in a source language considered by the translators to be the vehicle of a 'superior' culture becomes, as it were, a kind of 'feudal overlord exacting fealty from the translator' (Bassnett-McGuire 1991: 4).

The dynamic of power relations between the source language and target language texts is, and was, of course, considerably more different and paradoxical than this simple master–serf metaphor suggests. For example, when Greek texts (products of a superior culture in their translator's eyes) were translated into European 'vernaculars'—I use the term deliberately—during the European Renaissance, these were, so to speak, 'conquered' by the translator/s on behalf of a dominant readership even as they 'exacted fealty' from their translator/s.

Attitudes, of course, underwent change with the passage of time. An interesting 19th century debate on the desirability, or otherwise, of conquering a superior text was carried out between Francis Newman and Matthew Arnold, with Arnold wanting to 'English' Homer while Newman wanted to preserve his foreignness. This sort of controversy had important consequences for later translations of Western classical texts.[3] At any rate, paradoxical or not, the power relations between the source language and the target language text can be traced, and theorised, with a fair degree of confidence, when only two languages are involved in the process.

Consider what happens in our situation. Even if there seem to be, at first sight, just two languages involved in the translation in question, it is almost certain that at least one, if not several, more are exercising their influences on the process. An examination of a translation from Hindi to Bangla (or vice versa) would not only have to weigh in the balance the power (and other) relationships between the two languages, but would also have to consider the ways in which Sanskrit and English have impinged on the making of the source language and target language texts. This has to be done since both Bangla and Hindi trace their origins to Sanskrit, and have responded (positively and negatively) to the enormous influence, direct and indirect, of English on their formation. More of this later.

If one considers a translation where the source language text is in Assamese or Oriya and the target language text is in Hindi, the problem becomes even more complex. For, in addition to the influences of Sanskrit and English, there is also the question of the complicated and fraught relationship these languages have shared with Bangla, and the ways in which writers in these two languages, especially in the 19th century, sought to come to terms with the pejorative label of being mere 'inferior' versions/dialects of Bangla.[4] Such an Oriya or Assamese text may display, for example, at one and the same time:

a desire for affiliation with Bangla
a desire to shake off the burden of Bangla
a desire for affiliation with English
a desire to shake off the burden of English
a desire for affiliation with Sanskrit
a desire to shake off the burden of Sanskrit

Which of these sometimes conflicting desires are highlighted or foregrounded would depend on a variety of circumstances, including the time of a particular text's composition, the politics of that particular text's creator, the form of a text's composition, and so forth. And needless to say these desires may be used in diverse permutations and combinations for a variety of (intended or unintentional) reasons and effects.

At the level of praxis, a translator will have to deal with the vexatious issue of how to retain/indicate/communicate these effects in her translation. It is not possible, in the space of such a brief essay, to go into all the thorny theoretical issues such processes raise, but

I think it is necessary for us to at least recognise that the 'source language = target language' equation, or the 'author-text-receiver = translator-text-receiver' equation (Bassnett-McGuire 1991: 38) becomes a whole lot more complicated in our polyphonic multilingual situation.

Any consideration of translation, any attempt to theorise translation in the Indian context, must take into account not merely the relationship/s between the two languages directly involved in the translation process but also consider the several other languages whose ghostly presences hover around the margins of both, transforming them and their relationship/s to each other.

Orientalism as Doctrine Versus Translation as Emancipation

Ever since the publication of Edward Said's *Orientalism* (1978), there has emerged a large body of texts that seek to show—often in brilliant and subtly nuanced ways—the strategies by which the Oriental subject was reified by the hegemonic discourse of the imperial powers. Drawing on the work of Said and his intellectual preceptor, Michel Foucault, many excellent books and articles have appeared, laying bare the ways in which that largely fictitious/textual entity, 'The Orient', was created to serve the political interests of the Occidental powers.

However, it seems to me that far too much attention has been lavished on the methods by which Western/imperialist texts, including translations, appropriated Oriental texts, and not enough on the ways in which the 'Oriental subject' herself/himself appropriated those very same texts that sought to reify her/him. As Harish Trivedi puts it, 'as propounded so far, a critique of orientalism seems to be very much an ideological need of the Western academy than of an Eastern one, and to that extent for us a version of neo-orientalism in itself' (Trivedi 1993: 20). Trivedi rightly asserts that the need of the hour, as far as we are concerned, would be to study 'the assimilative or subversive strategies through which we coped with their orientalism' and to seek to understand 'our own *occidentalism*, which was a kind of comparable (mis-)knowledge with which we empowered ourselves to resist the West, and not entirely unavailingly either' (ibid., emphasis in original).

In short, doctrinaire orientalism is no longer sufficient. It is time we recognised the ways in which the entire Orientalist exercise was resisted, subverted, appropriated, assimilated, to serve indigenous, often nationalist, purposes. When it comes to our particular history, to see all translations from Indian languages to European languages (especially English), or vice versa, as serving the colonial enterprise is inadequate on several counts (Niranjana 1995). Such exercises (a) minimise, in fact erase, the resistance offered by Indian colonial subjects; (b) fail to recognise that foreign texts can have, and have had, salutary and, indeed, beneficial effects on Indian literatures, sometimes quite different from that intended by those who introduced/imposed these texts in the first place; and (c) reinforce the idea of the 'native' subject as a mere passive vessel incapable of (a) articulating her/his point of view, (b) resisting the 'civilising mission' of the colonial masters or, perhaps most importantly, (c) creating a new way of seeing which was/is, in a very real sense, an improvement on the earlier modes, whether Indian or European.

As Aijaz Ahmed points out, despite the fact of the imposition of English, 'the more remarkable fact is that in the entire history of Indian reformism, from Rammohan to Vivekanand to Sir Syed to Tilak and Gandhi, there is always an attachment to and competence in one or two Indian languages, but never any rejection of English as such; virtually all of them *wanted* it, not as a literary language but as a window on the most advanced knowledges of the world' (Ahmad 1994: 268, emphasis in original).

Quite apart from this *wanting* of access to the language of knowledge, and not just the language of power, the presence of the English language led to the enrichment of many (most?) Indian languages/literatures. Ahmad himself gives the examples of *Aaraish-e-Mehfil* and *Bagh-o-Bahar*, 'which eventually came to be included among the key classics of Urdu prose' even though both were 'initially composed as textbooks for British personnel who needed to learn the language and know its cultural ambience' (ibid.: 269).

This same point can be made by a brief look at the role played by translations in the creation of modern Bangla literature. As Jogesh

Chandra Bagal put it in the introductory remarks to his magisterial survey of 19th century Bangla translation-literature:

> *It is true that no literature can reach fullness without the help of translations.... A hundred and fifty years ago, intellectuals and educationalists paid particular attention to the development of this particular aspect of Bangla literature. The history of the development/shaping of Bangla prose-literature is, in fact, the history of this translation-literature.... A critical survey of the development of [Bangla] education and literature in the early years of the last century will clearly reveal the ways in which Bangla prose-literature was enriched by translations of [texts from] different branches of knowledge.... Institutional effort and individual enterprise contributed the raw materials and nourished this translation exercise...* (Bagal 1968, my translation).

This brings me to the second point I would like to make in this essay. To understand and appreciate that entity called 'Indian literature', it is absolutely essential to look at the vital role played by translations in the creation of literatures in the many Indian languages. Such an examination must treat with caution (Western academy-received) notions of the hegemony of the imperial masters' language/s and look closely at the ways in which texts in the masters' language/s were 'taken over' to serve a variety of emancipatory purposes in the different Indian languages.

Domesticating Texts Versus Foreignising Texts

In a lecture delivered in 1813 on the different approaches to translation, the German theologian and philosopher, Freidrich Schleiermacher, asserted that there are only two ways in which to go about translating a text. 'Either the translator leaves the author in peace, as much as possible, and moves the reader towards him; or he leaves the reader in peace, as much as possible, and moves the author towards him' (Venuti 1995: 19–20). As Lawrence Venuti comments:

> *Schleiermacher allowed the translator to choose between a* domesticating *method, an ethnocentric reduction of the foreign text to target*

> *language cultural values, bringing the author back home, and a* foreignising *method, an ethnodeviant pressure on those values to register the linguistic and cultural difference of the foreign text, sending the reader abroad* (my emphases).

To understand more precisely the difference between *domesticating* a text and *foreignising* it, I would like to take the help of an essay by Thomas S. Kuhn (1982) entitled 'Commensurability, Comparability, Communicability', where he differentiates between *translation, interpretation* and *language acquisition*. In this essay, Kuhn writes that:

> *...speakers of mutually translatable languages need not share terms.... But the referring expressions of one language must be matchable to coreferential expressions in the other, and the lexical structures employed by speakers of the languages must be the same, not only within each language but also from one language to the other. Taxonomy must, in short, be preserved to provide both shared categories and shared relationships between them. Where it is not, translation is impossible...*

Translation, then, according to Kuhn, is possible only when there is a homology of taxonomic structures between languages. When 'translation is impossible' the 'interpreter' (Kuhn would not call her/him a translator!) has to 'discover or invent meanings in order to render intelligible the texts on which he works. Interpretation is the process by which the use of those terms is discovered' (ibid.: 9). *Interpretation* is thus necessary when a homology of taxonomic structures does not exist between languages. In the absence of such homology, the interpreter can also become a 'language learner', introducing terms or sets of terms from the source language text to the target language text in order to facilitate communication. This process of borrowing terms from the source language to the target language is what Kuhn calls *language acquisition*.

Practitioners of translation, and even theorists of translation, do not generally make such rigorous definitional distinctions and the term 'translation' is often used to indicate all three Kuhnian processes—translation, interpretation and language acquisition. Since it is unlikely that a natural language will show perfect homology of taxonomic structure with another natural language, Kuhn's position can be reinterpreted to indicate that (in the sense in which we use the term) translation perforce partakes of interpretation as well as language acquisition.

Further, *even when* some homologous taxonomic structures/categories are available, translators frequently choose to interpret or introduce new terms (i.e., take the route of language acquisition) in their translations. What Venuti calls 'domesticating' a text comes close to Kuhn's 'interpretation' (interpreting the 'foreign' or the 'other' in familiar terms), while Venuti's 'foreignizing' is akin to Kuhn's 'language acquisition' (learning the terms of the foreign or the other in a process that defamiliarises the familiar terms of the target language).

When a foreignised text is introduced into a language system, the language itself undergoes fundamental change (subject, of course, to the wider acceptance and dissemination of the foreignised text). In turn, this new foreignised language becomes the vehicle for original works.

Histories of Indian language literatures would benefit from an examination of *when* and *how* they underwent their most radical phases of foreignising, and *how* and *when* they reverted to domesticating modes. Such an examination would also reveal *why* translators in these languages accepted or rejected terms/sets of terms from other (Indian and/or European) languages. This, in turn, would help us to better understand the cultural and linguistic politics that operated (and may, perhaps, still be operating) among these language systems.

Much modern Bangla writing, for example, can be seen to have its origins in early 19th century efforts to foreignise Bangla by pioneering writers, in genres as diverse as epic and lyric poetry, drama, and the novel, many of whom were directly inspired by European—and not merely English—models. Many of these genres did, of course, exist in earlier Indian literatures, notably in Sanskrit, but all of them underwent radical change as a result of European influence in the early 19th century. Once this phase of foreignising was completed, sometime in the early years of the 20th century, and the new, foreignised Bangla became the language of literature, if not always the language of daily use, Bangla writers reverted, with some significant exceptions, to a domesticating mode, a process that is still under way. And this brings me to the final point I want to make in this essay.

It is necessary for us to study the different kinds and modes of translations in the various Indian languages, in order to have a fuller picture of the role played by translation in the Indian context. This will allow us to theorise translation and practice it in our situation with a greater awareness and sensitivity to the diversity of our multilingual heritage.

Susan Bassnett-McGuire mentions how Brazilian translators have introduced the metaphor of 'the translator as cannibal, devouring the source text in a ritual that results in the creation of something new'. This metaphor is 'based on a revised notion of what cannibalism signifies, considered not from the perspective of the European coloniser who is appalled by it, but from the perspective of those peoples whose cannibalistic practices derive from an alternative vision of society' (Bassnett-McGuire 1991: 14–15).

Speaking of metaphor, I see Indian translators as revellers sitting down to a large celebratory feast where dishes from different parts of the country have been brought and are being consumed. There is a general air of excitement and many heated arguments about the novel sights, sounds, tastes, textures and fragrances that pervade the atmosphere. Once these have been discussed, the translators start exchanging recipes, enriching their culinary expertise even as they nourish their bodies and minds. As for me, I've always enjoyed a good *khana* myself.[5]

Notes

1. I am grateful to Bikash Chakravarty and Romit Roy for their comments and suggestions during the writing of this essay.
2. See Trivedi (1993: 45), where this quotation from Edward Fitzgerald appears and its implications are discussed.
3. See Venuti (1995: 118–47) for a comprehensive discussion of this debate.
4. See the chapter entitled 'Defining the Nation' in Chandra 1992 for a detailed discussion of this complex relationship.
5. In north India, the word *khana* in this context would probably be replaced by the word *daavat*, which seems to better convey the sense of 'a large celebratory feast', but in Bengal this term of Persian origin is more or less unknown, hence

the appropriate usage is indeed *khana*, illustrating again the enormous regional variations in the choice of 'translational equivalents' throughout the Indian subcontinent.

References

Ahmad, Aijaz, 1994. *In Theory: Classes, Nations, Literatures*. New Delhi: Oxford University Press.

Bagal, Jogesh Chandra, 1968. 'Bangla Anubadh Sahitya (1801–1860)'. *Ekshan*, vol. 6, no. 6, pp. 2–3. Also delivered as the Sarat Chandra Chattopadhyay Memorial Lecture at Calcutta University in March 1968.

Bassnett-McGuire, Susan, 1991. *Translation Studies* (revised edition). London: Routledge.

Chandra, Sudhir, 1992. *The Oppressive Present: Literature and Social Consciousness in Colonial India*. New Delhi: Oxford University Press.

Kuhn, Thomas S., 1982. 'Commensurability, Comparability, Communicability'. *PSA*, vol. 2.

Niranjana, Tejaswini, 1995. *Siting Translation: History, Post-Structuralism, and the Colonial Context*. Hyderabad: Orient Longman.

Trivedi, Harish, 1993. *Colonial Transactions: English Literature and India*. Kolkata: Papyrus.

Venuti, Lawrence, 1995. *The Translator's Invisibility: A History of Translation*. London: Routledge.

Three

Sources and Targets: Translation as a Cultural Filter

LACHMAN M. KHUBCHANDANI

A host of presuppositions prevail in different societies, and these have a significant bearing in portraying the role of a translator—or, in a broader context, 'communicator'—in a cross-cultural scenario. Indian mythology projects this dynamics through the celebrated character of Narada who is admired for his 'tempering' messages which are perceived as 'relevant' to the task of ferrying passengers across the cosmic universe. Charged with a positive mission, Narada's 'interventionist' approach, in transmitting the desired message to the other end, the target, can be viewed as a fine-tuning of the message, highlighting a subjective input in the role of an interpreter in intercultural settings. Chinese mythology, in turn, carries the image of an evercontented Buddha, rejoicing with raised arms, in his role as a transmitter of message: 'Yes, I know! It's always a great feeling to have delivered the message one has come to deliver!'

By contrast, in Western societies, the Hebraic story of the Tower of Babel as depicted, for example, in Brueghel's painting in Rotterdam has dominated its consciousness. This image presents 'linguistic diversity as a divine punishment' and the translator is burdened with the task of reversing this curse, the historic hubris that has been visited upon humankind. This orientation seems to have influenced many contemporary scholars in holding the stand that translation, in its ideal sense, is *impossible:* the words in which a statement is made are so much part of the statement itself that it cannot be uttered in any other words without some alteration of its meaning (Steiner 1975, Mulhausler 1991). The translator is, therefore, cautioned against the hidden danger of 'ruining' the message, and is confronted with a list of many do's and don'ts to achieve a degree of approximation in the altered text.

Since the premise is that only a certain degree of approximation is possible in translation, many language modernisation programmes envisage that languages could be developed on the scale of intertranslatability (Ferguson 1968; Khubchandani 1983). Taking a cue from the 'centre-periphery' hypothesis of politico-economic development, language planners suggest evaluating the development of 'premodern' languages by projecting an adequate rendering of lexical and grammatical features on the lines already accurately and easily expressible in one or the other crucial language of reference communities, or 'currently prestigeful' languages considered to be 'modern' (Fishman 1974). This so far has been the contribution of contemporary sociolinguistic theories to the notion of translation.

Multilingual Societies and Translation

What is translated, and from *which source* aiming at *which targets*? *How* are messages transformed from one code to the other in cross-cultural settings? In plurilingual societies answers to these questions are determined by the 'communication profiles' prevalent in individual regions. Reviewing a variety of such models of language pluralism on the global canvas elsewhere (Khubchandani 1983, 1991), I discuss the matrix of a 'plurality square' which presents a scheme of four types of pluralism under the rubrics: (a) Organic or Structural; and (b) Homogenising or Differentiating

Societies nurtured primarily in an *oral* milieu, such as India's, are guided by an overall 'communication ethos' which is significantly different from that of societies largely organised on the basis of the *written* tradition, as in the West (Khubchandani 1997a: 80–86).

Translation activity, in the classical sense, assumes a greater role in intergroup communications regulated through written cultures; here the transfer of a text from code A to code B provides a pivotal *interface* in meeting with the day-to-day requirements of adequate and efficient communication among diverse 'well-delineated' linguistic groups, such as, in Switzerland and Canada. A case of extreme *compartmentalisation* is found in the formal Canadian protocol, where the translation activity serves as a device of institutional parallelism and parity, leading to insulation or strategic distancing between French speaking and English speaking collectivities which even today are going through the agonies of transition and are yet to arrive at a mutually acceptable balance, as revealed in the 1995 Referendum over Quebec's aspirations for sovereignty (Khubchandani 1996).

Intergroup communications among predominantly oral societies in the Indian subcontinent, on the other hand, are characterised by an *amalgamative* approach through the various devices of dynamic language contact. These include cognate doublets: *dhan daulat*—'wealth', etc., in Hindi; *xush raazii parsanu*, 'happy and contented' in Sindhi (Khubchandani 1963); relexicalisations and loan translations; and the blending of phrases from diverse sources through language hybridisation and neutralisation, known as the *manipravaal* style of 'mixing gems and diamonds' from Sanskrit and Tamil in medieval Malayalam literature. Many compounds in Indian languages are also formed out of the reduplication of Sanskrit, Arabic, Persian and, sometimes, English cognates. Jawaharlal Nehru's public speeches were marked by this distinction: *mulk ke haalaat, de's kii sthiti* both meant, for example, 'conditions prevailing in the country'. In contemporary parlance, these instances of grassroots plurilingual discourses, in contrast to mandatory bilingualism and code-switching/mixing, are on the increase (Khubchandani 1992).

Multiculturalism, including multilingualism, and translation—considered in the wider context of language transformation and language dynamics—are, in an inalienable relation, variedly named as the 'linguistic turn', the 'interpretative turn' and the 'cultural turn' by scholars from different disciplines (Tirumalesh 1992: 15–30). It will be useful to prepare societal profiles of the translation activity in different regions to gain insights in understanding the dynamics of intergroup communications and language contact.

Multilingual societies, India being a glaring example, make a variety of claims on translation activity. These claims are often loaded with contradictory values:

1) Translation as a *cross-cultural* transmission of skills forms a bridge between two speech groups, and is judged by the degree of *gratification/acceptance* among the audience of the target language. It is taken as a *holistic* endeavour enacting the transfer from one source to another, negotiated in terms of code, audience, channel, context, and so on. In everyday life situations one spontaneously utilises this tool, guided by the dictates of *relevance*. The products of such transmission are identified by varied labels such as interpretation, paraphrase, rendering, adaptation, recapitulation, free translation and seed translation. The total impact of such transformation is judged by the *transpired message* of the discourse.

2) Translation as a *sacrosanct* endeavour, committed to the *authentic* transfer of language package in its entirety, demands a kind of sensitivity in both the source and the target codes/cultures. Such transmissions are identified by a close adherence to the source, evaluated on the aesthetic criteria of 'fine-tuning' (as in a literary discourse), on the demands of 'truth-value' in a scientific and technical text, and on the 'genius' of the original code (as in a literal grammar-bound translation). Hitherto, translation studies have, by and large, focused on the *techniques* of language transfer in different domains such as literary, scientific and literal translations.

3) Translation as a *privilege* is related to a power paradigm, based on parity or the donor–recipient arrangement, in a heterogeneous situation. It leads to a *cosmetic exercise*, a ritualistic propriety, of elaborating the target code through the coinage of domain-specific terminologies. The semiotic value of a product is judged on the assertion of its 'autonomy' even when it results in the blurring of the message and making it artificial or opaque. This phenomenon highlights an *adversarial* role for translation between two competing groups (as in the Canadian case discussed earlier), and undermines the efficacy of *trust*, an essential ingredient in human communication. Movements for language rights for minority speech communities in many countries thus foreground and assert the need for reciprocity in their own tongues of the translation and interpretation facilities made available to dominant languages (Leger 1996, Skutnabb-Kangas, et al., 1994, Khubchandani 1999).

The Indian Milieu

The Indian milieu is, by and large, characterised by many of the conflicting attitudes towards translation given earlier, but especially perhaps the third. Translation plays a rather unstructured, *complementary* role here. In this milieu, languages with a wider dispersal and those associated with greater politico-economic power acquire a greater access to the written domains. This in turn leads to differential paces of 'development' for different languages, related to their roles and functions in a plural society. The rhetoric of equality in language development is contained at the level of merely entitling these languages through legislation and allocating them funds in grandiose policy formulations, with little desire to really implement these policies in order to achieve the goals of 'autonomy' in communications across languages/cultures.

Considering these ground realities, translation activity in the Indian set-up is relatively scanty. Translation in India has grown as a supplementary endeavour, an incremental facility in inter-group communications. With the result that translation activity in many Indian languages has emerged more as a *privilege* with the claims of 'corporate' status (namely, Eighth Schedule languages and other accreditation devices, cf. Gupta, et al., 1995) rather than as a response to functional justification.

The Macaulay commandment, as recorded in his widely discussed 1835 Minute 'of *first* developing Indian vernaculars to qualify them for use in education and administration' has prevailed even after more than a century and a half, effectively postponing their introduction in formal domains (Khubchandani 1981). This has led to the demands for 'highbrow' artificial coinages of technical terms from classical stocks (Sanskrit, Perso-Arabic or old Tamil/medieval Telugu, etc.) to enable the 'vernaculars' to acquire an aura of sophistication and thus to join the comity of 'developed' languages (for a detailed discussion on this 'centre-periphery' model of language development, see Khubchandani 1969, 1983). Translations under this guise have inevitably developed a certain insipid and pedantic diction which is more *cosmetic* than serving the practical needs of communication, as is revealed from the sarcastic comments on the Hindi radio broadcasts during the sixties and the seventies: *ab samaachaar mein Hindi suniye* (Now listen to Hindi in the news), parodying the announcement *ab Hindi mein samaachaar suniye*, (Now listen to the news in Hindi).

Purposeful Activity

In the backdrop of the sociolinguistic perspective discussed here, it will be useful to probe the pragmatic considerations of translation, such as the purpose, attitudes and competence of target audiences or readers, requirements of different channels, including simultaneous interpretation, dubbing, print, mass media, computers, etc., and other contextual factors. One can identify two prominent orientations in handling varied tasks of translation: (a) *Source-directed*, namely close, literal translation; it concentrates on the *authenticity* of original discourse. (b) *Target-directed*, namely free translation, adaptation to another genre, channel (for instance, from a novel to a TV serial), rendering, interpretation, seed translation (i.e., conveying the idea); it puts a high premium on the *gratification* of the target audience.

The unifying influence of the epics (Ramayana, Mahabharata) and the Puranas on the Indian psyche can be gathered from the number of adaptations and renderings made of them during two thousand years from Sanskrit into various languages of the subcontinent. Tulsidas's Awadhi version of the Ramayana, the Ramacharitmanas, a transcreation of the epic, has even superseded Valmiki's original in popularity in most of northern India. In contrast, the copyrighted authorship in the contemporary communication order, often demands a close adherence to the original discourse (Khubchandani 1989).

Translation activity, in our context, has to be looked upon as a reconstruction device, a sort of recasting exercise, transferring from one language *tradition* to another. A language tradition does not confine itself to mere 'core' grammar in the conventional sense, i.e., the phonology, morphology, syntax or lexicon of a given code. Rather, it covers the entire gamut of cultural and communication ethos, including rhetorical systems (Khubchandani 1991).

When routed through 'filter' languages, mostly English and Hindi, it should be noted that translations in many Indian languages are removed one or more stages from the source language. Such 'twice-removed' texts obviously become less transparent and show the strains of ambiguity and opacity. The Council of Europe, for example, has introduced multilingual networks to ensure parity of member nations, and is seized with the issues of removing the barriers caused due to the dependence on filter languages, largely English and French.

In the Indian context, recent attempts to develop an inter-language called *Anusaaraka* at the Indian Institute of Technology, Kanpur, envisage a midway junction through a device for human-aided machine translation (HAMT) which allows a reader who knows one language to have direct access to a text in another language through the transfer of a skeleton blueprint. The issues of grammaticality and acceptability of the target language in this HAMT are to be handled at a separate level through post-editing. For example, the Akshar Bharati group in Hyderabad is presently engaged in preparing an *Anusaaraka* from Kannada and other Dravidian languages to Hindi, allowing a Hindi reader to read 'Hindi "*anusaar*" (following) Kannada' through a sort of Kannada-based Hindustani. (see Bharati, et al., 1994, Khubchandani 1995, 1997b).[1] The role of *Anusaaraka*, the language accessor is of course radically different from a single accomplished translator or *anuvaadak* as such. Yet, all these efforts show that practical efforts to 'intervene' in the prevailing dynamics of the 'natural' sociolinguistic processes of translation in our country are seriously under way.

Note

1. See also Chapter Fourteen, 'Language Barriers', on machine-translation where the progenitors of the *Anusaaraka* project speak for themselves.

References

Bharati Akshar, Vineet Chaitanya and **Rajeev Sangal**, 1994. *Anusaaraka or Language Accessor: A Translation Aid*. Kanpur: Indian Institute of Technology.

European Commission, 1996. *Euromosaic: The Production and Reproduction of Minority Language Groups in the European Union*. Brussels: European Commission.

Ferguson, Charles A., 1968. 'Language Development'. In F.A. Rice (ed.), *Study of the Role of Second Languages in Asia, Africa and Latin America*. Washington D.C.: Center for Applied Linguistics.

Fishman, Joshua A., 1974. 'Language Modernization and Planning in Comparison with Other Types of National Development'. In J.A. Fishman (ed.), *Advances in Language Planning*. The Hague: Mouton.

Gupta, R.S., A. Abbi and **K.S. Aggarwal**, 1995. *Language and the State: Perspectives on the Eighth Schedule*. New Delhi: Creative Books.

Khubchandani, Lachman M., 1963. 'The Acculturation of Indian Sindhi to Hindi: A Study of Language in Contact'. Ph.D dissertation. University of Pennsylvania, Philadelphia. Also University Microfilm Corp: Ann Arbor.

———, 1969. 'Equipping Indian Languages for New Roles'. In A. Poddar (ed.), *Language in Society*. Shimla: Indian Institute of Advanced Study.

———, 1981. *Language Education and Social Justice*. Pune: Centre for Communication Studies.

———, 1983. *Plural Languages, Plural Cultures: Communication, Identity and Social Change in Contemporary India*. An East–West Center Book. Honolulu: University of Hawaii Press.

———, 1989. 'Pragmatic Aspects of Translation'. Paper presented at the seminar Problems of Translation. University of Bombay, Mumbai.

———, 1991. *Language, Culture and Nation-Building: Challenges of Modernisation*. Shimla: Indian Institute of Advanced Study.

———, 1992. 'Relexicalisation and Communicability: Some Reflections'. *Osmania Papers in Linguistics*, Vol. 18, pp. 15–30.

———, 1995. '*Anusaarak*—An interlanguage: Its Acceptability, Learnability and Changes'. Paper presented at a workshop at the Indian Institute of Technology, Kanpur.

———, 1996. 'Organic and Structural Pluralism: A Review of Translation Activity in India and Canada'. In S. Ramakrishna (ed.), *Translation and Multilingualism: Indian and Canadian Experiences*. New Delhi: Pencraft.

———, 1997a. *Revisualizing Boundaries: A Plurilingual Ethos*. New Delhi: Sage.

———, 1997b. 'Human-aided Machine Translation: A Case of Anusaarak'. Paper presented at the seminar Natural Language Processing. Indian Statistical Institute, Kolkata.

———, 1999. 'Philosophical Issues of Contact Language Planning: Response to the Prevailing Tendencies of Linguistic Hegemonism'. In A.F. Christidis (ed.) *"Strong" and "Weak" Languages in the European Union: Aspects of Linguistic Hegemonism*. Proceedings of an International conference in 1997. Vol. 1, pp. 42–57. "Language and Nation: A Symposium" Vol. 2, pp. 936–39. Thessaloniki: Centre for the Greek Language.

Leger, Sylvie (ed.). 1996. *Towards a Language Agenda: Futurist Outlook on the United Nations*. Proceedings of a conference in 1995. University of Ottawa, Ottawa.

Mulhausler, Peter, 1991. 'Babel Revisisted'. *The Unesco Courier,* no. 2.

Saberwal, Satish and **L. Khubchandani,** 1972. 'Social Sciences: The Audiences', *Seminar,* September, vol. 157, pp. 33–36.

Skutnabb-Kangas, Tove and **Robert Phillipson** (eds.), 1994. *Linguistic Human Rights: Overcoming Linguistic Discrimination*. Berlin: Mouton de Gruyter.

Steiner, George, 1975. *After Babel: Aspects of Language and Translation*. New York: Oxford University Press.

Tirumalesh, K.V., 1992. 'Translation and Multiculturalism'. *Bulletin of the Central Institute of English and Foreign Languages,* vol. 4; 1–2, pp. 15–30.

Four

Post-colonial Representation: Translation as Disruption

TEJASWINI NIRANJANA

Historical materialism… blasts open the homogeneity of the epoch. It saturates it with ecrasite, that is, the present…. The events surrounding the historian and in which he takes part will underlie his presentation like a text written in invisible ink.

Walter Benjamin, *Passagen-Werk*

Looking again into Charles Trevelyan's *On the Education of the People of India*, I find the colonising gesture repeatedly performed by a move that translates as it inscribes history. Describing the benefit derived by the Indians from the British, Trevelyan presents a bizarre analogy whose paradoxically inverted structure betrays the overdetermination of the field of translation. Trevelyan's narrative of colonisation suggests that the precursors of India and England (standing in for Asia and Europe) are Greece and Rome: a cradle of civilisation, once glorious and mighty but now fallen and decadent, is conquered by a younger, more vigorous race, which proceeds to imitate and translate the literature of its subjects as well as take over the leadership of the world.

In its crude construction of an Indian Golden Age and its subsequent decline, the origin story of the 'founding' of the West functions in Trevelyan's text as an analogy for, and therefore as a justification of, the inevitability of the British conquest of India. Here Trevelyan runs into a problem. He has to account in his book not just for the British desire to learn Indian languages but for what he sees as the native clamour for 'English knowledge'. So he inverts the analogy, turning Greeks into Romans and Romans into Greeks. The Indians who demand to be taught English are like the Romans who learned the language of those they had conquered in order to become 'modern'. The 'English book' displayed to the boys from Comercolly by the gentlemen on the boat was, after all, Plato's *Republic*. The 'profound speculations' of the Greeks drove out the 'doting superstition' of the Etruscans, whose language the Romans used to employ. A similar revolution, argues Trevelyan, is taking place in India (Trevelyan 1838: 38). England now takes its place in colonialism's narrative as the mother country, the place of civilisation. India, through the English language, draws strength from it to be able to turn away from 'useless knowledge' and re-enter the story of humankind. The colonised are wrenched from 'history' in order to be inserted into history-as-progress.

English as the Language of a 'Universal History'

The curious shuffling between 'Greeks' and 'Romans' reveals an incoherence at the very centre of the discourse of improvement. It is an incoherence that marks a simultaneous recognition and disavowal of difference, which also makes possible the double inscription of the colonial encounter in a homogenising universal history—as a version of Greeks-and-Romans, and as a necessary moment in history-as-imperialism. The universalising move, which is, after all, part of the West's constitution of itself as subject, contributes to erasing the violence of colonialism. Non-Western peoples attain to maturity and subjecthood only after a period of apprenticeship in which they learn European languages and thereby gain a 'voice'.

Inserting the encounter with the language of the coloniser into universal history permits Trevelyan to imply that a knowledge of this history promotes the widespread use of English. The order of mimesis presiding over the notion of translation that enables Trevelyan's text helps domesticate the colonised and repress their heterogeneity by dismissing it as 'fantastic' and 'barbaric'. The material for Trevelyan's dismissal comes not just from what he calls his 'experience' as an administrator in India but, more important, from the discourse on 'the Hindoos'—evoked by such proper names as William Jones, William Ward and James Mill—which provides a matrix for the experience in 19th century colonialists, and allows translation to function as translation-into-history.

As Derrida points out, 'History and knowledge, *istoria* and *episteme* have always been determined (and not only etymologically or philosophically) as detours for the purpose of the re-appropriation of presence' (*Of Grammatology*, p. 10). *Istoria* and *episteme* claim to 'represent', and the idea of translation circulating in Trevelyan's treatise on education proposes representation as adequate to a pre-given 'reality', as being translation that functions as an originary philosopheme, for according to Derrida, the notion of a transcendental signified takes shape 'within the horizon of an absolutely pure, transparent, and unequivocal translatability' (Derrida 1981: 20). Translation, as I have contended, is thus brought into being in the colonial context in a complex field structured by law, violence and subjectification, as well as by determinate concepts of representation, reality and knowledge.

To see the overdetermined nature of translation is to complicate our response to the construction of the 'Hindoo'. Under the sign of Western liberalism, a certain kind of moral indignation has condemned colonial representations as simplistic and has demanded 'better' representations in their place. This kind of response, although partially aware of the intersections of power and knowledge, can be seen, in its argument for a simple reversal, to be as much a response to a 'command' as that of Trevelyan's 'natives' asking to be given history.

The call for reversal also informs the discourses of nationalism and nativism that circulate in the colonial and post-colonial situations, and that participate in what Said calls a 'politics of blame', a politics of lamentation for a lost precolonial past combined with a denunciation of the colonisers. The nationalist and the nativist, whose class provenance are usually that of the indigenous elite created in part by colonialism, often end up colluding in the denial of history and the occlusion of heterogeneity. In the interests of constructing a unified national identify that will challenge colonial domination, the discourse of nationalism suppresses marginal and non-elite people and struggles. Claiming to counteract Western domination, nativism (or its more familiar and frightening face, religious revivalism and fundamentalism) advocates a return to lost origins that completely obscures the violent history of the colonial encounter. Fanon points out that the 'passionate search for a national culture which existed before the colonial era finds its legitimate reason in the anxiety shared by native intellectuals to shrink away from that Western culture in which they all risk being swamped' (Fanon 1967; 1968: 168). Confronted by European descriptions of a history of decline, degradation and bestiality, the 'native intellectual' attempts to discover a counter-history of a 'wonderful past' that will provide the basis for a post-colonial national culture. However, to quote Fanon again, 'the attitude of the native intellectual sometimes takes on the aspect of a cult or of a religion' (ibid., p. 175) and the tendency is to forget that the creation of culture in colonised space often involves techniques and languages 'borrowed' from the coloniser (ibid., p. 180). The reformist native response, on the other hand, is to accept the story of the fall into barbarism and to put forward programmes that will turn the colonised into 'civilised' imitators of the colonisers. Both the nationalist and the nativist discourses converse, therefore, in an acceptance of the paradigm of representation provided by the colonising culture.

They accept thereby the incoherent analogy with Greeks and Romans provided by Trevelyan, whose liberal discourse makes room for a period of learning or apprenticeship as a time of imitation necessary in the history of nations. The Indians will imbibe, along with the English language, models of national culture. 'We must... give a liberal English education to the middle and upper classes, in order that we may furnish them with both the materials and models for the formation of a national literature' (Trevelyan 1838: 175)[1].

Post-colonial Translators as Anti-essentialists

The post-colonial translator must be wary of essentialist anticolonial narratives; in fact s/he must attempt to deconstruct them, to show their complicity with the master narrative of imperialism. This is a crucial task, especially at a time when the myths of nationalism—secularism, tradition, nationhood, citizenship—are invoked to suppress heterogeneity in a decolonising country such as India, for example. The translator must participate in what Fanon spoke of as 'a complete calling in question of the colonial situation', and this includes the re-examination of liberal nationalism as well as the nostalgia for lost origins, neither of which provides models of interventionist practice or 'grounds' for ideological production that challenges hegemonic interpretations of history (Spivak 1987: 271–313). As Homi Bhabha, using the model of literary criticism, maintains, when nationalism takes over 'universalist' criticism's 'mimetic view of the text's transparent relationship to a pre-constituted reality', it 'represses the ideological and discursive construction of difference, reducing the problem of representing difference to the demand for different and more favorable representations' (Parry 1987: 46).

The political and theoretical discussion of non-essentialising representation must, therefore, avoid replicating the moves of Western imperialism and metaphysics. It might be useful to remember here Walter Benjamin's remark that 'the state of emergency in which we live is not the exception but the rule. We must attain to a concept of history that is in keeping with this insight' (Benjamin 1986) as also Bhabha's suggestion that 'the state of emergency is also always a state of emergence' (ibid.). The state of emergency/emergence that is the post-colonial condition demands a disruptive concept of history that, by problematising the striving for adequatio in the ways shown by Derrida, de Man and Benjamin, will also contribute to formulating a notion of representation/translation to account for the discrepant identities of the post-colonial 'subject'.

Analysing the collusion of *istoria* and *episteme*, I have emphasised the need to examine the political aspects of representation along with the linguistic. We ought to keep in mind both these notions of representation, as Gayatri Spivak suggests in 'Can the Subaltern Speak?' In Marx's *The Eighteenth Brumaire*, for example, the need to keep the two notions together shows how 'both in the economic area (capitalist) and in the political (world-historical agent), Marx is obliged to construct models of a divided and dislocated subject whose parts are not continuous or coherent with each other' (CSS,

p. 276). This is because Marx takes representation to mean, on the one hand, *Darstellung*, or the philosophical concept of representation as 'staging' or 'signification', which, 'computed as the sign of objectified labor', is related to the production of value, and, on the other hand, *Vertretung*, which for Marx is representation in the political context (ibid., p. 278). Spivak sees these related notions of representation ('representation or rhetoric as tropology and as persuasion') being run together by certain post-structuralists (her targets are Michel Foucault and Gilles Deleuze) in the interests of 'an essentialist, utopian politics' that would require that 'oppressed subjects speak, act, and know for themselves' in a situation beyond representation (ibid., p. 276). Spivak's position is that we cannot afford to overlook the double meaning of representation if we are to account for the 'micrological texture' of the geopolitical and economic dimensions of neocolonial domination. '[We] must note how the staging of the world in representation—its scene of writing, its Darstellung—dissimulates the choice of and need for "heroes", paternal proxies, agents of power—Vertretung' (ibid., p. 279). Here Spivak sounds a useful cautionary note against a nationalist discourse that arrogates to itself the position of proxy (representative and speaking for) after constructing itself as portrait (representative and speaking as), erasing thereby the heterogeneity of the post-colonial subject.

But the problem remains. How does one represent difference without privileging the role of the Western intellectual or the post-colonial intellectual? How can we extend the meaning of representation while calling it into question? Meditating on the translation of repraesentatio in *Vorstellung*, *Darstellung*, representation, representation, and Reprasentation, Derrida points out that before we know 'how and what to translate by "representation", we must interrogate the concept of translation and of language which is so often dominated by the concept of representation' or a 'presupposition or the desire for an invariable identity of sense' (Derrida 1982: 302–03) Derrida asks if translation is 'of the same order as representation', or whether 'the so-called relation of translation or of substitution' escapes 'the orbit of representation' (ibid., pp. 297–98). I would argue that to rethink a practice of translation regulating and regulated by the horizon of metaphysics involves a use of translation that shatters the coherence of the 'original' and the 'invariable identity of sense'. This coherence is constituted in part through the operation of history and knowledge in the colonial context. To deconstruct these essentialising discourses, therefore, is to disrupt history in the Benjaminian sense. The Derridaean critique of 'representation' combines *Darstellung* and *Vertretung* in 'translation', not in any simple collapsing of the economic and the political but in a practice in which we constantly interrogate ourselves and our right to speak as and/or speak for.

The problematic of translation exists uneasily on the interface between the post-colonial context and post-structuralist theory.[2] For some, this is also a version of the decolonisation debate, and to use 'Western' theory in deconstructing colonial texts is to reproduce the conditions of neocolonialism. This attitude, which can be seen to be part of a nativist discourse,[3] seems to me to deny history in at least two ways: first, in arguing for a return to a lost purity, it not only employs a discredited realist epistemology but also ignores the pervasiveness of a colonial violence that renders impossible even the positing of a mythical uncontaminated space; second, in denouncing post-structuralism as Western, the nativist does not realise the extent to which *anti-colonial* struggles have intervened in changing the trajectory of Western thought by demanding a non-exploitative recognition of difference.[4] To accept the need for 'theory' in the post-colonial setting is not to uncritically accept the totalising narrative of global capitalism but to make the best use we can of the tools available for deconstructing that narrative and showing the infinitely varied inflections of the post-colonial condition. As I have argued elsewhere, the Western subject is constituted not only through a repression of the non-Western other but also through a marginalisation of its own otherness. Post-structuralism's attempt, therefore, to dismantle the hegemonic West from within is congruent with post-colonial praxis.

Literary theory contributes to that praxis through its focus on the rhetoric of representation. In '*The Resistance to Theory*', Paul de Man emphasises that 'what we call ideology is precisely the confusion of linguistic with natural reality, of reference with phenomenalism. It follows that, more than any other mode of inquiry, including economics, the linguistics of literariness is a powerful and indispensable tool in the unmasking of ideological aberrations, as well as a determining factor in accounting for their occurrence'. (De Man 1986: 11) de Man's meticulous unravelling of literary and philosophical texts, and his serious engagement with questions of ideology, representation and history provide to the post-colonial intellectual, even when s/he may not agree with de Man's conclusions, an important reminder of the salience of rhetorical structures in hegemonic discourses.

Walter Benjamin writes: 'An image is that in which the past and the present moment flash into a constellation.... The image that is read, I mean the image at the moment of recognition, bears to the highest degree the stamp of the critical, dangerous impulse that lies at the source of all reading' (Benjamin 1983–84: 1–40). Reading, because it is interventionist, is both critical and dangerous. Taking a cue from Derrida, I have argued that post-colonial interpretations or readings 'will not be readings of a hermeneutic or exegetic sort, but rather political interventions in the political rewriting of the text and its destination' (Derrida 1985: 32). Benjamin troped his theory of translation into a theory of writing history; the deferred epistemological desire of translation, the attempt to reach a realm of 'pure' language, was refigured as the need for political intervention, in the realm of world history. Reading then is a model for the historian as well as for the translator who chooses to read certain past 'texts' over others. The choices of the translator/historian, I suggest, are prompted by the *historicity* of these texts; they are constellations or conjunctions of past and present, they lay claim to us, as Benjamin would put it. They may also be emblematic of technologies of colonial power.

Retranslation and the Rewriting of History

The post-colonial desire to *retranslate* is linked to the desire to *rewrite* history. Rewriting is based on an act of reading, for translation in the post-colonial context involves what Benjamin calls 'citation' and not an 'absolute forgetting'. Hence there is no simple rupture with the past but a radical rewriting of it. To read existing translations against the grain is also to read colonial historiography from a post-colonial perspective, and a critic alert to the ruses of colonial discourse can help uncover what Walter Benjamin calls 'the second tradition', the history of resistance.[5] The act of remembering, as Bhabha has pointed out, 'is never a quiet act of introspection or retrospection'. Rather, it is 'a painful re-membering, a putting together of the dismembered past to make sense of the trauma of the present' (Bhabha 1986). This is not to say that the past can, simply, be made whole again. An Benjamin suggests in his ammetaphor of the amphora, the fragments that are pieced together in translation were fragments to begin with. Deconstructive practice shows us that we need, as Spivak indicates, 'provisional and intractable starting points in any investigative effort' (Spivak 1987: 180). It insists that 'in disclosing complicities the critic-as-subject is herself complicit with the object of her critique', and also acknowledges 'that its own discourse can never be adequate to its example'. The use of post-structuralism in the decolonising world, although fraught with the anxieties and desires of representation, brings to legibility areas of contradiction, difference and resistance.

Just as Benjamin's awareness that the Babelian performance could not, perhaps, be dominated by what Derrida calls 'theorization' appears to motivate his troping of translation into historiography, I turn from theorising to a translation of translations. To be able to reject the signifying systems of imperialism, we need 'a cartography of imperialist ideology more extensive than its address in the colonialist space' (ibid.). I turn, therefore, to an analysis of two post-colonial translations that, in very different but related ways, participate in the production of the Orient. I initiate here a practice of translation that is speculative, provisional and interventionist.

I shall provide here the 'original' in transliteration and three translations, the last one being my own. The exemplary poem or *vacana*[6] (Parry 1987: 45) is a fragment from a lengthy spiritual text 'produced' in south India in the 12th century but codified only in the 15th century. One of the reasons I choose a 'sacred' poem to retranslate is to emphasise that what Benjamin would call a 'profane' reading is of great significance in a context dominated by nationalist and nativist discourses that, in seemingly opposed but related ways, essentialise religions and thereby endorse communal violence. As Benjamin puts it: 'In every era the attempt must be made anew to wrest tradition away from a conformism that is about to overpower it' (TH, p. 255).

Transliteration

nimma tejava nodalendu heresari noduttiralu
satakoti suryaru mudidantirdudayya
mincina balliya sancava kande
enagidu sojigavayittu
Guhesvara, ninu jyotirlingavadare
upamisi nodaballavarillyya

Translation A

As I stepped back and looked
To see Thy light,
It seemed a hundred million suns
Came into sight;
A cluster of creeping lightnings I
With wonder saw.
O Guhesvara, if Thou become
The effulgent Linga, there be none
Thy glory to match
(Nandimath et al. 1960).

Translation B

Looking for your light,
I went out:
It was like the sudden dawn
Of a million million suns,
A ganglion of lightnings
for my wonder.
O Lord of Caves,
if you are light
There can be no metaphor
(Ramanujan 1973: 168)

Translation C

Drawing back
To look at your radiance
I saw
The dawning of a hundred million suns.
I gazed in wonder
At the lightning's creepers playing.
Guhesvara, if you are become the *linga* of light
Who can find your figuration (*My translation*).

A brief introduction to the proper name that is usually designated as the author of this text: Allama Prabhu was a 12th-century saint born in Balligave (in present day Karnataka state), a small village in one of the kingdoms of south India. Allama was one of the 'founders' of what became (and still is) a powerful sect devoted to the worship of the god Siva. Virasaivism launched an attack on the Vedic tradition of orthodox Hinduism, demanding the abolition of caste and gender distinction in the access to worship. Its saint-poets disregarded Sanskrit, the traditional religious language of Hinduism, in favour of the local language, Kannada. In addition, the *vacana* poets used for the first time the local 'non-standard' dialects of the areas they came from, whereas others poets of the time employed 'a highly stylized archaic language'.[7] For more than two hundred years, the *vacanas* circulated as part of a strong oral literature, until the Vijayanagar Empire revived Virasaivism in the 15th century and underwrote the codification of its sacred texts. So the text comes to us (even in Kannada) always already disarticulated, environmental-coded.

The Virasaiva movement, commonly known in Karnataka as the *vacana* movement, has been examined primarily by students of religion or of literature. Very little material exists on the sociocultural history of the period, and even that which is available is a welter of contradictory assertions. What appears certain, however, is that the Virasaivas or Lingayats came from different castes and occupations, and successfully challenged both priest and king, or temple and palace—the traditional centres of power. Although the influence of Jainism, Buddhism and Islam on the Virasaiva movement has been remarked upon, some writers see the Virasaiva movement as resulting in a reformed Brahminism strengthened by the adherence of different castes (Narayanan & Kesavan 1987: 45, 53).[8]

The Bhakti Movement (to give it its pan-Indian name) in general is seen by some historians as not really anti-Vedic, and ultimately as performing the function of incorporating the non-Brahmin, non-Aryan population into the Vedic hierarchy.[9] However, a retranslation of the *vacanas* can show, for example, that bhakti, or Virasaivism, was neither monolithic nor homogeneous.

Given the lack of material on medieval Karnataka, we can only ask a series of questions: Why is it that the *vacana* movement did not come into being until the 12th century in spite of Saivisim having been a strong religious current for four centuries before that? Did the movement present a radical challenge to the established religious and economic order, or did it actually strengthen feudalism and the Vedic tradition? What was the significance of the participation of people from different castes? How did this undermine existing notions of caste boundaries? Why was the notion of ritual purity/impurity abandoned by the Virasaivas? Did a great number of women really take part in religious discourse, or was it just a highly visible minority? What is the relationship between the Virasaiva movement and social transformation in the 12th century? What does the Lingayat consolidation of caste and socioeconomic power in later centuries tell us about the Virasaiva tradition's impulses? How do questions like these inform our contemporary translations of the *vacanas*? My inability to provide even provisional answers forces me to devise other strategies of interpretation. These strategies, however, are profoundly marked by the questions I have just raised.

Parameters of Reading and the Afterlife of Texts

The parameters of my reading/translation of Allama's text are provided, on the one hand, by the consistent and disarticulated imagery of Saivite mystic poetry and, on the other, by my 'theorisation' about translation in the post-colonial context. That is to say, on the one hand, by the notion of figure in Saivite poetry, which undoes the insistence on *linga*, meaning and representation; and, on the other hand, by the consideration of the afterlife, the *living* on of a text, and the task of the translator.

In his attempt to assimilate religious experience into everyday life, in his concern with propagating the new path to salvation,

Allama emerges in this fragment and others as a poet deeply interested in issues of articulation and representation. The fragment comes from *Sunyasampadane* (achievement/attainment of nothingness). A work written around Allama's life, *Sunyasampadane* incorporates Allama's *vacanas* as well as those composed by the other Virasaiva saints, and is presented as Allama's dialogue with those saints. It was first compiled by Sivagana Prasadi Mahadevayya in the early decades of the fifteenth century and included 1,012 *vacanas*. The edition in use today is based on the fourth compilation, made by Gulura Suddhaviranarya, and includes 1,543 *vacanas* (Narayanan & Kesavan 1987: 45, 53).[10]

The fragment we read belongs to Allama's 'spiritual autobiography'. It is part of a dialogue with a saint-to-be in which Allama tries to convey a sense of the 'ultimate' experience, the experience of the 'void', or *sunya*. The eye of god (Siva) has opened up the eye of fire in the soul of Allama's foot, and Allama sings praises of this eye, calling it 'radiance', 'lightening', 'a hundred million suns'.

If we are to have a privileged 'figure' for this text, it is the *linga*, which in fact offers itself as the 'originary' figure for the entire corpus of Saivaite poetry. The *linga* is/is not Siva or God; it is a form for formlessness, a shape for shapelessness. It is an attempt to articulate that which cannot be articulated in the mystic experience, and in the the poem-fragment it eventually turns out to be an articulation of a disarticulation.[11]

The thematisation of light in Allama's poetry is always bound up with the possibility of articulation. Images of light are always connected here to those of sight. In the short space of six lines, Allama uses 'look' or 'see' three times; and 'light' appears five times (radiance, suns, dawning, lighting, the *linga*). In Allama's spiritual biography there is a description of his meeting with the saint Animisa (literally, 'one who does not blink', that is, a god; one who, therefore, sees steadily). Animisa transmits the unutterable experience to Allama's heart through his eye alone. A single look transforms Allama, and the *linga* on Animisa's palm is transferred to Allama's.

Allama has now experienced the void, and is in a state of *Jivanmukta* (free from life), which means to live in the world and be out of it at the same time, like 'light in a crystal bowl'. There are a number of light images in this part of *Sunyasampadane*: burning charcoal, lighted camphor, lamps, fire, the refractive crystal. Allama has become form, though formless; he is body, though bodiless.

He is *sunyamurthi*, void taken on form, image or figure of the void. Jangama, the saint, is himself *linga*, proclaims Allama. *Nodi kudi saiveragada/sukhavanenendupamisuvenayya, guhesvara*? asks Allama. 'How can I figure this joy of looking at and mingling with you?' He adds, *Nimma suluhina sogasanupamisabaradu*! 'I should not/ought not to figure the splendor of your passing'. *Suluhu* can mean 'motion', 'turning', 'going' or 'passing'. It shades off into 'glimpse', 'transitory perception', and eventually into 'trace'. 'I ought not to figure the splendor of your trace'. *Suluhu* can also mean 'sign'.

The traces left by Allama's experience are always already there in the conception of this kind of experience in the bhakti or devotional tradition. The failure to find figures is an expected failure of language, a failure of articulation because of the disarticulation at the centre of what demands articulation. Allama cannot finally believe that his figure represents his experience. 'The undoing of the representational and iconic function of figuration by the play of the signifier' (De Man 1979: 61) is indicated by the *linga* (neither signified nor signifier, but that which can move with ease from one position to the other), which makes a mockery of all attempts to figure its glory. These attempts are seductive insofar as they lead us to believe that we have somehow captured in language the shadows of the cave (Guhesvara, Allama's god, is lord of the cave). But the movement of Allama's poem is a step beyond 'traditional conceptions of figuration as modes of representation', and is therefore a movement toward 'the undoing and erasure of the figure'. The arrest of articulation (recalling Derrida's speculations on Maurice Blanchot's *L'Arret de mort*) is actually a triumph of articulation, for a *jangama* is shown to be the *linga*, and death (or Benjamin's mortification) or attainment of the void is seen as survival or a living on.

Economies of Translation and Textual Difference

Let us return to the different translations of Allama's poem, keeping in mind Derrida's comment that any translation contaminates the text with meanings, which it imports in turn and which rework the text. As he suggests, a text in translation trails more than one language behind it (Derrida 1979: 76). Because the poem has what Benjamin calls translatability, because it is not untranslatable, although it presses for constant deformation and disfiguration, there is an economy of translation—which does not exclude the political—that regulates the flow of medieval Kannada into modern English.[12]

My contention is that Translations A and B fail to comprehend the economy of translation in this poem because they fail to understand 'the specific significance inherent in the original which manifests itself in its translatability' (Benjamin 1969). Attempting to assimilate Saivite poetry to the discourse of Christianity or of a post-Romantic New Criticism, these translators reproduce some of the 19th-century native responses to colonialism. Accepting the premises of a universalist history, they try to show how the *vacanas* are always already Christian, or 'modernist', and therefore worthy of the West's attention. Their enterprise is supported by the asymmetry between English and Kannada created and enforced by colonial and neo-colonial discourse. This is an asymmetry that allows translators to simplify the text in a predictable direction, toward English and Judeo-Christian tradition and away from the multiplicity of indigenous languages and religions, which have to be homogenised before they can be translated.

The first Western-style dictionary of Kannada was prepared in 1817 by William Carey, a polyglot colleague of William Ward and one of the most prolific of the Serampore missionaries (Benjamin 1969: 71). The first translators of the *vacanas* were Christian missionaries in the 1860s (Carey 1817), attracted to Saivite poetry, according to Ramanujan, by its 'monotheism', which 'lashes out in an atmosphere of animism and polytheism'.[13] This is, by the way, the same paradigm that allows James Mill to differentiate Islam, which he calls monotheistic, from the barbaric polytheism of Hinduism. The missionaries are said to have made sarcastic references to the failure of the Virasaiva saints' prophecies that they would return from the 'west', for they, the Christians, had instead arrived. Even according to the terms of the Saivites' own texts, they argued, the Christians represented a more evolved religion. We see here one of the typical moves of a colonial discourse that translates indigenous religious texts, castigates the natives for not being faithful to the tenets of their (translated) religion, then claims that the native religion is incapable of sustaining its devotees, and proposes 'conversion' as a path to salvation. The missionaries even speculated that 'bhakti attitudes were the result of early Christian influence' (Ramanujan 1973: Introduction, 27), another move that seamlessly accommodates the idea of a former Golden Age and the present fallen, degraded state of the 'Hindoos'.

Both European and Indian commentators persist in discussing Virasaivism in terms of Puritanism and Protestantism, suggesting that the poems of the Virasaiva saints are part of a Pilgrims' Progress. Speaking of the fact that the Virasaiva saints came from all classes, castes and trades, Ramanujan adds in parenthesis "like Bunyan, the tinker" (ibid., p. 27, note 4). Ramanujan's version of the *vacanas* emphasises that they are 'deeply personal' poems, that they use the language of 'personal conversion', that they embody the conflict of 'real persons'. There is a corresponding stress on the similarities between Virasaivism and European Protestantism: the privileging of 'individual', 'original', and 'direct' experience; 'monotheism' and 'evangelism'; and distrust of 'mediators' such as priests (ibid., pp. 54). This combination of emphases allows Ramanujan to produce a post-Romantic translation of Allama's *vacana* that presents it as a 'quest for the unmediated vision', (ibid., pp. 53–55), a project deconstructed so skilfully in Paul de Man's 'The Rhetoric of Temporality'. This reading of Ramanujan's, I argue, cannot account for the instability of the 'original'.

Translations A and B both translate *teja*, the first significant noun in the *vacana*, as 'light'. I translate the word as 'radiance', because the poem is a movement toward the ostensible simplicity of light. Allama goes from 'radiance' to 'hundred million suns' and 'lighting' before he approaches *jyotis*, or 'light' in the fifth line. The word 'effulgent' in Translation A is superfluous for this reason. We cannot, however, gloss over the fact that *jyotis* is a Sanskrit word embedded in the Kannada poem, and that *jyotirlinga* refers to a special kind of *linga*, functioning therefore as a figure of condensation. Translation B has 'light' for both *teja* and *jyotis*, since Ramanujan claims that Allama begins with a traditional metaphor of light and denies it at the end of the *vacana*. In the first place, the 'original' does not suggest any such denial of light. Second, it seems to be in Ramanujan's interests to confer on the *vacana* a circularity of movement, or rather to suggest that the Saivite poets tell cyclical stories like those narrated by Ramanujan himself when he writes of protest against the 'establishment' followed by its ultimate institutionalisation, which appears to have for its premise a metaphysical concept of history, associated, as Derrida points out, 'with a linear scheme of the unfolding of presence, where the line relates the final presence to the originary presence according to the straight line or the circle' (*Of Grammatology*, p. 85). The concept of representation underwriting this notion of history participates, as I have argued, in colonial practices of subjectification.

Heresari in the first line is translated as 'stepped back' in A and as 'went out' in B. The dictionaries do not list the meaning provided by B, but instead list 'drew back' or 'drawing back' to 'stepped back'. I use 'drawing back' since it seems to more clearly indicate the context where Allama looks at the eye on the sole of his foot. Why does B use 'went out' almost completely contradicting the sense of *heresari*? One possibility is that B mistakes *here* (back) for *hora* (outside).[14] Or else, the translator is playing a variation on the theme of the linear 'unfolding of presence', suggesting that it is only by a 'going out' that Allama can see the figurative suns and lightning; in fact, the poet is made to go out 'looking for your light'. The notion of 'drawing back' in order to see goes so much against his sense of what the poem means that he refuses to grant to the poem what it is saying. *Balli* refers to creeper, as in flowering vine, so the 'cluster' in A is superfluous and the 'ganglion' in B improbable. *Mincina* qualifies *balli* and is adjectival, referring to the lightning. A key word that both A and B leave out of their translations here is *sancu* (*mincina ballya sancu*: the lightning's creepers' play)—'flash' or 'play'. The play of signifiers sets in motion all the images of light in the *vacana*, and B responds by removing the verbs 'gazed' and 'playing' from the English version, setting in their place the word 'ganglion', taking the 'play' from the realm of meaning and placing it firmly within the nervous system of the individual body.

Guhesvara is the name of Allama's god and remains untranslated in A as well as in C. It is a name that recurs in every *vacana* that Allama wrote, and force of repetition allows it to function as a unique proper name that is not obscured by simple translation. Given that colonialism's violence erases or distorts beyond recognition (as witnessed in innumerable colonial texts) the names of the colonised, it seems important *not* to translate proper names in a post-colonial or decolonising practice. Ramanujan's rationale for translating Guhesvara is oddly significant. He argues that since the god's names are 'partly Sanskrit' (interestingly, both *Guhe* and *esvara* would be of Sanskrit origin), and since 'the transparent Kannada' ensures that the Sanskrit is 'never opaque or distant for long', the etymologies quicken in the poem and demand the translation of 'attributive proper names into literal English'. In attempting to smooth over the heterogeneous text, Ramanujan assigns to Kannada, and by implication to English, the ability to make and the transparent.

I have already suggested that Translation A's use of an adjective in place of a noun, 'effulgent' instead of 'light', does not work within the economy of the poem. B's version—'if you are light'—ignores the conception of *linga*, which is not only crucial to this *vacana* but also to the entire Virasaiva tradition. Ramanujan's refusal to translate or inscribe the *linga* is, therefore, a refusal to interrogate the most significant image in Allama's text. My version translates *jyotis* as 'light' and retains *linga* to complicate the notion of light as signification, since *linga* may be said to function in the *vacana* as the figure of dissemination that authorises the use of 'figuration' in the last line.

Translation B's trick of making verbs disappear is matched by its habit of constantly reducing and simplifying them. In the penultimate line, for example, *adare* ('if... are' in the sense of 'to be' and also 'if... to become') is turned into 'are', and in the last line, *nodaballa* ('find', 'to be capable of') is translated simply as 'be'. Translation A, on the other hand, retains only the sense of 'become'. In comparison, my version uses a somewhat archaic phrase 'if you are become', in order to be able to translate both meanings, 'be' and 'become'.

Trying to find a suitable translation for the structuring statement in the *vacana, ninu jyotirlingavadare/upamisinodaballa-varillayya*, A takes the easy way out by turning *upama* into a negation (*an-upama*) to mean 'incomparable' or 'matchless', so that 'there be none/Thy glory to match'. This misses the problem entirely, for the question is not one of finding other gods or mortals to 'match' the glory of Guhesvara, but one of finding someone capable of representing the *linga*. *Upama* is figure of speech, simile, metaphor, never merely or simply 'metaphor', as Translation B has it. B in fact turns the last line (which I translate as 'Who can find your figuration') into 'there can be no metaphor', thereby reinforcing its conception of the circularity of the *vacana*: 'Sometimes in the *vacanakara*'s [the author of the *vacana*'s] quest for the unmediated vision, there comes a point when language, logic and metaphor are not enough: at such points, the poet begins with a striking traditional metaphor and denies it at the end'. (Ramanujan 1973: Introduction, 47) Ramanujan refuses to acknowledge that the poet-saint does not deny the need for figuration. He merely recognises its ineffectualness, marking thereby its possibility/impossibility, like that of representation or translation.

The deliberate roughness of my version of the *vacana* allows the text to 'affect', as Benjamin would have it, the language into which it is being translated, interrupting the 'transparency' and smoothness of a totalising narrative like that of Ramanujan. Seeing 'literalness' as an 'arcade', I privilege the word over the sentence, marking thereby what Derrida calls in 'Des Tours de Babel' a 'displacement' from the syntagmatic to the paradigmatic level, and inserting my translation into the attack against homogenising and continuous narratives.

The strategies of containment typical discourse operate in Translations A and B through the diction and 'absences' in the former, and the insistence on the 'light' motif and metaphor in the latter. The emphasis on metaphor seems to be 'interpreted and over determined' here as 'a representation of representation'. (Ramanujan 1973: 52) The use of 'figuration' and the reinscription of *linga* in my version is part of an attempt to resist containment, to re-mark textuality, to dislodge or disturb the fixation on any one term or meaning, to substitute translation for representation in the strict sense. The *linga* functions as a 'supplement' in my translation, exposing polysemy to what Derrida has called the law of dissemination, and the last line—'Who can find your figuration'—is neither a question nor an affirmation, but both at the same time.

Conclusion

This essay has shown how the *vacanas* 'claim' the post-colonial translator by problematising the issue of representation, which is crucial in a context where nationalist myths of identity and unity are collapsing. It seems more urgent than ever to be aware of the instability of the 'original', which can be meticulously uncovered through the practice of translation. The arbitrariness of what is presented as 'natural' can be deconstructed by the translator or her/his alter ego, the critical historiographer. The drive to challenge hegemonic representations of the non-Western world need not be seen as a wish to oppose the 'true' other to the 'false' one presented in colonial discourse. Rather, since post-colonials already exist 'in translation', our search should not be for origins or essences but for a richer complexity, a complication of our notions of the 'self', a more densely textured understanding of who 'we' are. It is here that translators can intervene to inscribe heterogeneity, to warn against myths of purity, to show origins as always already fissured. Translation, from being a 'containing' course, is transformed into a disruptive, disseminating one. The deconstruction initiated by re-translation opens up a post-colonial space as it brings 'history' to legibility.

Notes

1. We must remember here that the notion of culture itself evolved into a tool for nation-building during the period of European Imperialism.
2. For stimulating explorations of this idea, see Dhareshwar (1990: 231–50) Tharu (1987: 157–86).
3. The suspicion of the post-structuralist theory also marks the responses of sections of non-nativist 'left' which do not want to give up their versions of the history-as-progress narrative.
4. Descombes suggests that the 1960s talk in France about the end of philosophy indicated a 'philosophical examination of conscience' that was 'contemporaneous with the disappearance of the European colonial empires (1962, the end of the Algerian war)'.
5. See Guha (1983), which demonstrates brilliantly how a post-colonial historiographer can construct a tale of resistance through a new reading of texts by British officials engaged in suppressing uprisings by Santal tribals in north eastern India in the early part of the 19th century.
6. Pronounced *vachana*.
7. By far the most though-provoking Kannada book on *vacana* poetry is Kalgudi (1988). See also Murthy (1975).
8. I am grateful to Gauri Dharampal for pointing out that the images of light, the void and the cave, which are crucial to an understanding of Virasaiva poetry are typical images in Vedic texts as well.

9. See Thapar (1966, 1: 216) for the influences on Virasaivism, and Dumont (1980: 190) for the notion of Brahminism being strengthened by a movement like that of the Virasaivas. The problem with Dumont's theory is that it seems to rest on the same kind of essentialised and unchanging Hinduism and Brahminism that we find depicted in Orientalist texts.
10. For more information about the different editions, see the translators' preface to Nandimath et al., 1960.
11. Although Western commentators have suggested that the *linga* is a phallic symbol, there is no indication in any of the surviving *vacanas* that this was the case. Ramanujan explains that the *linga* is 'the only symbol of Siva' and is 'to be worn inseparably on his body by the devotee' (Ramanujan 1973: 42). Female devotees of Siva wear the *linga* too.
12. Medieval Kannada is comprehensible to a speaker of modern Kannada. A discussion of this and of how the punctuation, syntax and vocabulary of present-day Kannada have been affected by English, is beyond the scope of this chapter.
13. I have not been able to locate these early translations of the *vacanas*. It would be interesting to speculate what direct or indirect influence they might have had on the diction of Translation A.
14. One of the Kannada versions available has *herasari* for *heresari*; this could be one of the source of the confusion.

References

Benjamin, Walter, 1969. 'The Task of the Translator' in Hannah Arendt (ed.), Harry Zohn (trans.) *Illuminations*. New York: Schocken Books.

———, 1983–84. 'Theoretics of Knowledge, Theory of Progress'. trans. L. Hafrey and R. Sieburth. *Philosophical Forum* vol. 15, nos. 1–2, emphasis added.

———, quoted in Bhabha's foreword to the 1986 English edition of Fanon's *Black Skins, White Masks*, p. 11.

Carey, 1817. *A Grammar of the Karnata Language*. Serampore: Mission Press.

De Man, Paul, 1979. 'Shelley Disfigured' in Harold Bloom et al. (eds) *Deconstruction and Criticism*. New York: Seabury Press.

———, 1986. 'The Resistance to Theory,' in *The Resistance to Theory*. Minneapolis: University of Minnesota Press.

Derrida, Jacques, 'Sending: On Representation'. *Social Research*, vol. 49, no. 2, pp. 302–03.

———, 1979. 'Living On: Border Lines' in *Deconstruction and Criticism*, Harold Bloom et al., (eds) New York: Seabury Press.

———, 1981. *Positions*. trans. Alan Bass. Chicago: University of Chicago Press.

———, 1985. 'Otobiographies', in *The Ear of the Other*. trans. Peggy Kamuf. New York: Schocken Books.

———, 'Sending: On Representation,' p. 299.

Descombes, Vincent, 1980. *Modern French Philosophy*, trans. L. Scott-Fox and J.M. Harding. Cambridge: Cambridge University Press.

Dhareshwar, Vivek, 1990. 'The Predicament of Theory' in Martin Kreiswirth and Mark A. Cheetham (eds) *Theory between the Disciplines*. Ann Arbor: University of Michigan Press.

Dumont, Louis and **Gulati, Basia**, 1980. *Homo Hierarchicus: The Caste System and its Implications*, trans. by Mark Sainsbury, Louis Dumont and Basia Gulati. Chicago: University of Chicago Press.

Fanon, 1967, 1986. *The Wretched of the Earth*. trans. Constance Farrington. Hamondsworth: Penguin Books; New York: Grove Press.

Guha, Ranjit, 1983. 'The Prose of Counter-Insurgency', in *Subaltern Studies II: Writings on South Asian History and Society*. New Delhi: Oxford University Press.

Kalgudi, Basavaraja, 1988. *Madhyakaaleena Bhakti Matthu Anubhaava Sahitya haagaoo Charitrika Pranje*. Bangalore: Kannada Sahitya Parishat.

Murthy, M., Chidananda, 1975. *Vacana Sahitya*. Bangalore: Bangalore University Press.

Nandimath, S.C., Menezes, L.M.A., and **Hiremath, R.C.**, 1960. *Sunyasampadane* (ed. and trans.), Dharwar: Karnatak University 1:240. Reprinted by kind permission of Karnatak University.

Narayanan, M.G.S. and **Kesavan, Veluthat**, 1987. 'Bhakti Movement in South India' in S.C. Malik (ed.) *Indian Movements: Some Aspects of Dissent, Protest and Reform*. Simla: Institute for Advanced Study.

Parry, Benita, 1987. 'Problems in Current Theories of Colonial Discourse'. *Oxford Literary Review*, vol. 9, nos. 1–2.

Ramanujan, A.K., (trans.), 1973, *Speaking of Siva*, Harmondsworth: Penguin Books.

———, 1973. Introduction to *Speaking of Siva*. Harmondsworth: Penguin Books.

Spivak, Gayatri C., 1987a. 'Can the Subaltern Speak?' in Cary Nelson and Lawrence Grossberg (eds) *Marxism and the Interpretation of Culture*. Urbana: University of Illinois Press, Cited hereafter as CSS.

———, 1987b. Translator's foreword to 'Draupadi,' by Mahasweta Devi, in *In Other Worlds: Essays in Cultural Politics*. London: Methuen, 1987.

Thapar, Romila, 1966. *A History of India*. Harmondsworth: Penguin Books.

Tharu, Susie, 1987. 'Tracing Savitri's Pedigree', in Kumkum Sangari (ed.), The Politics of the Possible. *Cultural Critique*, no. 7, pp. 157–86.

Trevelyan, 1838. *On the Education of the People of India*. London: Longman, Orme, Brown, Green & Longmans.

2. Historical Perspectives

Five

Classical Idiom: Translating Sanskrit Critical Terms

KRISHNA RAYAN

Nearly all of the more important Sanskrit literary theory was produced around the 11th century or earlier, with the result that finding equivalents in English for its terminology presents certain problems. One problem which is not directly relevant to translation and is probably more apparent than real has been described thus by Owen Barfield, now a little-remembered critic:

> *The meanings of the fundamental terms used by Plato and Aristotle are different from their established meanings in our civilization, and to avoid the error of interpreting Plato and Aristotle in the light of subsequent thought and getting them all wrong, it is necessary to unthink our meanings and to feel, by poetic imaginative sympathy, how their terms came into being out of Greek consciousness. The meaning of such a term is not deducible from the context or expressible in definitions and the like. It is only indirectly expressible in metaphor and simile. That is to say, it is suggestible; for meaning itself can never be conveyed from one person to another; words are not bottles; every individual must intuit meaning for himself, and the function of the*

poetic is to mediate such intuition by suitable suggestion. (Barfield 1928: 132–33)

In the first place, the chasm assumed here between ancient Greek civilisation and modern Western civilisation is illusory, because the latter is after all sprung from Hellenic-Hebraic origins. Similarly, we might argue that there is recognisable continuity from Bharata's and Anandavardhana's civilisation to our own today. Further, although a word is set up as a technical term by 'fixing' its meaning by means of definition, its becoming modified 'in the light of subsequent thought', as Barfield puts it, is more or less inevitable, so that being obsessed with the original meaning serves no purpose. In any case, the solution proposed, i.e., accessing this meaning through intuition, is quite impractical. When translating *catharsis* into Sanskrit or *rasa* into current Greek or English, the deciding factor is not what Aristotle or Bharata meant in their time but what they mean to us today.

The second problem is: Can the term 'suggestion', for instance, which is used by Barfield above and is common enough in Western criticism, be accepted as the equivalent of *dhvani* in Sanskrit? Most comparatists are agreed that it can. Yet the two terms are not identical in meaning. 'Suggestion' as understood in 19th and 20th-century theory has to do with polysemy, undecidability and indeterminacy, while *dhvani* signifies unstated but definable meaning. As S.K. De puts it:

> *We must not mistake suggestion to be a form of quiet hinting, or of absolute silence, such as we find in some modern poetic mystics, or that particular train of thought which holds that all things have their being in the unexpressed or resolve themselves into the indeterminable. Sanskrit poetry does not aim at leaving the unexpressed to be darkly gathered, nor does the theory of poetics regard it as indeterminate.* (De1925: 221).

It is because the similarities between 'suggestion' and *dhvani* so overwhelmingly outweigh the divergences which De speaks of that it is reasonable to say that *dhvani* very strongly resembles 'suggestion', that, in a manner of speaking, it *is* 'suggestion'. Thus when we translate *dhvani* as 'suggestion', we are introducing a metaphor; we are, that is to say, asserting that the terms have a high degree of similarity amounting to near-identity.

Purists, it is true, reject this procedure, and by focusing on dissimilarities, they perceive distortion where what is in fact being effected is a maximally close approximation almost tantamount to identification. A metaphor, so created, establishes itself and in course of time extends and enlarges the original concept. Knowledge thus grows through metaphoric activity enabling concepts to cross the borders of languages, disciplines and cultures. If, for instance, the social sciences have achieved so much expansion, differentiation and sophistication today, it is mostly through acquisition of concepts from the physical sciences by metaphoric action involving the incorporation or 'translation' of terms.

However, the disparity between the hinterlands of connotations and associations of the two terms involved in the translation act continues to survive it and remains suspect in the eyes of pedants as a source of error and distortion. I would hold that it is these very 'inaccuracies' that extend and refine knowledge on both sides of the fence by adding to or honing the content of the two concepts that have been brought together. Thus once you translate *sringara* as 'love', the Sanskrit term begins to enrich itself by attracting the semantic nuances, extensions and cultural ramifications of the English term, so that the word *sringara* is never the same again; you cannot read or hear it without awareness of the traditions and mores clustering around the word 'love'—courtly love in medieval and Renaissance literatures, Romantic love in the 19th century and the explicit presentation of sex in the 20th century. The English word 'love' for its part experiences a comparable agglutination and becomes host to the *leitmotifs* of several kinds of Sanskrit poetry—that of 'love-in-union', of 'love-in-separation' and that of liaison and guilty intrigue. Even more widely, and more importantly, in the modern Indian languages, the theme of profane love as a metaphor for sacred love in Bhakti poetry and the theme of romantic love in the *ghazals* enrich the connotations of both 'love' in English and *sringara* in Sanskrit.

If the translation of literary terms has these positive, enabling potentialities, it also has its problems and constraints. These problems are indeed the main concern of this essay, but as the essay is a relatively short one, it would be realistic to limit its scope by offering case studies of four or five major terms in Sanskrit literary theory to serve as examples of the risks and rewards of translation. These terms are *rasa, vibhavadis, dhvani, laksana* and, very briefly, *vakrokti*.

Rasa and *Vibhavadis*

The two most important concepts in Sanskrit literary theory are *rasa*, which is the end, and *dhvani*, which is the means to it. *Dhvani* I have mentioned briefly already and will return to, but what is *rasa*? As an answer, K. Krishnamoorthy offers an awesome string of possible translations: '…sap, essence, taste, mercury, poison, emotion, interest, mood, feeling, passion, sentiment, enjoyment…' (in Narasimhaiah 1982: 70). The three terms in this list which are most directly relevant to literary theory, and also the most widely used, are 'sentiment', 'mood' and 'emotion'.

'Sentiment', which is seldom used today, has nevertheless had the longest history in translated Sanskrit theory. A.B. Keith, for instance, referred to 'the interrelations of the sentiments, their possible combinations, their harmonies and conflicts' (Keith 1924: 325). Pravasjivan Chaudhury said: 'the eight or nine sentiments only denote classes—the particular shade of a sentiment expressed is uniquely determined by the expression' (Chaudhury 1953: Chapter 1). And K. Krishnamoorthy added a cautionary note: 'When the sentiment is presented *principally* (viz., by suggestion), compound words should be avoided' (Krishnamoorthy 1955: 66). Manomohan Ghosh, translator of Bharata's *Natyasastra*, which was the first to enunciate the concept, also used the same equivalent (Ghosh 1967). Despite this impressive pedigree, 'sentiment' as a translational equivalent of *rasa* has now fallen into disuse, not only because the zeitgeist of the late 20th century militated against it, but also presumably because it had been realised that it was misleading to equate these two terms. 'Sentiment' denotes an emotional tendency or view or attitude that the reader, in a sense, brings to the text, whereas *rasa* is a for-the-nonce *etat d'ame* either induced in the reader/spectator by the written/performed text or—to mention two alternative explanations no longer accepted—'expressed' by the author or 'contained' in the text.

Ananda Coomaraswamy, the Sri Lankan savant, translated *rasa* as 'aesthetic emotion' and *bhava* as 'mood' (Coomaraswamy 1948: 53). Daniel Ingalls, the Harvard Sanskritist, turned this around and translated *rasa* as 'mood' and *bhava* as 'basic emotion' (Ingalls 1965: 11–17)! *Bhavas* are of two kinds—*sthayibhavas* (corresponding to the eight or more *rasas*) which in *Indian Theories of Meaning* (1963) K. Kunjunni Raja translates as 'permanent moods', and *vyabhicharibhavas* which he translates as 'transient moods' (in Seturaman 1992: 302). 'Mood' in current use denotes a state of mind which is subject to swings and would therefore correspond to *vyabhicharibhavas* but not to *sthayibhavas;* and it does not seem to correspond at all to *rasa,* despite Ingall's provocative switching around the translations of *bhava* and *rasa*.

Coomaraswamy's more inoffensive use of 'aesthetic emotion' as the equivalent of *rasa* is shared by Kunjunni Raja (ibid.: 288). However, we have here an illustration of the dangers of matching technical terms from disparate cultures. While Coomaraswamy's use of the phrase is explicable both in terms of the period in which he wrote and his own interests which were primarily in art criticism and cross-cultural aesthetics, it is easy to see in hindsight how inappropriate his translational choice for *rasa* was. 'Aesthetic emotion' was a concept popularised by Clive Bell, Roger Fry, T.E. Hulme and others in the early decades of the 20th century. They defined it, in Clive Bell's words, as 'a peculiar emotion provoked by works of art' (Bell 1914: 25) by virtue of what they called the 'significant form' which works of art possess; and they maintained that 'significant form' was itself defined by 'the rather uncommon emotion which it causes'(!). This circular definition was fatal to the concept, and although support was available to it from Freud's theory of aesthetic pleasure, I.A. Richards had little difficulty in rejecting it as 'a caprice of the fancy'. And even if the concept were still in business, it would in any case, I think, be inaccurate to equate it with *rasa*. 'Aesthetic emotion' is a unique emotion roused by the non-representational features of a work of art, 'lines and colours... certain forms and relations of forms...' (ibid.). *Rasa*, on the other hand, is the product of representations in art of causes and effects in life and is differentiated into eight or more emotions.

In the very first chapter of *Studies in Comparative Aesthetics*, Pravasjivan Choudhury translates *rasa* as 'sentiment'; in Chapter

Six, however, he equates it with 'emotive meaning' (Chaudhury 1953). It is true enough that the reader's emotional response is the meaning of a work. But to call the response 'emotive meaning' can be misleading, because this again is a term established in quite another cultural context by I.A. Richards as the opposite of 'referential meaning'. 'Emotive meaning' thus corresponds, if at all, less to *rasa* and more to *dhvani* or *vyangyartha* (i.e., suggested meaning, which is often emotion-related) as opposed to *abhidha* or *vachyartha* (which is unstated, lexical, logical meaning) than to *rasa*.

Writing in 1972, I had said: '...*rasa* can be described as the response to art... it is emotion objectified...' (Rayan 1972: 35). I have repeated this translation of *rasa* more recently: 'The emotional response is the meaning of the work.' As Abhinavagupta says, *kavyartho rasah* (Rayan 1991: 18). The assumption that *rasa* is *kavigata* (located in the author) does not hold any more, as expressionism has been given up; and the other assumption that *rasa* is *kavyagata* (contained in the work) ceased to be tenable when New Criticism was superseded. *Rasa* today is accepted as the *sahrdaya*'s (i.e., the competent reader's) affective reaction to the work. 'Emotional response' is clearly thus the equivalent term for *rasa*.

A *rasa*, which is a subjective state, is evoked by its phenomenal equivalents, the sensible constituents of the written or performed text. These have been named *vibhavas* (conventionally translated as 'determinants') and *anubhavas* ('ensuants' or 'consequents'). *Vibhavas*, in turn, are divided into *uddipanavibhavas* ('excitants') and *alambanavibhavas* ('attractants'). These conventional translations are well meant and, I suppose, literally accurate, but what is important is how the assembly of *vibhavas*, etc., (describable as *vibhavadis* or *rasasamagri*) generates the *rasa*. In order to explain the process, *vibhavadis* has to be equated with a term in English.

When T.S. Eliot's famous phrase 'objective correlative' was first set beside *vibhavadis*, it brought into focus the whole operation in which 'the external facts, which must terminate in sensory experience', i.e., 'a set of objects, a situation, a chain of events', evoke the emotion of which they are the equivalents (Eliot 1932: 145). A.K. Ramanujan (1985) proposes 'correlative object' as a term that would apply where the objective equivalents are not those found by the poet, as envisaged by Eliot, but those given in the culture. But perhaps the most accurate translation of *vibhavadis* is the simplest—just 'objects'. The relation between emotions and their objects has been, for a long time, an important inquiry in Western philosophy, and 'objects' seems to me to define for non-Sanskritists the content of *vibhavadis* more clearly than any other term can.

Dhvani, Laksana and *Vakrokti*

The emergence of the *rasa* from its *vibhavadis* is not by the operation of causation, nor is it by inference or reference, but is akin to the emergence of complex subtextual meaning from an utterance by a process of loose, variable signification. Rich unspoken meaning, which is the product of this process, is called *dhvani*, and the process itself is also called *dhvani*. The literal sense of *dhvani* is 'sound', which tempted Daniel Ingalls to translate it as 'overtone', on the grounds that, being a technical term in music, it would be closer to the Sanskrit word. The same sonic factor made Krishnamoorthy translate one kind of *dhvani*, i.e., *samlaksyakrama*, as 'resonance'. But *dhvani* really has more to do with meaning than sound.

I.A. Richards' concepts of referential meaning and emotive meaning correspond roughly to *abhidha* and *dhvani*. Pravasjivan Choudhury, in 'Emotive Meaning in the Light of Indian Aesthetics' (Choudhury 1953: Chapter 6), equates *dhvani* with, but does not translate it as, emotive meaning. His translation for *dhvani* is 'suggested meaning' or quite simply 'suggestion'.

Suggestion is one of the longest-standing critical terms in English, its first observed occurrence being three hundred years ago in Dryden's comment on Virgil who, he said, 'loves to suggest a truth indirectly' (Dryden 1697). It is not known when and by whom *dhvani* was first translated as suggestion, but whoever did so was not just translating a word but was joining the *dhvani* theory, by harnessing the harmonising, unitive force of metaphor, as pointed out earlier, to the pre-Symbolist, Symbolist and post-Symbolist theorising in the West by Edgar Allan Poe, Mallarmé and others.

In addition to *abhidha* and *dhvani*, a third kind of signification was assumed, namely, *laksana*. S.K. De translated *laksana* as 'the transfer of sense' (De 1925). Krishnamoorthy translated it as 'indication' (which does not tell us much) but also offered a twofold translation or description of it as 'secondary sense' and 'metaphorical attribution of identity' (Krishnamoorthy 1955). K.C. Pandey offered the translation 'secondary meaning' (Pandey 1959), and Kunjunni Raja 'secondary metaphorical sense' (Raja 1963). Yet I am afraid none of these translations are satisfactory, chiefly because the word 'secondary' does not define the nature or function of *laksana*.

Krishnamoorthy and Kunjunni Raja, however, seem to have a sense of the dual nature of *laksana*. *Laksana* consists in the transfer of meaning and has two forms, depending on the relation between the primary and the secondary referent. In *gauni laksana* it is a relation of similarity; in *suddha laksana*, it is relations other than similarity. The two can be translated as 'metaphor' and 'metonymy', thus equating the Sanskrit dichotomy with the well-known pair of contraries defined by Roman Jakobson. Thus Russian Formalism/ Structuralism and the *laksana* theory are brought together.

Likewise, when *vakrokti* was translated as 'deviation', Russian Formalism and Kuntaka's theory were brought in line with each other. It is significant that Kuntaka in *Vakroktijivita* on the one hand and, on the other hand, Jan Mukarovsky in *On Poetic Language* (1976), not to mention Geoffrey Leech in *A Linguistic Guide to English Poetry* (1979), developed very similar lines of thought on how deviation operates on the phonetic/phonological, lexical/ semantic and syntactic/grammatical levels.

Again, whoever translated *anukrti* as mimesis or imitation joined the poetics of Plato and Aristotle to Bharata's, and whoever translated *aucitya* as 'decorum' joined this dominant concept in Latin, Renaissance and Neoclassical criticism to the expositions by Ksemendra and others.

Conclusion

In this essay, it has been my submission that in such theoretically informed translations from the Sanskrit, what is achieved is not just a superficial or arbitrary pairing of concepts from different systems but some success in taking important insights from within a closed body of theory and making them accessible to non-Sanskritists by availing of existing correspondences between two formulations. Indeed, it is not often that formulations rub shoulders thus. Usually, one makes do with straightforward run-of-the-mill, off-the-shelf equivalents: for example, 'figure of speech' for *alamkara*, or 'style' for *saili/riti*. Sometimes, the translator has to be content with a long explanatory phrase, like Krishnamoorthy's 'illustration of the universal with the particular and vice versa' for *arthantaranyasa*. Where this is ruled out, one has to resort to a clumsy approximation and risk misleading the reader. It is this last that makes the Sanskrit-into-English literary lexicographer regret on occasion a career option that is otherwise profoundly challenging and often intellectually invigorating.

References

Barfield, Owen, 1928. *Poetic Diction: A Study in Meaning*. London: Faber and Gwyer.

Bell, Clive, 1914. *Art*. London: Stokes.

Chaudhury, Pravasjivan, 1953. *Studies in Comparative Aesthetics*. Shantiniketan: Visvabharati.

Coomaraswamy, Ananda, 1948. *The Dance of Shiva*. Mumbai: Asia Publishing House.

De, S.K., 1925. *Studies in the History of Sanskrit Poetics*. London: Luzac.

Dryden, John, 1697. 'Preface' to the translation of Virgil's *Pastorals, Georgics* and *Aeneid*. London.

Eliot, T.S., 1932. 'Hamlet and His Problems' in *The Sacred Wood*. London: Methuen and Co.

Ghosh, Manomohan, 1967. *The Natyasastra: A Treatise on Indian Dramaturgy*. Kolkata: Manisha Granthalaya.

Ingalls, Daniel H.H., 1965. *An Anthology of Sanskrit Court Poetry*. Cambridge, Massachusetts: Harvard University Press.

Keith, A.B., 1924. *Sanskrit Drama*. London: Oxford University Press.

Krishnamoorthy, K., 1955. *Anandavardhana's Dhvanyaloka*. Pune: Oriental.

Narasimhaiah, C.D. (ed.), 1982. *Ananda Coomaraswamy: Centenary Essays*. Mysore: Prasaranga, University of Mysore.

Pandey, K.C., 1959. *Comparative Aesthetics*. Varanasi: Choukhamba.

Raja, Kunjunni, K., 1963. *Indian Theories of Meaning*. Chennai: Adyar Library.

Ramanujan, A.K. (tr.), 1985. *Poems of Love and War*. New Delhi: Oxford University Press.

Rayan, Krishna, 1972. *Suggestion and Statement in Poetry*. London: The Athlone Press.
———, 1991. *Sahitya, A Theory*. New Delhi: Sterling.
Richards, I.A., 1924. *Principles of Literary Criticism*. London: Routledge.
Seturaman, V.S. (ed.), 1992. *Indian Aesthetics*. Chennai: Macmillan.

Six

Premodern Negotiations: Translating between Persian and Hindavi

ADITYA BEHL

As its title indicates, this essay deals with premodern Indian strategies for translating and interpreting texts and cultural practices. Given that the act of translation implies a mediation between different languages, we appear to be singularly blessed with a multiplicity of tongues in India. Yet there has been little scholarly attention paid to the intellectual practices involved in translating between one Indian language and another. This apparent neglect is not surprising, as I hope to show in this essay, for there is a vexed philosophical problem at issue here. Put simply, it is this: What is the relation between the intellectual framework for understanding difference in language and its cultural or social placement? In other words, if I translate Allah into Ishwar, or Ram into Rahim, then I am not only translating between Arabic and Sanskrit, but also making a statement of equivalence over what some would say is an unbridgeable social and ideological difference. That the statement has a social relevance and that its timing in this context is important, few would deny.

If translation, or indeed interpretation, is the production of familiar knowledge from unfamiliar facts, then the act involves a process of cultural and social comparison, of weighing different social and semantic inflections to convey finally such a supposedly 'equivalent' message. The inadequacy or adequacy of this equivalence to cultural differences is not at stake here. Rather, the issue revolves around the terms for its intellectual justification. To stretch my example a little further, what does it mean that Allah is equal to Ishwar? What is my justification for talking about it? Do I want to prove something else besides the equality of Ram and Rahim? If I use God instead of any of these terms, what sort of linguistic equivalence is that? All these questions imply a wider theoretical framework of comparison, of understanding different cultural and religious identities and their social interactions.

In this paper, I would like to discuss pre-colonial Indian translation strategies and the wider comparative frameworks in which they are embedded. I shall be looking mostly at interactions between Persian speakers and those who spoke in a north Indian variety of Hindavi, whether Punjabi or Awadhi or Brajbhasha or Khari Boli. To complicate the linguistic scene a little more, let me add that the scriptural sanctions for these groups were classically in Arabic and Sanskrit, languages in which the production of knowledge was tightly controlled and which did not serve as a spoken idiom. (I hope that this will suffice to convince even the most doubting sceptic among my readers that there is a crying need to look at intra- and inter-linguistic modes of translation in pre-colonial India.) Most of my examples will show how linguistic interactions are bound up with larger ideological concerns such as the presence of Islam as a powerful cultural system, the formation of new languages and modes of religious experience, and the always hotly contested issue of who is right and who is not.

For the sake of convenience, I distinguish six different textual modes for comparing and representing linguistic difference:

(1) synthesis
(2) translation
(3) compendia
(4) Sufi poetry
(5) ethnographic works
(6) polemics

If, after the linguistic turn, 'equivalence in difference is the cardinal problem of language' (Jakobson 1987: 260–66), these classes of texts can be seen to map out a spectrum between identity, synthesis (they're the same as us) and otherness (polemics—they are so different, they are off the map). What I hope to do is call attention to the intellectual and linguistic strategies used in these classes of texts, as well as their wider religious and social implications. In our secularised post-colonial setting, we tend to think only of translations between languages. However, linguistic identities in pre-colonial India come bound up with wider religious and literary self-definitions, putting to the question our academic policy of dividing up isolated domains of cultural practice. Translations can also be seen as attempts to define social groupings within cultural difference, as I hope will become clear from my paper.

Synthesis

Perhaps the most famous attempt to synthesise two different religious and linguistic systems is by Prince Dara Shikoh (1615–1659), who wrote among other things a work entitled *Majma-al Bahrain* (The Mingling of the Two Oceans) as well as the *Sirr-i-Akbar* (The Greatest Secret), which consisted of his translation of fifty Upanishads into fluent Persian. Appropriately enough, the latter work became the basis of Europe's idealist philosophers' discovery of the East after Anquetil-Duperron translated it into Latin in 1801. What we are interested in here, however, is the wider intellectual frame employed by Dara and its implications. If we turn to the preface of the *Sirr-i-Akbar*, we find the prince detailing his quest in lucid Persian. He relates that for some time his mind had been disturbed by assertions of difference between Islam and the religious practices of the Indian subcontinent. Therefore, he began to look for a common truth between Muslims and Hindus. Due to the encouragement of a Sufi Shaikh in Kashmir, he realised that the key to bridging this difference in belief was the idea that for Hindus there was no revealed book, i.e., they had not received divine revelation (*wahi*) from heaven.

Notice how the terms of selection are set up. We have the truth because it came down from heaven and is present in the form of a book; therefore, in order to prove that they have a truth and it is the same truth, we must prove that a similar condition obtains among the Hindus. In order to do this, Dara Shikoh has merely to point out that there are many such heavenly books (*asmani kitab*) among the Hindus which also come from the same mystical truth (*haqq*). Therefore the prince chooses the *Upanishads* to translate, fully expecting to find the same mystical truth.

The aim of Dara's translation is a synthesis, social and religious, based on the intellectual synthesis he is carrying out on every page of his rendition of the *Upanishads*. If one looks at the *Majma-al Bahrain*, one finds the theoretical attempt to flesh out equivalences in technical terminology between two pantheistic systems: *Wahdat-ul wujood* and *Vedanta*. Again, the aim is to effect a synthesis by mapping out and reducing difference, to tackle translation's basic problem of trying to send equivalent messages in different languages. Dara Shikoh's mystical synthesis of equivalence is perhaps the first place to start considering the state of translation, theoretical and practical, in premodern India. He stands at the 'identity' end of the spectrum, in marked contrast to other translators who found that cultural differences obstructed their enterprises.

Translation

Translation is often accompanied by an ethnographic encounter, or by the institutional deployment of state power, as we know from colonial times. In the 16th century, Emperor Akbar set up a *maktab khana* or translation bureau in order to make available the classics of Indian thought in Persian. The emperor's purpose seemed to be edification and entertainment, as well as promoting understanding between the two major religious systems of the day, although with not very much success. Among the works translated are the *Mahabharata*, rendered into Persian as the *Razm-nama*, the *Yogavasistha*, the *Harivamsa* and the *Bhagavata* as the *Tarikh-i Krishna-ji*, the *Singhasan Battisi*, works on Indian music and, last but not least, the *Ramayana* of Valmiki.

Very rarely has the *Ramayana*, which has been translated and reworked in dozens of versions in as many Indian languages, found such an unwilling translator. Mulla Abdul-Qadir Badayuni was ordered by Akbar to do the translation in order that the work might finally be available in Persian. The Mulla, much as he hated the imperial command, had to comply with what one scholar has called 'a veritable spiritual punishment'. In 1580 he completed his translation of Valmiki. We have his words written on the occasion.

> *I seek God's protection from the cursed writing which is as wretched as the parchment of my life. The reproduction of infidelity* (kufr) *does not mean infidelity. I utter words in refutation of infidelity, for I fear lest this book written at the order of the Emperor entirely might bear the print of hatred.*

The problem that Badayuni had to face in his translation was that he hated to transmit pagan stories, especially those that had to do with polytheistic faith in embodied gods. In marked contrast to Dara Shikoh, the Mulla presented Hindus as idolaters and heretics. The notion of embodying God so that human beings might touch God, talk to God, feed God, eat God's leavings, entertain God, wake God up and put God to sleep was anathema. What was especially problematic about translating the *Ramayana* was also the multiplicity of gods. For Badayuni, Valmiki and the Hindus in general commit the sin of *shirk*, or 'associationism' (believing that there is more than one Allah). The cultural difference and the problems notwithstanding, he completed the translation while condemning it in the same breath. For his pains, however, the emperor rewarded him with his next project: a complete Persian translation of the *Atharvaveda*!

Compendia

So far, we have been considering the problems which attend the translation of works from the Indic language into Persian for mystical or educational goals, with varying degrees of success in bridging cultural gaps and differences. What about movement in the reverse direction, from Persian into another Indian language, the Hindavi of my title? Here the scene is more complicated, and I have chosen two different kinds of examples from the masses of texts that can legitimately be discussed here. First, I'd like to talk about the form and content of some of the Sikh scriptures, in particular the *Japu Sahib* and the *Guru Granth Sahib*. To take the *Japu Sahib* first, it forms part of the daily gutka, or 'little book of observances', along with the *Japji Sahib, Shabad Hazare, Asa di War, Sukhmani Sahib*, and so on. The *Japu Sahib* is a recitation of the names and attributes for God in Punjabi, written in rhyming lines:

> arup hai, anup hai/aju hai, abhu hai//29//
> anil hai, anadi hai/aje hai, ajadi hai//33//
> amik hai, rafiq hai/adhandh hai, abandh hai//36//
> nirbujh hai, asujh hai/akal hai, ajal hai//37//
> agamm hai, ajanm hai/abhut hai, achhut hai//40//
> aman hai, nidhan hai/anek hai, phiri ek hai//43//

All of these names for God have to do with the divine transcendence of all known qualities and embodiments, and I am not going to translate them here. What I would like to draw attention to is the similarity of the form and content of this daily ritual with the Sufi *wird* or the recitation of the 99 names of Allah, also done in rhyming attributes:

> *Ya-Qayyum Ya-Waajid Ya-Maajid Ya-Waahid Ya-Ahad Ya-Samad*
> *Ya-Qaadir Ya-Muqtadir Ya-Muqaddim Ya-Mu'akhkhir*
> *Ya-Awwal Ya-Akhir Ya-Zahir Ya-Batin*

It is clear that an entire mode of religious practice is being appropriated and recreated in a different language, Punjabi. The textual form is equivalent, but different messages are encoded in the two languages. These different messages are part of different frameworks for comparing cultural activity and making social statements about it.

In the Sikh case, the wider framework for comparing and translating between cultures and languages lies in the *Guru Granth Sahib*. The text contains the hymns of the Sikh gurus as well as a range of appropriations from different sources such as Kabir, Mirabai and Baba Farid Ganj-e Shakar. On the level of textual strategy, the *Guru Granth Sahib* uses translations, paraphrases and straightforward quotations from these sources, but with a commentary on how these items are to be viewed. In other words, there is a sort of compendium or collection being presented here, where some bit of each source of contemporary religious truth is represented, translated and interpreted. Of course, this means that the compiler of the collection controls the placement and hierarchy of each item within it. It should be clear that this process of translating and creating scripture implies the social definition of a Sikh religious community with its own source of religious truth, distinct from all other social groups. Such compendia as the *Guru Granth Sahib* illustrate the premise that, in cultural terms, not only is it important what something is translated from, but what it is fitted into.

Sufi Poetry

The second case of translation into Hindavi I should like to consider are the Sufi romances called *premakhyanas* in different Indian languages, along the lines of the Persian romances of Nizami Ganjavi and his imitators. Sufis were responsible for creating new languages, literatures and religious forms in India. In the Sufi *premakhyana* literature, we find that our concern with language and translation is complicated by the fact that many Sufis present the seeker's most important experiences and states of feeling (*maqamat, hal*) as beyond the reach of language. As the writer of the romance *Madhumalati*, Shaikh Manjhan Shattari, put it in 1545:

parihari suddhi, buddhi au gyaana, kaya bevarjit laavanhi dhyaana.
nirgun jahan niranjan sunaan, tahan aapu son aapu bihunaan.
gyaan paara jahvaan agyaanaan, tahan appu seun apu ayaanaan.
sahaj samadhi laav tain tahan, appu seum aapu paav sudhi jahaan.

Abandon consciousness, wisdom and knowledge,
focus on meditation, not your body.
In the place of the pure absolute, void of qualities,
you will find your self detached from selfhood.
Past all knowledge, unknowing rules
where your self will not know itself.
Focus on Sahaj, the simple mystery,
and you'll awaken to knowing your self.

The inadequacy of language, of ordinary concepts of self, mind and body, to deal with the highest level of mystical experience or metaphysical 'otherness', is clearly in the foreground here. Within the linguistic complexities of the Indian scene, Sufis have produced a richly imaginative mystical literature. These poets adapted religious terminology from the *Nath Panth* and the *nirguna bhakta* poets in order to (1) translate Persian Sufi metaphysics into Indian languages, as well as (2) translate through figurative or narrative discourse the most important experiences of the *salik* or seeker.

Thus, Sufi theological terminology translates Persian and Arabic notions of the Godhead into terms common mostly with *nirguna bhakti* poetry in Hindi. The Creator, *khaliq*, is here called the *karta* or *vidhata*, and He is the author of the created world. Divine Being is placeless (*lamakan*) yet at play everywhere, formless, yet in every created form. The *nirguna Rama* of Kabir and the *ik oankar* of the Nanakpanthis are both echoed here, but with different valences. The Lord (*gosain*) is exemplified in the *ek oankar*, which among Sufis refers to the Quranic injunction which created the world, 'Be! and it was' (*kun fayakun*). Allah is represented as a Being or Reality which is *nirguna*, or beyond qualifications, and constantly at play (*kasrat and wahdat*).

The major thrust of this act of theological translation is to present a narrative language for a style of Sufi practice. All the terms translated from Indian religious practice are fitted into the narrative frame of love stories such as those of Ratnasen and Padmavati or Manohar and Madhumalati. This Hindavi language of poetry or narrative is the wider framework within which Sufis express their distinctive mystical agendae.

In the act of translating from Persian to Hindavi, the new language takes on an importance of its own. Thus, in the eastern Hindavi tradition, the language and poetic form forged by the Sufis is used again most notably by Tulsidas in his *Ramcharitmanas*. No other 'Hindu' religious work in Awadhi predates the *Manas*. It is clear from this that translation between Persian and Hindavi has been an act constitutive of an entirely new language for poetry and religious experience.

Ethnographic Works

Till now, we have discussed two examples of translation from Indian languages into Persian (Dara Shikoh and Akbar's translation bureau), and two examples of translation from Persian into another Indian language (Sikh and Sufi texts). These translations assimilate linguistic and religious difference into their language implicitly, as a necessary concomitant to cross-cultural understanding and/or social definition. Any reading of them has to sort out the levels and layers of translations, appropriations, reinterpretations and paraphrases by careful close reading. But there are examples of texts from pre-colonial India where the entire problem of social definition has been taken up theoretically. In such texts, someone has gone around and done something akin to modern ethnography by asking various groups how they define themselves, reading and translating their most important scriptures, describing their most important practices, and putting it all together in massive encyclopaedic works. Perhaps the most famous of such works is Al-Biruni's *Kitab al-Hind*, written in Arabic in the 11th century A.D. and dealing with the cultures of India. Another such work is the *Dabistan-i Mazahib* (School of Religious Faiths) of Mulla Mubad Shah, written in Persian in the 17th century and unjustly neglected.

Recent work in anthropology and in cultural studies has underscored the primacy of translation in projecting cross-cultural understanding. Whether one is an ethnographer or a translator, or both, one highlights what appears to be different within another culture and brings it into familiar terms. Mubad Shah, our 17th-century ethnographer, was a Zoroastrian about whom little is known. Writing in Persian, he begins his encyclopaedic work with a metaphor calculated to organise all religious and theological thinking: 'knowledge of God', he says, 'is the supreme knowledge, the *mobid* [a Zoroastrian priest] is the teacher, and the world is a school [*dabistan*]'. Mubad's *Dabistan* is divided into sections, chapters and sub-chapters. Each religion—Islam, Hinduism, Zoroastrianism, etc.—is the subject of a large section, with different sects and religious groupings divided into chapters and sub-chapters.

What I shall focus on here is the conceptual exposition of each sect's beliefs and practices in Mubad's presentation, the organisation of topics, criteria for making distinctions, and so on. Within each section, Mubad Shah concentrates, in turn, on a group's description of God, (judged 'true' or 'untrue'), their account of the creation of the world, the physiological division of the world into four elements, the origins of a religion, its stages of evolution (reckoned dynastically, as in the *Shah-nama*), its cosmology, and units of time.

The most important criterion for judging between sects and ranking them is two-fold: (a) whether their religion is revealed or non-revealed, and (b) whether a distinction can be made between the manifest form and the concealed meaning of a phenomenon. For example, there is the problem of Hindu gods (this always seems to be a problem for ethnographers). What Mubad Shah will try to claim is that the external form of an idol conceals a hidden intellectual operation accessible to him. Either he makes a god into an allegory for a Quranic concept, or, an analogy can be drawn between the god and something familiar in terms of function (we have this way of dealing with x, they have that way), or content. Or, in certain cases, gods are familiar cultural concepts (agricultural fertility, say) taken over by Indians from Muslims, but that somehow the lines of communication got muddled and a substitution took place. In all these cases—in common with a basic precept of modern ethnography—the distinction between latent and manifest form is used to fill in a Persian meaning which probably would not have occurred to Mubad's informants.

As an example of premodern translation/ethnography, the *Dabistan* is a fascinating text because it shows how different linguistic processes are used to translate social reality from one language to another. Space does not permit a detailed coverage, so I will confine myself to two remarks: (a) here we have a reflection of the terms of cultural comparison within the wider framework of access to the lived reality of social others, and (b) the process by which the *Dabistan* is written seems to be a combination of two modes of writing about other cultures which were historically separate in the West—eyewitness ethnography (what I saw or heard them doing); and translation of written authorities (the best sources). As a reflection on cultural contact, it takes us further than the previous four examples because it shows us a text full of the different intellectual operations involved in producing knowledge across the gap of cultural difference in premodern India.

Polemics

This last mode of translation is actually an admission of defeat or a position of 'no compromise' over linguistic and ideological differences, since it says that social others are so different that we cannot mix and match them, or translate them into our terms. This is the classic philosophical position of 'strong' cultural relativism which holds that the languages we use and the cultures we inhabit so determine our world views that we must remain enclosed within our 'own' solipsist universes and cannot ever hope to understand how meanings are construed within another culture (see, for example, in this connection, Mandelbaum 1921). None of the operations I have described in the modes of translation above are permissible here, as cultural difference is proclaimed to be absolute. Following from this, various polemical charges can be made, such as naming the putative other heretic, *kafir, mlechcha,* and so on. I do not really want to spend much time on this, except merely to note that it exists and is opposed to the position of identity or synthesis that we started from. The ultimate justification for this position, at least in Indian cultural history, seems to be religious purity and the attempt to define culture as single, unique and limited rather than multiple, changing and open-ended. No translation is possible here, only ineradicable difference.

Conclusion

This brings me to the task of trying to sum up this range of cultural practices and to reflect on the question I started with: What is the relation between the intellectual framework for understanding difference in language and its cultural and social placement? I hope that I have been able to show that in the multilingual Indian case, various discursive strategies have been employed to make sense of linguistic and cultural plurality. Two conclusions seem to flow from this: translation as cultural comparison is inextricably linked both with interpretation as well as with the social and historical interaction between groups. Translating Allah into Ishwar has been tried before, and if we wish to make sense of some of our past it behoves us to pay attention to how people have tried to do this. Whether it is in the encounters of Al-Biruni and Mubad Shah with the bewildering diversity of India, or the captive Mulla Baduyuni in Emperor Akbar's *maktab khana*, or the Sufis who evolved new languages, or the Sikhs or *bhaktas* who assimilated differing religious truths into new religious frameworks, it is clear that rich intellectual and cultural resources exist for grappling with multiculturalism in the Indian context. The recent violence around is a pointed reminder that we have to focus on what is positive in our past, on what has allowed different cultural ideals to live together rather than cut each others' throats.

Second, there is the larger question of the placement of academic knowledge—our own place, writing in English, in a post-colonial setting, trying to read the cultural monuments of the past and translating them into a language accessible to us. The task is made more difficult by the intervention of colonial and nationalist attempts at redefining the past. Whether one talks about translating from the past into the present or from one language to another, there is a play between identity and otherness which is linked to our social and historical positions. I hope that my attempt to deal with intellectual practices of translation in premodern India will focus more scholarly attention on a field that needs fresh work and fresh insights urgently. If we can place the translation of cultural differences in today's social arena, perhaps we can convert our multiplicity of tongues into a strength instead of a weakness, and establish an equivalence between Ram and Rahim.

References

Jakobson, Roman, 1987. 'On Linguistic Aspects of Translation' in *Selected Writings, Volume II*. The Hague: Mouton.

Mandelbaum, D.G. (ed.), 1921. *The Selected Writings of Edward Sapir*. Berkeley: University of California Press.

Seven

Contemporary Textual Politics: Translating a Sacred Text

K. AYYAPPA PANIKER

I start with the assumption that the nature of a source text imposes various kinds of limitations on the translation process. A purely literary text is basically 'secular' in the range of meanings that the words used in it can evoke; a sacred text in this sense is a multi-layered one, with a non-secular level over and above the possible minimum secular level. When the text to be translated is both literary and sacred, the problems that the translator runs into are not merely multiplied, but are of a different order. There is on the one hand the temptation to read and render it as a literary text, which has to be resisted if one has to bring out the religious associations embedded in the text. On the other hand, one is also led to think of the text as a hermetically sealed document, like the word of God, the revealed word, the Word. The Word so charged with meaning, once it is identified as such in any language, may not easily find its exact equivalent in any other language.

Divine Language, Sacred Text

The concept of a divine language or *devabhasha* takes the text out of the purview of the linguist and makes it part of theology. It assumes the status of liturgy, and the belief-system makes it so sacrosanct that any attempt to re-word could be construed as a sacrilegious act. This has been a potent factor in discouraging the translation of sacred texts in all parts of the world: the Vedas, the Bible and the Koran were kept out of the hands of the common people, who were considered incapable of understanding the works in the proper way. In Europe, the Reformation was in essence a movement, among other things, for breaking the holy seal over the Word of God and making it accessible to everybody. In India, the Bhakti Movement of the Middle Ages promoted the translation of the sacred *puranas* and other works from Sanskrit into the actual spoken languages of the millions to whom they had been inaccessible for long.

Thus, every act of translation became on the one hand a sacrilege, but on the other hand, an act of intellectual as well as religious revolution. The energies released by the Reformation in Europe and the Bhakti Movement in India, almost at the same time, paved the way for a great literary efflorescence in both places. The modern European languages came into their own, breaking the barriers imposed by medieval feudalism and superstition, exactly in the same way as the modern Indian languages entered the threshold of creativity, resulting in unprecedented productivity in almost all branches of literature. There were of course social, economic and political forces, which together brought about this massive transformation of the intellectual and cultural ambience of whole peoples.

Consequently, it may be argued that the old languages which had served as the medium of literary expression in the past tended to become obsolete and defunct—if not wholly dead, at least shunted to the back seat. They had to seek a new lease of life from those who began to wield the new languages. The translation of religious classics had a good deal to do with the entire transformation of the people's understanding of the world about them. The word of the Creator re-created by man opened up new vistas of our understanding of the universe and its laws.

It is no wonder, therefore, that most Western theories of translation are themselves inextricably bound up with the history of Biblical translation in particular. The multiple reincarnations of the Old and New Testaments in a way led to the establishment of multiple denominations of the once universal or catholic Church. God could now speak in as many languages as the speakers of those languages wished; He Himself moved closer to them and began to hear their prayers in human languages, instead of in any one privileged language. With the decline of linguistic centralism arose the importance, the responsibility and the empowerment of translation itself as a mediator between countries and cultures.

Translator's Compulsions, Reader's Truths

In this context, the anxiety to be 'true' to the original author or source text has often resulted in a certain disregard for the potential reader of the translation; that the translation has to be truthful to the target reader seldom appears to have been the concern of the Western translators of the Bible in Eastern languages. The conscious or unconscious imposition of a foreign idiom, resulting perhaps from an assumption of superiority on the part of the source text or, at least, the source language (maybe a carry-over from imperial or colonial authority) has bedevilled these early translations. As a consequence, post-colonial translations had to be made in which the native idiom was given preference over the foreign-flavoured one of earlier translations. The importance of the target language and the target reader has, to a large extent, been reinstated in post-colonial translations. This is closer to the position of the translators of Indian classical texts, including scriptures, during the Middle Ages. In spite of the veneration in which sacred texts were held in medieval India, the translators ventured to capture the spirit rather than the letter of the original texts. The result was that these translations came to be seen as classics in the respective languages into which they were translated.

Reader acceptance becomes easy when the speakers of the source language and the target language operate within the same broad culture. This is perhaps one of the reasons why medieval translations of the Bible into the modern European languages became popular and important texts, capable of influencing later writings in those languages. The authority of the 1611 King James or Authorised Version of the Bible in English is probably based not on the royal seal of approval but the public avowal of acceptance.

In the same way, the two great Indian epics were rendered into the modern Indian languages by devout poets in whom the poetic power of invention matched the fervour of religious devotion and their works were wholeheartedly 'received' by readers who could not read these sacred texts in the original Sanskrit. They did not worry too much about linguistic exactness, but wanted to ensure an emotive response in the right measure. But today, unfortunately, translations are evaluated not so much by devotees carried away by emotion as by cold-blooded scholars who have linguistic tools to scrutinise levels of accuracy and equivalence. No wonder the reading public is often put off by such inane enterprises.

The way I came to translate selections from the *Granth Sahib*, the holy text of Sikh scripture, was a matter of accident. When I agreed to translate from English to Malayalam the monograph on Guru Nanak published by the Sahitya Akademi in its series *Makers of Modern Indian Literature*, the biographical and critical part did not pose much of a problem, but the poems included in the text made me aware of the seriousness of the task I'd undertaken. Very little had been written in Malayalam on Punjab and Sikhism, let alone on Guru Nanak or his writings. The proper names were often improperly transliterated and, perhaps until the Bhindranwale phenomenon surfaced, there was little understanding about the nature of Sikhism in the popular imagination.

Although many people from Kerala had lived and worked in Punjab and had close associations with the Sikhs, Punjab and Punjabi literature had had very little impact on the literary imagination of the Malayalis. Translation, if it existed at all, had to resort to a circuitous route via Hindi and English, and that had had no success worth mentioning. I could not lay my hands on any book on Sikhism in Malayalam, nor on any Malayalam translation of the works of Guru Nanak. This meant that I had no usable model before me. Even the English versions of these hymns appeared to be substantially different from the other versions by Sikh and non-Sikh translators. This meant that I had to devise my own strategies for translating scriptural texts of a religion not quite familiar to me from a language not known to me, but available in different versions in English done by faithful followers as well as those not so faithful.

There was yet another big hurdle, which perhaps the English translators by and large could, and did, ignore: the musical structure of the text. These hymns are meant to be sung aloud; they are composed in various ragas, well known to the devotees. Thus, the works of Guru Nanak were scriptural texts with the emotional intensity of mantras, where sometimes the number of syllables had an esoteric meaning too, which the translator could not just totally ignore. These linguistic, literary, religious, musical and esoteric elements appeared to make the work of translation next to impossible. I had to put off the translation of the hymns until I had prepared myself for the unenviable task.

Methodological Issues, Musical Harmonies

The first thing I did was collect all the available translations of the hymns in English and make a comparative study of these versions in order to arrive at an estimation of the range of freedom one could legitimately hope to take in this regard. I felt both encouraged and disheartened to find the widest divergences one can imagine: encouraged because I felt I did not have to worry too much about mere verbal exactness, and discouraged because these divergent versions appeared to keep me away from the texts, making me think that the only way to get beyond this problem was to study Punjabi. But then I also realised that these differences had cropped up in so-called authentic versions made by people who were reputed scholars, both of Punjabi and Sikhism.

I decided to read about the language used by Guru Nanak and to also, at the same time, try to understand the doctrines of Sikhism as well as its history. Still, I didn't feel competent enough to take up the task. Then came an opportunity for me to go to Punjab, live in Kasauli and Chandigarh and get to speak to a few Sikhs about Nanak and the Sikh religion. Going into a Sikh household, crossing the threshold, as it were, and sharing food and talk with several Sikhs, men and women, was both an education and a confidence-building experience. To feel like an insider was very necessary—almost a prerequisite—for attempting something so unusual as translating Sikh scripture into Malayalam. To bury ignorance, to live down prejudices of all kinds, to grasp the religious and literary associations, to cross the barrier of language: in all these I had to depend upon the friendship and affection of many Sikh acquaintances, who at the time did not know that they were transmitting so much of their conviction and confidence to me. (Some of them may not be quite aware even now that they have been unconscious collaborators in a great endeavour.)

And yet, all this was not enough. The underlying musical structure was part of the inner meaning of the hymns which were regularly chanted. One had to listen to the chanting in the authentic and orthodox style, not with the intention of carrying over the original score at all, but to relive the intuition that for medieval Bhakti poetry the aural-oral dimension was integral. In this matter I received generous help and assistance from friends who made recorded discs and cassettes available. Listening to these chants actually resolved some of the difficulties I had encountered while going through the printed texts. Now the chanting style sounded familiar: it was not too far from the way medieval hymns or *kirtanas* were recorded in my own language in Malayalam. But I also warned myself against rendering these compositions as merely equivalent to the Malayalam *bhajans* or Bhakti songs. Their difference had to be maintained.

Linguistic similarities were another trap. Many of the words repeatedly used in these songs are of Sanskrit origin. While this could be of some help, it could not always be taken for granted. The cognate forms could not be taken to mean the same in the literary contexts of the two languages. But the fact that many words which sounded unacceptable in the different versions in English could be used with more or less identical connotations in Punjabi and Malayalam was certainly a matter for consolation—within certain limits, of course. The translation of the monograph along with the illustrative poems was thus completed with reasonable satisfaction although there were still some nagging problems; these became more formidable when I undertook the translation of a whole book of selections from Guru Nanak for the *World Classics Retold* series published by D.C. Books, Kottayam, as their

128th volume in July 1987. The Guru Nanak volume was to be the last in the series.

A decision was also taken to publish the original versions in the Malayalam script on the left hand page so that Malayalam readers could not only see the similarity or dissimilarity between the original and the translation, but also move on to the original after reading the Malayalam version. The translation was not intended to replace the original; it was to be used as a stepping stone only, as a mediator. Now this was possible only between languages which are similar in many ways, especially in terms of their sound systems and vocabulary. This also helped preserve the musical structure, which was difficult to transfer to another language without loss or distortion of meaning. The text was made available in Devanagari and then transliterated into the Malayalam script. Perhaps, more importantly, it helped to keep intact the mantra-like mystical quality of the original, where the order of the syllables and the length of the vowels could be retained without any substantial change. It cannot be claimed that this was a fool-proof method, since fools have their own ways of circumventing scholarly efforts.

The opening *moolamantram* was first given in Malayalam transliteration. This was immediately followed by a paraphrase in Malayalam, with the translation on the right hand page facing it. The translation had to be longer than the original because of the latter's highly tight and profound nature. The paraphrase does not take more space than the original, but the translation had to bring out the extended meaning of the original in full. This was not felt necessary in the case of the other poems, although some concessions had to be made to suit the requirements of an apparently metrical structure natural to Malayalam. We might take a quick comparative look at Song no. 12, reproduced here in the Roman script:

Transliteration	Translation
manne kii gati kahii na jaii	mananattin gati parayaan kazhiyaa
je ko kahai pichhai pachhutaaii	parayunnavanu varum paritaapam
kaagadi kalam na likhanahaaru	katalaasu, leekhakar, peenakal poora

manne kaa bahii karani vichaaru	mananamahatvam velivaakkaan
aisa naamu niranjanu hoii	atra niranjanamee tirunaamam
je ko manii janai manikoii	mannanattaalariyunna manassil.

One can see here the preference for cognate forms of words, wherever feasible: *manne, gati, katalaasu, likhanahaaru, niranjanu, mani (koii)*, etc. Here, an effort has been made to retain the tight formal structure of the original. Song no. 17 shows the repetition of key words which are part of the stock diction of medieval Bhakti poetry common to most Indian languages:

Transliteration	Translation
asankh jap asankh bhaaii	asankhyam japikunnasankhyam bhajikkunnu
asankh puujaa asankh tap taauu	asankyam puujikunnasankhyam tapikkunnu
asankh granth mukhii vedapaath	asankhyangal granthangal veedangal chollunnu
asankh jog mani rahahi udaas	asankhyam yoogattaal udaasiinachittar
asankh bhagta guna gyaan vichar	asankhyam bhaktanmaar gunajnaanasiilar
asankh satii asankh daataar	asankhyam satyajnar asankhyam daataakkal
asankh suur muha bhakh saar	asankhyam suuranmaar urukku neerkkunnoor
asankh monii liva laaii taar	asankhyam mounikal aaraadhikkunnavar
kadarti kavan kahaa vichaaru	engane ninne prakirttikkuveen jnaan
vaariaa na jaavaa ek vaar	ellaamoradbhutam etra vichitram
jo tudhu bhaavai saaii bhalii kaar	ninte abhiishtam atu tanne shreshtham
tuu sadaa salaamati niran kaar	nii nityanalloo sadaa niraakaaran

Conclusion

There is perhaps no need to multiply examples to show that the bilingual model, that is, transliteration plus translation, can go a long way to eliminate or overcome the limitations of translation. If the main objective is to bring the original text closer to the reader, or the reader in the target language closer to the source text, then this approach may be suitable. However, it is obvious that this method has its limitations. It is most successful only within the same culture and between languages having the same or a similar sound system and a shared vocabulary. Especially when a text is charged with mystical or religious meanings, using such a methodology seems almost inevitable. The translator has to take on the role of a mediator, with only limited opportunity to display his verbal skill, scholarship or cleverness at interpretation. The translation and the translator have to keep a low profile. Yet it can be claimed that this process significantly shortens the distance between the original text and the target reader. It is also true that the English translators of Guru Nanak cannot resort to this bilingual approach with the same degree of success as an Indian translator may hope to achieve.

3. Pragmatic Considerations

Eight

Intimate Alienation: Immigrant Fiction and Translation

JHUMPA LAHIRI

A letter recently came to my father's office from a Bengali gentleman in Kolkata. The author of the letter, unknown to my family, explained that he was a lifelong writer of fiction, adding that his 'pen was never still'. This prolific gentleman, impressed with the fact that I, with my recognisably Bengali name, had won the Pulitzer Prize, wanted to know how he himself might apply for the honour. On the phone from New York, I explained to my parents that it hadn't been a matter of applying, that it had actually been the single greatest surprise of my life, something like winning the lottery without ever having bought a ticket. When my father asked whether Indian nationals were eligible for the Pulitzer, I told him what I knew: that the book had to be by an American citizen, and deal, preferably, with 'American life'. At this point my mother interjected that the judges had made an exception in my case. I might have been naturalised as an American citizen when I was eighteen (I was born in London), but in her eyes I am first and forever Indian. Furthermore, my book, in her opinion, wasn't about American life. It was about people like herself and myself—Indians. I suppose I should be grateful that my mother wasn't on the Pulitzer committee.

I draw attention to this anecdote because it exemplifies the perplexing bicultural universe I inhabit, the expectations and assumptions I have always shuttled between. My mother has lived outside India for nearly thirty-five years; my father, nearly forty. Since 1969 they've made their home in the United States. But there were invisible walls erected around our home, walls intended to keep American influence at bay. Growing up, I was admonished not to 'behave' like an American, or, worse, to 'think' of myself as one. Actually 'being' an American was not an option.

Freedom and a Bilingual Identity

I believe what first drove me to write fiction was the desire to escape the pitfalls of being viewed as one thing or the other. As an author, I could embody any individual my imagination enabled me to, of any origin. This sense of freedom is one of the greatest thrills of writing fiction, and for a person like me, who has never been confident of what to call herself or of where to say she is from, it is a solace. But what I have discovered upon publishing my book—*The Interpreter of Maladies*—is that authorial freedom is limited to the process of writing itself, in the private sphere of creation. Once made public, both my book and I were immediately and copiously categorised. Take, for instance, the various ways I am described: as an American author, as an Indian-American author, as a British-born author, as an Anglo-Indian author, as an NRI (non-resident Indian) author, as an ABCD author (ABCD stands for American born confused '*desi*'—desi meaning Indian—and is an acronym coined by Indian nationals to describe culturally challenged second-generation Indians raised in the US). According to Indian academics, I've written something known as 'diaspora fiction'; in the US, it's 'immigrant fiction'. In a way, all of this amuses me. The book is what it is, and has been received in ways I have no desire or ability to control. The fact that I am described in two ways or twenty is of no consequence; as it turns out, each of those labels is accurate.

I have always lived under the pressure to be bilingual, bicultural, at ease on either side of the Lahiri family map. The first words I learned to utter and understand were in my parents' native tongue, Bengali. Until I was old enough to go to school, and my linguistic world split in two, I spoke Bengali exclusively and fluently. Though I still speak Bengali, I have lost this extreme fluency. I was stunned, listening a few years ago to a cassette tape that had recorded the wedding of one of my parents' friends, in 1970. There I was, three years old, prattling confidently on in a way I no longer can. Still, my ability to speak the language made me feel less foreign during visits to Kolkata every few years. It also made me feel less foreign in the expatriate Bengali community my parents socialise with in the United States and, on a more quotidian level, in my own home.

While English was not technically my first language, it has become so. My knowledge of Bengali is spoken, colloquial—above all, familial. It's hard for me to understand the formal elocution of a Bengali television newscast or the literary diction of a poem. I read with the humble prowess of a struggling young child. (Standard typeset letters are easier for me than penmanship). My writing is at about the same level. Putting these skills to use was an isolated, occasional need: 'Write a letter to your grandfather,' my father would say. And then, 'Try to read his reply'. Still, my basic aptitude allowed me, in graduate school, to translate six short stories by a Bengali writer named Ashapurna Devi. The process was as follows: My mother would read the story aloud in Bengali, and I would simultaneously write a rough translation in English. Then I would go back and read the story to myself, at a snail's pace. The painstaking process made me realise that while I'd always liked to consider myself bilingual, this was hardly the case.

The Consequences of Writing in English

When it came to my own writing, English was, from the beginning, my only language. The very first stories I wrote, in the second grade during recess, were imitations of what I'd learned to read in the classroom. I proceeded to write throughout my childhood, always in English, never about anything to do with India. If writing may be seen, in part, as an impulse on the author's behalf to control the world, then this was my youthful attempt to maintain order: to write about one sort of life without letting the other sort seep in and complicate things.

In my twenties, I began to complicate things. My first 'adult' attempt at a story took place in India, as did a few others that followed. I had come to regard India as a place both in which and about which to write fiction. During visits there I was idle, unmoored, intensely curious about what I saw: an alternate life, which, had my parents chosen not to live their lives abroad, would have been mine. The main resource for any writer was suddenly, abundantly available to me uninterrupted by time and relative isolation. (I say relative because in fact I was always literally surrounded by my relatives.) It was in India that I discovered that given a stretch of time in which I had nothing to do, and given pen and paper, I would write something.

The earliest story in *The Interpreter of Maladies*, 'A Real Durwan', was written soon after returning from a visit to India in 1992, in my bedroom in my parents' house in Rhode Island. This story and another, 'The Treatment of Bibi Haldar', have been attacked by Indian reviewers as having a 'tunnel vision' of India. My only defence is that my own experience of India was largely that of a tunnel—the tunnel imposed by the single city we ever visited, by the handful of homes we stayed in, by the fact that I was not allowed to explore this city on my own. Still, within these narrow confines, I felt that I had seen enough of life, enough details and drama, to set stories on Indian soil. An Indian man I met at a dinner party in New York, speaking of 'A Real Durwan', disagreed with me. He felt I had misrepresented the plumbing technologies of Kolkata. 'All houses in Calcutta have sinks,' he informed me, indignantly, assuming that I had never been there myself, or at best had been there once or twice as a child. I did not argue to the contrary, in spite of the fact that my maternal grandparents' house—the house the story was based on—had no sinks but rather a series of plastic and metal buckets from which we washed our hands and bathed. I realised that, according to this man I had carelessly construed the city from which he originally hailed. Mistranslated it, if you will.

What this gentleman was suggesting is something that has been stated more explicitly in certain reviews of my book in the

Indian press. And that is that I, being an ABCD, lack the cultural ambidexterity to write about Indian life and characters in an authentic way. I have been accused of setting stories in India as a device in order to woo Western audiences with exotica. Non-Bengali reviewers make noises about the fact that I only write about Bengalis, only one of India's numerous regional populations.

Even after I won the Pulitzer, *India Today*, a national news magazine, wrote that my setting stories in Kolkata was 'an unwise decision'. Most disturbing of all was a review in an Indian paper called *Business Standard*, in which the reviewer, discussing *The Interpreter of Maladies*, comments upon the infatuation of Mr Kapasi, a part-time Indian tour guide, with the Indian-American Mrs Das. In this story, Mr Kapasi is intoxicated by the sight of Mrs. Das's bare legs and short skirt, things I had safely assumed many of the world's men found arousing. But Mr Kapasi's intoxication was not universal in the reviewer's mind; it was 'appalling[ly]' stereotypical—severe condemnation for a fiction writer. The review continues: 'This could be understandable if the writer were a complete foreigner, but not from someone who flaunts her Indian lineage'. In other words, had I no hereditary connection to India, the story's 'stereotypical' premise would be an excusable offence. But given my family tree, and given the fact that I chose India as a subject matter, different rules apply: I should know better. And yet, given the fact that I was raised in the US, the review also implies that I cannot know better.

To avoid this sort of review in the future, I suppose I could decide to play it safe and never write about India or nonimmigrant Indians again. I am the first person to admit that my knowledge of India is limited, the way in which all translations are. I am impeded not only by my own lack of proximity but by the fact that my parents' impressions—one of my main resources when writing about India—are also arrested in time; the country they left in the sixties is, in many respects, unrecognisable to them today. Still, my translation of India has evoked, for some readers and reviewers here and there, the illusion of cultural accuracy, and resonance. One of my mother's cousins, now living in West Virginia, even went so far as to thank me for taking her back to the Kolkata of her childhood, all its requisite details, in her opinion, intact.

The Rewards of Speaking Bengali

Rendering an Indian landscape into English, with or without sinks, is one thing. Dialogue is wholly another. Because Bengali is essentially a spoken language for me, because it occupies such an aural presence in my mind, forcing my Bengali characters to speak a tongue they either can't or wouldn't speak in a given scene is one of my most daunting challenges. It is a disorienting and at times highly dissatisfying thing to do. I must abandon a certain sense of verisimilitude in the process, a certain fidelity. It is something of a betrayal, for example, to have the family in 'When Mr. Pirzada Came to Dine' speaking English when they are at home. For in my imagination, these characters are conversing in Bengali. Were I to tell this story to myself, I think I would narrate the expository passages in English while preserving all the dialogue, where appropriate, in Bengali. Such tactics aren't feasible for a general audience, except in very short doses. In some instances I do retain Bengali words in my stories. The 'durwan' of 'A Real Durwan' is one example. I liked the sound of the word in Bengali, and the full phrase, with the two English words in front of it, sounded perfectly normal, just as it is normal for me and even for my parents to slip the occasional English word into Bengali conversation. (Even the coinage ABCD betrays a similar linguistic hybridisation.) The word *bechareh*, an epithet used to designate a pitiable person, also appears in 'A Real Durwan'. I included it not out of any need to be culturally accurate, but due to the whims of my own quasi-bilingual brain.

Incorporating Bengali words into my stories is something I have stopped doing. This may be attributed, in part, to a healthy artistic impulse: My writing, these days, is less a response to my parents' cultural nostalgia, and more an attempt to forge my own amalgamated domain. Writing 'When Mr. Pirzada Came to Dine' was a turning point. I say turning point not because it was the first time I set a story on American soil or because it was the first time I had an Indian-American protagonist. Both of these things I had already done. But in this story I felt I was, for the first time, conveying that intimate Bengali of my upbringing, both spoken and otherwise, into English. Here I incorporated no foreign words or expressions. What concerned me more was the precise explanation of certain gestures and details—the manner in which the family eats, for example, and their preoccupation, while living in a small New England town, with the Pakistani civil war. My focus in this story wasn't the unilateral translation of a place or a language. Instead it was a simultaneous translation in both directions, of characters who literally dwell in two separate worlds. This story was recently translated and published in a Bengali literary magazine. While I can easily comprehend the dialogue, much of the story's vocabulary is inaccessible to me. At the same time, because the English 'translation' is something I've already written and largely committed to memory, it's relatively easy to guess what an otherwise foreign word means.

Conclusion: Translation as Character

Looking at my stories as a whole, I am aware that I am preoccupied with language, as if this concept, this fact of human life, were itself an element of drama. I seem especially preoccupied with the presence in any given character's life of two languages and sometimes more, in different sorts of equations. Almost all of my characters are translators, insofar as they must make sense of the foreign in order to survive. The failed linguist in the title story literally makes his living off his knowledge of English and other languages.

In 'Sexy', Miranda's curiosity about Bengali is a way for her to gain access to her married and increasingly unavailable lover. In 'The Third and Final Continent' the last story in the book to be written, the protagonist notes that when his wife arrives in Boston, he speaks Bengali in America for the first time. Yet there is no discernible change in the style of his dialogue; he speaks to his wife in the same manner that he speaks in English to Mrs. Croft. For the ancient Mrs. Croft, meanwhile, modern life has itself become a baffling foreign language, one she neither participates in nor understands. The protagonist in this story also fears that his son will no longer speak in Bengali after he and his wife die. This is displaced anxiety on my part—my own fear of my parents' death. For if I am to survive them, it is I who will suffer that linguistic loss.

In my dictionary, the biblical definition of translate is 'to convey to heaven without death'. I am struck by the extent to which this decidedly Western, nonsecular definition sheds light on my own personal background of Eastern origin.

In my observation, translation is not only a finite linguistic act but an ongoing cultural one. It is the continuous struggle, on my parents' behalf, to preserve what it means to them to be first and forever Indian, to keep afloat certain familial and communal traditions in a foreign and at times indifferent world. The life my parents have made for themselves here has required a great movement, a long voyage, an uprooting of all things familiar in exchange for an immersion into all things strange. It has required, moreover, an endless going back and forth, repeated travelling, urgent telephone calls, decades of sending and receiving letters. Somehow they have conveyed the spirit of their former world to the here and now, where it exists for them, still thriving, still meaningful.

Unlike my parents, I translate not so much to survive in the world around me as to create and illuminate a nonexistent one. Fiction is the foreign land of my choosing, the place where I strive to convey and preserve the meaningful. And whether I write as an American or an Indian, about things American or Indian or otherwise, one thing remains constant: I translate, therefore I am.

Nine

Authorial Submissions: Publishing and Translation

Ritu Menon

The scene that greets me when I enter Aini Apa's room is truly amazing. She's sitting on a divan in her room, in front of her is an open VIP suitcase crammed with sheets of paper, there is another pile by her side, and sorting out assorted loose sheets is Rehana, her young assistant.

'Accha, now look for Chapter Eighteen,' Aini Apa tells her. Rehana rifles through the suitcase and fishes out a chapter. Aini Apa peers at it, then slaps it down next to her and says, 'No, no, not this, this is the old one—give me the corrected one—I've changed it, you see,' she says to me in an aside. Rehana rummages some more, then produces another, newer looking version, and Aini Apa declares triumphantly, 'Han! This is it. Here—"Sir Cyril Ashley in Sydney Sussex College". Now, this is final!'

'This' is none other than an English translation of *Aag ka Darya*, Qurratulain Hyder's magnum opus in Urdu, her great novel on 'Life!'. 'History. Civilisation. India. Human striving. Everything!' A great river of a novel, majestic in its sweep, grand in its vision, an acknowledged masterpiece, and published to widespread critical acclaim in 1960. In 1966 it was translated into fourteen Indian languages by the National Book Trust, in a version abridged by the author herself. But it had never been available in English. Till 1997, that is.

Qurratulain Hyder was 29 when she started writing *Aag ka Darya* in 1956–57, and it took her a year to complete. She began translating it in 1960, finished it within a year—and has been translating it ever since. 'Don't call it a translation,' she says, 'I've changed quite a lot. A translator can't do that, naturally. But when I work in English, it's another language. I have to change. Nobody else can do that!'

If it was translated as far back as 1960, I ask her, why has it never been published?

'I forgot about it!' she says ingenuously. Then, seeing a look of utter incredulousness on my face, adds hastily, 'You can call it laziness—you know, I'm so disorganised! I lost many chapters, I had to do them again. Every time I shifted I found something else was missing—anyway, now it's ready!'

And so, 40 years after it was written, and 37 years after it was first translated, *Aag ka Darya* was published in English for the first time in 1997, the 50th anniversary of India's independence. In some ways a most appropriate time for what many people regard as Qurratulain Hyder's 'Partition' novel, although she herself says she has never stopped writing about it.

At the same time as we were working on Aini Apa's translation of *Aag ka Darya*, chapter by chapter, we were also discussing the publication of three novellas by her (*Sitaharan*, *Housing Society* and *Sound of Falling Leaves* under the rubric, *Season of Betrayals*) in a translation by the Urdu scholar, C.M. Naim. This would be almost the first time that a fairly substantial offering of Aini Apa's writing, not translated by herself, was being published, for Qurratulain Hyder is well known for preferring her own translations (transcreations?) to anyone else's.

The Role of the Publisher

The anecdote I've just related, concerning a phenomenon one might describe as 'creative chaos', illustrates many of the conundrums of publishing creative writing in translation from other Indian languages into English, in India. *Aag ka Darya* is a particularly appropriate example because it compels us to consider not only the interplay of author and translator in translating, but also the role of the publisher, hitherto seldom taken into account in this enterprise.

Let me elaborate. The systematic identification, translation and publication of regional writing in English was first undertaken by the state-supported Sahitya Akademis in the 1950s and 60s. Since this essay is concerned mainly with the post-Independence period, it is important to start by noting that these initial efforts provided us with what we may call 'base line' translations of award-winning novels from one regional language into another, and into English. For the most part, the Akademis' has been a pioneering activity, and to some extent, it has served—and still serves—the purpose for which the Akademis were set up to begin with: namely, to encourage cross-cultural exchange within India and present the best of our literary output to those whose mother tongues are not the same as the works translated. In a country where twenty-two languages are officially recognised, if, as Sujit Mukherjee points out, the Akademis were to take only one title from each language and translate it into twenty-one others, they would produce four hundred and sixty-two translated books! One can imagine the scope and size of the task if such an ambitious programme were to be carried out in a comprehensive manner.

From a publishing perspective, the setting up of regional Sahitya Akademis with the objective of 'linking literatures' may be considered the first phase of translation activity in India. In this phase, non-commercial considerations were primary; quality of translation and production values were secondary, while marketing, distribution and critical attention were, and continue to be, disappointing. The selection of titles, too, favoured what was called 'representative' Indian writing, although then, as now, no one is agreed on what exactly qualifies as either 'best' or truly 'representative'.

A little later, around the 1960s, commercial publishing began to test the water gingerly. I remember first reading many translations published by Jaico and Hind Pocket Books and then, in the 1970s and 80s, by Sangam Books, Vikas, Arnold Heinemann, Oxford University Press and Bell Books. The selection of titles by these publishers was eclectic and contemporary. Vikas, for example, in its *Library of Modern Indian Writing*, published Bhisham Sahni's *Tamas* (as *Kites Will Fly*) in a translation by Jai Ratan; Kiran Nagarkar's *Seven Sixes are Forty-three*; Agyeya's *Island in the Stream*; Rajinder Awasthi's *The Red Soil*; and anthologies of Assamese, Hindi, Oriya, Sindhi, Tamil, Gujarati and Malayalam short stories. In all, it published thirty translated works in a space of about five years.

Bell Books, Vikas' paperback imprint, published Mathampu Kunhukuttan's *Ashwathama*, Indira Parthasarathy's *River of Blood*, K. Shivaram Karanth's *Whispering Earth* and Krishna Sobti's *Blossoms in Darkness*, among others. Oxford University Press's imprint, Three Crowns, published much fine poetry and drama in translation, and some excellent playscripts were published by the little magazine, *Enact*. Girish Karnad, R. Parthasarathy, A.K. Ramanujan, Mohan Rakesh, B.V. Karanth were among the brightest writers. In the late 1970s, too, was launched a very significant literary journal, *Vagartha*, with Meenakshi Mukherjee as chief editor. It appeared for a regrettably brief six years, but its twenty-five issues presented some of the most exciting and innovative writing in the languages at the time. Gieve Patel, Gauri Deshpande, Arvind Mehrotra, Moti Nandy, U.R. Ananthamurthy, Kiran Nagarkar, and many others were featured in a discerning and sophisticated selection. Years later, the best of *Vagartha*'s writing was published by Penguin India in an anthology by the same name.

This period could be said to mark the second phase of translation activity in India, characterised by the presence of more 'commercially' oriented publishers for whom presenting writing in translation was no doubt important in itself, but it also had to be economically viable. This important difference made for two further departures from the earlier state-subsidised activity: an improvement in distribution and marketing, and much greater attention to the quality of translation. As much as this second phase represented an advance on the first in terms of its range and quality, both of content and production, it was still a sporadic activity, and the books proved quite difficult to sell. Indeed by the early 1980s, Oxford University Press, Vikas and Bell Books had discontinued publishing translated books altogether, *Vagartha* had ceased publication, Sangam's list became so thin as to be almost invisible, and for a while, it looked like the whole experiment would revert to the Akademis and the National Book Trust.

Then, quite suddenly, in the late 1980s, writing in translation received an unexpected fillip through what I can only call sheer happenstance. Certainly, no one can say it was a planned or predictable development. Three publishers, independently of each other but aware of what the others were attempting, set about publishing fiction and poetry in translation with a clearly defined editorial focus, a carefully worked out acquisition and selection process, and a distinct marketing strategy. The three were Kali for Women, Penguin India and Katha, set up in 1984, 1985 and 1988 respectively; together they initiated what I would like to call the third phase of publishing translations. Of the three, one is the Indian division of the oldest and most famous paperback imprint in the world; Kali is a non-profit feminist press; and Katha, a non-governmental organisation working on sustainable learning (as Kalpavriksham) and as a story research and resource centre, Katha-vilasam, through which it fosters translations, especially of short stories.

Penguin India is a trade publisher which brings out a wide range of general interest fiction and non-fiction titles. From its very inception its publishing policy has been to develop quality translations of the best regional writing in an accessible idiom for a general readership. Kali publishes in an area generally called 'women's studies', and most of its publishing is in the social sciences, but a small amount of fiction each year, almost entirely in translation, has always been an important part of its objective of providing a forum for women's creative writing. Katha alone publishes, on the whole, only fiction in translation.[1]

The Growing Support for Translations from Publishers

Around this time, too, discussions, debates, seminars and conferences on the subject of translation grew from a slow trickle to a veritable spate. In an attempt to theorise it, academic and cultural institutions, reviewing periodicals, writers' and translators' workshops, analysed and reflected on every aspect of translation, from the production of meaning and the role of the translator as a 'translator of culture', to the politics of translation; the relationship of regional languages to metropolitan ones; and the place of the literary establishment, teaching institutions, akademis and mass media in the dissemination of translated literature. Publishing translations in this context is thus a markedly different exercise from what it was even two decades ago. My concern in this essay is to examine the place of the publisher in the creation and dissemination of Indian writing in translation, and what the different projects of the three publishers mentioned earlier tell us about how translations are commissioned, edited and published—in other words, about the politics, aesthetics and economics of publishing translations.

The commissioning of translations by a publisher—that is to say, the selection of the work to be translated, the identification of a competent and good translator, the painstaking editing and checking of the translation and finally the marketing and selling of the translated book—are part of a long-term investment in literature, and may justifiably be considered a developmental activity in every sense of the word. Each of the three publishers mentioned (joined now by Manas, Disha, Rupa and, most recently, Macmillan) commissions almost all its translations and is unique in the methods it has adopted to profile its authors and books.

Katha invites translators to enter a competition which is judged by a panel of eminent writers and litterateurs in each language. Prize-winning entries are then published as Katha Prize Stories, and the translators honoured with an award and a cash prize. At the time of writing it had published six anthologies of stories from several languages; one authology of stories, *Southern Harvest*, from the four southern languages; and two single-author anthologies, to wide acclaim. The activity of Kathavilasam has extended to holding workshops and seminars on translation and to interacting on a long-term basis with universities and colleges. This itself is an extension of conventional publishing activity (hitherto undertaken by the Akademis and other cultural outfits, rather than publishers) and an indication of the much greater awareness Katha has of its role in the ramified world of translation.

Kali's purpose in publishing the work of less known women writers from the languages is statedly political. It is part of its overall objective of presenting the totality of women's contribution to the arts, literature and scholarship in general. To this end its attempt is to uncover work previously unknown; anthologise writing by women from different languages and literatures, thus exposing better known as well as less known writers from the same language; and to publish important work previously unavailable in English, or reissue work that may have been translated but is offered afresh in a new translation that reveals other aspects of the original.

So far Kali has published anthologies of writing from Malayalam, Urdu and English (as just another Indian language!) with Tamil in the pipeline; two mixed anthologies with stories from ten languages; the major works of Ismat Chugtai, including *Terhi Lakeer*, which have been published in English for the first time; M.K. Indira's *Phaniyamma*; Qurratulain Hyder's *Aag ka Darya*; Mahadevi Varma's *Ateet ke Chalchitra*; and Taslima Nasreen's autobiography, *My Girlhood*. It is undeniable that women have been translated far less than men, even though they have been writing for as long and as powerfully, albeit against formidable odds, as pointed out, for example, by Susie Tharu and K. Lalitha in the preface to their impressive edited collection *Women's Writing in India* (Oxford University Press, 1995). By focussing on women writers exclusively (and not, as is sometimes thought, on stories about women by men) Kali's endeavour is to explore the richness of women's writing and their contribution to literature from every part of the country, but also to initiate critical enquiry into the politics of women's writing and so arrive at a gendered reading of it.

Penguin India is, quite straightforwardly, engaged in presenting the best of Indian writing, contemporary and classical, in translation, and translated works form a substantial part of its list. To them we owe O.V. Vijayan's masterly *The Legend of Khassak*, Srilal Shukla's *Raga Darbari*, Rahi Masoom Raza's *Aadha Gaon*; anthologies of Hindi and Urdu poetry, the reissue of Bhisham Sahni's *Tamas* and scores of other works from contemporary as well as classical literature. Penguin's success in marketing its books all over the country and the strong association of the imprint with quality publishing, has helped enormously in popularising Indian writing in translation, particularly over the last decade.

More recently, Manas, an imprint of East-West Books, has started to publish a series of translations from the four southern languages: Tamil, Malayalam, Kannada and Telugu, and Macmillan (India) has a most remarkable and ambitious project to publish 50 or 60 English translations of post-Independence novels from eleven Indian languages. Twenty-four have already been published, and sold out within six months of publication. All the Macmillan novels are well-known in the original, so that its editorial priority is clear: a work of acknowledged merit is chosen by the general editor for each language (well-known writers or academics themselves) and a translation commissioned. The general editor, author (if living) and translator work closely to ensure fidelity to the original and fluency in English, as well as accessibility to as wide and varied a readership as possible, within and outside India. Macmillan's long-term expectation that their translations will be used as prescribed texts is clear from the way the works have been presented, and the deliberate appending of glosses, notes and sometimes, annotations. One is reminded here of the Arden Shakespeares, and indeed Macmillan, which is basically an educational publisher, knows the value of such long-term planning. This is reinforced by the identity of its sponsor for this series, the A.R. Educational Society, Chennai.

All round then, we see a much more varied and purposeful translation activity in the third phase than we did in the earlier two, and editorial biases that will obviously have an impact on the works translated.

The Text, its Interpretation and the Politics of Publishing

At the heart of the matter lies the text: how one reads it, how one represents it and, for the purposes of this essay, how one presents it. This takes me back to the anecdote I began with, and a second one that I am about to relate. In 1986, Kali published the first translation in English of Mahasweta Devi's short story, *Stanadayini*, which appeared as 'The Wet Nurse' in the anthology *Truth-Tales*. In the same year, 1986, the well-known literary scholar Gayatri Spivak too translated the story which she called 'The Breast-Giver', and presented a 'reading' of it at a conference in Kolkata. Mahasweta Devi, who was also at the conference, presented her own reading of her story, and upon hearing Spivak's is rumoured to have exclaimed, '*Eta ki*? Is this my story she's talking about?'

Purists may well react similarly to Qurratulain Hyder's own translation of *Aag ka Darya*, for it is certain that she has departed from the original and rewritten or dropped sections of it while translating. Not even the author, they will argue, can tamper with the text after it has been published—although we are all familiar with revised, abridged, condensed and edited texts, translated or otherwise, and accept them without demur. India is unique in its multilingualism, which actually enables an author to translate his or her own work into English with confidence and flair. Can one even imagine Marquez, Kundera, Proust, Tolstoy, Mahfouz, or any other non-English-speaking writer, translating themselves? Yet we have not only Qurratulain Hyder and O.V. Vijayan insisting that they are their own best translators, but authors such as Ajeet Cour, Gauri Deshpande and Indira Goswami, for example, whose translations of their own writings *are* often better than anyone else's. And yet again there are those such as Ismat Chugtai, Lalithambika Antharjanam and Thakazhi Pillai and, yes, even Mahasweta Devi, who weren't really concerned about whether they were translated at all, let alone concerned enough to do it themselves.

The examples of Qurratulain Hyder and Mahasweta Devi assume relevance in the publishing—and translating—context today for two reasons: the volume of translations now being undertaken and in circulation, and the experience of post-coloniality which has raised important questions regarding the relationship of the centre to the periphery, the local to the global. The role of the publisher as intermediary between the author, translator and reader, and as disseminator of translated texts, is now a decisive one in the selection of translator and translation, and therefore on the impact it has outside its original language and region. So, a valid consideration could be: which translation of *Stanadayini* or *Aag ka Darya* should be privileged, and what criteria should a publisher consider in making that decision? Fidelity to the original? A politically astute representation or interpretation? An imaginative transcreation that serves the original better or a faithful rendering?

In her presentation of Mahasweta Devi's 'The Breast-Giver', Spivak offered no less than eight possible interpretations of the original: as a historian and teacher of literature; from the author's subject position; the teacher and reader's position; a Marxist feminist reading; a liberal feminist reading; and a gendered subaltern reading. Each of these might make for a different translation of it. Both translation and interpretation have an important bearing on how the story may be used by a teacher of texts, she explained, especially one concerned with the production of meaning and with the 'gendered subaltern', the protagonist of Mahasweta's story.

It is not my intention here to discuss this particular issue, important as it is, but to direct attention to a factor that may affect a publisher's decision regarding a prospective translator. In this connection, a recent development has been the use of translated texts from Latin America, Africa and Asia in courses of study in the West, and various publishers are aware of this development. Some have been supplying books for just this purpose. This is a relatively new 'market' since, hitherto, fiction made for retail sales primarily, unless prescribed for undergraduate or graduate study within India. Even today there is a very marginal requirement here. However the export potential can be significant, and for this the choice of text and translator is often carefully deliberated. Which text will ultimately be used then, and how that represents a writer, a literature, a region and a culture are the issues at stake.

Not just these, obviously. Not every anthology or novel is intended for the classroom. Indeed the majority are not and we will always have multiple readings, and consequently translations of the same text, that take their place alongside each other. Perhaps we will even develop the sanguinity of 'translators' of yore, who simply adapted texts to suit the times without unduly worrying about being 'true' to the original.

Conclusion: The Publisher as a Critical Intermediary

Rupantar, anuvad, tarjuma—none of these commonly used terms implies a literal translation, nor do they sanctify fidelity to the original. Yet such has been the anxiety surrounding the question of how to communicate or 'translate' cultural nuance, that the language and words one uses to do so come under close scrutiny. Each time the issue of Indian English—or Indo-Anglian—versus regional writing is raised (and somehow, it's always *versus*), the importance of having 'good', 'competent' or 'reliable' translations is reiterated. For, whereas regional writing is self-referencing, its translation into English immediately requires that it be judged on terms other than its own. Then the question of whether it has been *represented* faithfully or brilliantly enough becomes critical. The regional is always having to pass muster in another language (which many believe is not native to us, although this belief has been challenged), and the translator has to prove her or his credentials for being up to the task. Original writing in English however has no such hurdles to cross: its 'translatability' is not seriously at issue, no matter how local or regional its context and content.

For a publisher this makes for some poignant and problematic situations. Since we are generally agreed that there is no such thing as a 'standard' Indian English, that we may be translating and publishing from ten or more different Indian languages into 'one' English, in a single anthology, how do we achieve minimum consistency in the translation? Should we even strive for such a thing? There are two schools of thought on this: one that believes a translation should read like one, that is, it should remind the reader that it is *not* an original work; and the other that says a translated work must read like an original, fluent and graceful, with no awkward acknowledgement of being a mere approximation. Neither position really helps a publisher since, in the final analysis, the translated work will have to rely on its own strengths in the market, and its readers, whether in India or abroad, expect a certain readability in 'good' English. If they do not find it, they simply will not take the trouble to read the work in question, no matter how good or important the original may be. Nor, to be honest, will they assess the merits or demerits of the two positions mentioned earlier.

Publishers and editors have a special responsibility here precisely because they are working with many languages simultaneously, and English is only one of them and yet they function in a market where English is an international language. Hence their translations have to take their place not only with original Indian English writing, but with every other English as well. They have to be true to the spirit of the regional, and to the letter and spirit of the national or international as well. Moreover they need to take into account the native English translator of our texts who has an advantage over us in practically every respect except, perhaps, familiarity with the culture. No wonder then that the links between literatures are so difficult to forge.

Who are we translating and publishing for? If we accept the hypothesis put forward earlier of the three phases or streams in the development of translation activity in the last 40 years, then we might say that in the first continuing phase, the emphasis was on inter-regional or cross-cultural exchange within India. The endeavour was socially and culturally important in the interest of 'national integration', so to speak, and merited state support. We were translating for society and the good of literature. The second phase saw the beginnings of a more commercial orientation with greater attention being paid to economic viability—in other words, the individual reader and the 'market' figured more prominently than before, catered to by a more eclectic selection of translations. The earlier concern with promoting good writing and fostering cultural exchange was still present but this was now also tied in with the search for a market.

The third and current phase has seen a far more politically conscious and editorially focussed activity, clearly articulated marketing strategies, much wider circulation, and an informed and active involvement by publishers in the whole translation enterprise. The objective now, in addition to the other two, is to be seen, recognised and attended to in the many overlapping spheres in which we operate as writers, translators and publishers. As we saw in the opening anecdote about Qurratulain Hyder, it is now amply clear that a writer or author does not merely submit her work to a publisher and remain content. She may actively intervene and even 'subvert' her own text. Translators, too, are today often in the Spivak mould; they may actually choose self-consciously to foreground certain aspects of the text they are translating. Authorial submissions and translation subversions are part of the same increasingly sophisticated discourse that is developing around the interchange of texts on the Indian subcontinent.

Indeed, it must be said in conclusion that even as publishers have sought to 'develop' or discover a market for translations, the context itself has changed quite a bit in the last fifteen or twenty years. It is now more hospitable to this kind of publishing than it has ever been, for a number of reasons. These include the growth of Indian writing and curiosity about ourselves; the spiralling cost of imported books which actually enabled, to an extent, the spurt in creative writing in the last decade or so; much better production and packaging, and a marked increase in the export of Indian books; media attention and interest in Indian authors; a new generation of readers who have not grown up on colonial classics; and, of course, the growing confidence of publishers and translators tackling this difficult genre.

Note

1. This has changed since this essay was written. The Katha ACT programme now also publishes non-fiction in translation, as does Kali, occasionally.

Ten

Classroom Constraints: The Pedagogy of Translation

VANAMALA VISWANATHA

Translation Studies (TS from now on) is a young discipline still in the process of mapping its territory. Attempts have been made to define its boundaries and develop its terrain by scholars working in disciplines as varied as Anthropology, Comparative Literature, Culture Studies, Linguistics and Literary Theory. The challenge before us is to build up an integrated and holistic picture of TS which draws from these different perspectives. In the first section of my essay, I attempt to provide a road map of approaches to the study of translation, an upcoming academic discipline.

Introduction: Mapping the Territory

Viewing translation as a transaction between two languages, the dominant linguistic paradigm has treated it merely as a matter of grammatical and lexical transfer from the source language (SL) to the target language (TL). The work of Jakobson, Catford, Nida and Newmark exemplify this approach to TS with minor variations.

Drawing from the Firthian model of linguistic theory, Catford (1965), for instance, defines translation as 'the replacement of textual material in one language by equivalent textual material in another language'. Newmark offers a more inclusive model which takes in the contextual factors. Nida's concept of 'dynamic equivalence' is a further refinement of the notion of equivalence, albeit within the minimalist linguistic framework.

While there is no denying the fact that translators in actuality have to deal with the nitty-gritty of the two languages involved, the linguistic perspective is a reductive, partial account of the extraordinarily complex activity of translation. Often this model deals more with the product of translation than with the process, which is what practitioners of translation have to face. Further, this model which views translation as a serial process moving from the first sentence in the text to the last ignores the sociocultural setting which governs the function of the text. Perhaps because of its claim to scientificity and respectability gained by the use of jargon, and the security offered by quantifiable data and procedures, this perspective has been particularly influential in translator training programmes. And yet trainees have often felt unable to relate these theories to their own experience of translating—a factor that keeps theory out of the practitioners' orbit.

Yet another significant attempt at defining translation has traditionally come from literary criticism. The views of practising translators such as Jerome, Dryden, Pound and Nabakov constitute the bulk of some curricula at the advanced levels. The prefaces and translations done by these writers are often taken as guidelines. George Steiner's (1975) hermeneutic model which visualises four moves as essential for translation is the clearest articulation of this literary orientation: an initial trust in the meaningfulness of the text; aggression, the second move which sees interpretation as an unavoidable mode of attack; the third move is incorporative, referring to the act of importation which is bound to be unbalanced; and finally, restitution, a process in which the translation restores the equilibrium between itself and the original. However, this model, which predominantly addresses literary issues, ignores translation outside this sphere, limiting its range of applicability.

More recent attempts in Literary Theory and Cultural Studies have come from scholars such as Derrida, Spivak, Venuti, Niranjana, Toury and Lefevere. This writing has made for a valuable, radical rethinking on translation. Lefevere (1988), for instance, has argued for a shift from the epistemological question: 'What is translation?', which has only lead to an impasse in our inquiries, to a more functional one: 'What do translations do?' as a more potent and revealing way forward. These attempts have focused attention on translation as an ideological negotiation between two cultures, often unequal and hierarchically placed. Post-colonial thought has highlighted the essential violence and the politics of power implicit in translating texts from a colonised culture to the coloniser's, and has argued for 'foreignizing' translation strategies that can resist appropriation and homogenising of differences by the dominant culture. In their zeal to offer a corrective to the aesthetically oriented, politically naïve textual models, these post-colonial approaches have veered to the other extreme of ignoring the text altogether, thereby creating a gap between the translator and the text. They often obscure rather than illuminate the reading and interpretation of texts.

As Schulte (1996) observes, there has been a conspicuous movement away from the text while interpretive scholarship is dominated by metalanguage that appears to be separated from an accessible internal thought progression. Hence a translator who has to essentially work with the text feels disempowered in the face of this kind of user-unfriendly theory.

We can now gainfully turn to the translation scenario in India, for any knowledge about translation is inextricably bound up with the culture of the land. Location is crucial for the project of developing the discipline of Translation Studies. For a 'translation area' like India—a country that has lived in and through translation for centuries—and for a nation in which translation happens to be a daily business countrywide, the translation scholarship in the country is woefully meagre. Translation is such an all-pervasive and all-permeating phenomenon that we have not looked at it seriously enough as an object of academic enquiry. The work of Sujit Mukherjee, Harish Trivedi, G.N. Devy, Tejaswini Niranjana, Ayyappa Paniker and Aijaz Ahmed is noteworthy. However, one cannot ignore the goldmine that exists in the form of stray articles, prefaces, interviews and reviews in journals such as *Sethu, Indian Literature* and *Literary Criterion*. Given the absence of infrastructural facilities for publishing, it is important that teachers and scholars of TS give value to the work that is being done through these less known channels. For, these views and insights, which have been shaped by the socio-cultural ethos and the varied linguistic contexts of India, have a lot to offer to our students. One also needs to keep an eye on current debates on issues in translation published in newspapers and magazines. For instance, the polemics regarding Indian Literatures versus Indian Writing in English set off by Rushdie's assessment in the *New Yorker* (23 June 1997) and the reactions it has naturally spawned (Nabanaitha Dev Sen in *The Indian Express*, 16 July 1996) are a case in point.

When we set out to survey the field, what we have is a puzzling array of writing which looks at different aspects of translation, from totally different orientations, using widely varying metalanguage. This makes for a very confusing scene in which the choice seems to be between adopting a single approach with the attendant problems of minimalism and reductionism, and eclecticism with its attendant problems of lack of rigour, clarity and coherence.

The work of James S. Holmes (1975) and Susan Bassnett-McGuire (1991), two scholars devoted to Translation Studies, has been seminal in establishing the nature and scope of TS. They have addressed the issue of the disciplinary formation of TS in a most explicit form, with vision and foresight. Drawing on a scientific model of epistemology, Holmes describes the emergence of a new discipline thus: when a new problem comes into view, there is an influx of researchers from adjacent fields, who bring with them paradigms that have proved successful in their areas of research. In some cases this exporting is successful and therefore, the area of study is subsumed under a larger discipline; in other cases, the paradigms fail to produce results and there is a need for creating new methods. Holmes places the complex problems clustered round translation and translating in the second category.

Discussing the two major impediments to the development of TS as a 'disciplinary utopia', Holmes mentions (a) the confusion about its proper designation, and (b) the lack of a general consensus about the scope and structure of the emerging discipline. Though the first of these seems like a trivial matter, Holmes cautions us against taking it for granted. Reminding us that the map is not the territory, he argues that we cannot call a discipline by its subject matter. He is referring here to the use of the word 'translation' in conjunction with words such as art, craft, principles, philosophy—each choice of term reflecting the attitude, point of view or the scholarly fashion of the times. There have also been attempts at creating more 'learned' terms such as 'translatistics' and 'translatology', which have hardly been acceptable. Two further terms that have been used in recent years are 'the theory of translation' and 'the science of translating', which has been used by Nida (1964). While 'translation theory' is not satisfactory as it excludes the entire body of practice, the term 'science' was found to be too precise to capture the open-ended, multiple being of translation. However, 'studies' tends to be a word that describes the disciplines which fall under the Humanities or the Arts. On the analogy of Women's Studies, Holmes argues for 'Translation Studies'. And Bassnett-McGuire's book *Translation Studies* (1991) has helped establish this name as a satisfactory choice reflecting the nature of the field.

According to Holmes, the second and greater impediment to the growth of TS is the lack of any general agreement as to the nature of the field. What constitutes the discipline of TS? As we saw in section one, the answers are bound to be many, varied, incomplete and not easy to connect. Acknowledging this one-sidedness of the answers, Holmes approvingly quotes Werner Koller: 'TS is to be understood as a collective and inclusive designation for all research activities taking the phenomena of translation as the basis for focus.' Holmes privileges the idea of TS as an empirical discipline which can be categorised as 'pure' and 'applied'. He posits two main objectives of TS (Holmes 1975): (a) Descriptive TS (DTS), which aims at describing the phenomena of translating and translations as they manifest themselves in the world of our experience, and (b) Theoretical TS, which aims to establish general principles by means of which these phenomena can be explained and predicted.

DTS would include three kinds of work: product-oriented research, which describes existing translations—synchronic and diachronic, culminating in a general history of translations; function-oriented DTS, focusing on the function of the translated work in the receiving socio-cultural situation—in short, a study of context alongside the text; and process-oriented research, which deals with the act of translation itself, probing exactly what takes place in the 'little black box' of the translator's mind as s/he creates a new, matching text in another language for a detailed explanation of the psycholinguistic aspect of translation, see Kiraly 1995.

Under the other main branch of pure TS, viz., Theoretical TS, Holmes offers two categories: General Translation Theory, which aims to explain and predict all phenomena falling within the terrain of translation; and Partial Translation Theory, which specifically deals with one or a few of the various aspects of translation. Even while foreseeing that a general theory of translation would be highly formal and complex, Holmes expresses scepticism about the achievability of such a theory. While most attempts at a general translation theory have been little more than prolegomena, partial translation theories have made significant advances.

Work in this area can be characterised as: Medium-restricted, depending on whether it is machines or humans who are involved; area-restricted, depending on which languages or cultures are being talked about (Comparative Linguistics, Stylistics and Anthropology have contributed to this); rank-restricted theories, which are limited to dealing with lower linguistic ranks/levels (the rank of the word); text type-restricted, dealing with specific types or genres; time-restricted, dealing with texts belonging to contemporary and older periods; problem-restricted, focusing on a specific problem area such as translating metaphors, puns, etc.

It is possible to see the limitations even within this well-worked out framework. Holmes' model is essentially informed by the principles of positivist, empirical science—this accounts for his preference for a certain objectivity—which has since come in for questioning. Further, his notion of a general translation theory, however sceptically put forward, smacks of a universalism which again has been critiqued by post-colonial theory for its homogenising and appropriative tendencies. On the other hand, the value of this framework lies in its comprehensiveness and inclusiveness.

This framework brings together the various strands of work—linguistic, literary and cultural studies—into one interdisciplinary frame. It has the further value of establishing the relationship between these perspectives with a clarity of vision that conceives of the discipline in complex ways that are reflective of the contours in the field. Furthermore, a young discipline such as Translation Studies can easily get incorporated into already established disciplines such as Linguistics, Comparative Literature and Literary Theory, with their attractive and sophisticated articulation which can sway us easily, thereby undermining the autonomy of the new discipline. In addition, if a discipline has to take root and grow healthily, it has to enlarge, assimilate and reconcile the old and the new in ways similar to Eliot's model of tradition and the individual talent; it has to have the strength to resist the strong winds of fashion which can uproot it, even while keeping itself open to them. Holmes' work offers a comprehensive and critical map of the interdisciplinary terrain of translation on which we can plot the various old and new approaches.

However, the framework falls short of specifying just how the interdiscipline of TS functions—in what proportion, in what particular chemistry and in what kind of ambience, to serve what kind of politics. Yet it is important for us to ask ourselves if that is a fair expectation of any framework. Wouldn't it then require a degree of prescriptivism which would inevitably weaken the generalisable power of the framework? We shall return to this question later. Yet another TS scholar who has sketched the contours of the field is Susan Bassnett-McGuire. In her introduction to the revised edition (1991) of *Translation Studies*, Bassnett-McGuire discusses four general areas of interest within TS, each with a degree of overlap.

> History of Translation: This includes investigation of the theories of translation at different times, the critical response to translations, the role and function of translations in a given period, the methodological development of translation and analysis of the work of individual translators.
>
> Translation in the Target Language Culture: This includes work on the influence of a text, author or genre on the absorption of the norms of the translated text into the TL system.
>
> Translation and Linguistics: This includes work done at the phonemic, morphemic, lexical and syntagmatic levels, as well as problems of translating non-literary texts.
>
> Translation and Poetics: This includes literary translation in theory and practice—general and genre-specific studies investigating particular problems of translating poetry, theatre texts or sub-titles of films.

As Bassnett-McGuire points out, the first and third categories are relatively more popular than the second and the fourth. However, there is hardly any systematic study of translation history while the work in translation and linguistics remains rather isolated from mainstream TS. Like Holmes, Bassnett-McGuire also offers a way of seeing all the work within TS in some kind of interrelationship. She also underlines the need to be aware of work done in all the four categories in order to avoid fragmentation.

Developing the Terrain

Having acquainted ourselves with the terrain and territory covered by TS in the West, the task before us now is to see how a syllabus for TS could be made to reflect the essential interdisciplinarity of the field. Distilling the significant developments in the field, one can propose two aspects for inclusion in a syllabus—one, strengthen the knowledge base of the students and the second, enhance the skills required for translating. The names of texts or authors given under each heading is by no means exhaustive, it is only indicative of the rationale for selection. This proposal is offered in the spirit of an exploratory description of content rather than as an authoritative prescription. It could be used as source material for drawing up an actual syllabus, which will have to be responsive to local factors.

A Syllabus Proposal

I. Knowledge Component

(a) Translation theories: varied perspectives

Linguistic: Jakobson, Nida, Catford and Newmark.

Literary: Dryden, Goethe, Pound, Steiner, A.K. Ramanujan, Ramachandra Sharma and D.R. Bendre (the last three are famous Kannada poets and translators).

Cultural/Post-colonial: Venuti, Lefevere, Spivak, Sujit Mukherjee, G.N. Devy, Harish Trivedi, Tejaswini Niranjana, Homi Bhabha, Susan Bassnett-McGuire, Gideon Toury and Johar.

(b) Case studies from different contexts: The production and reception of literary translations.

International: Marquez, Tolstoy and Milan Kundera

National: Orientalist and Resistive Models

Classical Literature: Excerpts from rewritten versions of Vyasa's *Mahabharata*, Sudraka's *Mrichchakatika*, Kalidasa's *Shakuntalam*.

Modern Literature: Tagore, Premchand, Bashir and Mahashweta Devi.

Bhasha Literature (for example, Kannada)

From other languages to Kannada:
Mohan Rakesh's *Ashad Ka Ek Din*
Bankim Chandra's *Anandmatha*
Shakespeare's *Hamlet* (multiple versions)
B.M. Srikanthaiah's *English Geethahalu*
D.V. Gundappa's *Omar Khayyam*

II. Skills Component: Translation Practice

(a) Translation and analysis of texts from the following domains: literary discourse, scientific discourse, legal writing, officialese, journalistic writing, advertisements, children's literature and sub-titles of films.

(b) Study of multiple translations:

Lankesh's poem *Avva*
Yeats' *Leda and the Swan*
Vacana poetry—three samples
Shakespeare's sonnet *Shall I Compare Thee*

(c) Student Project:

Producing a translation of 20–30 pages from either Kannada or English, along with comments on the process of translating.

Producing a term paper on a translated text in context.

Evaluation Schema for a Translation Pedagogy

50% for theory questions comprising two essays (15 + 15) and two short notes (10 + 10). 50% for practice comprising five 10-mark questions covering a wide variety of texts.

* * *

The previous section offered a list of topics and authors that could form the content of a TS programme in very general terms. The first component has the views of both theorists and professional translators since both have as much to contribute to the development of translation thinking among students. This proposal, which is by no means a fully developed syllabus, needs to be adapted to suit the local conditions in different academic settings. The first crucial consideration that will determine syllabus design is the larger aim of the teaching programme.

Brian Mossop (1992: 402) has, for instance, discussed three types of programmes with differing aims: one focussing on methods of translation; the second on training researchers and translation teachers; and the third on training professional translators. Even while the thrust and orientation of each programme will be different, it is possible to posit some common goals for teaching TS.

On the analogy of Chomsky's notion of 'linguistic competence' and Culler's (1975) extension of it—'literary competence'—as a viable goal of literary pedagogy, one can argue for 'translation competence' as the minimal goal of a TS programme. The phrase has been variously used as 'translational competence' and 'translator competence', reflecting slight changes in orientation. Thus scholars differ in their perceptions about what constitutes translation competence. Wilss (1982: 58) describes it as the amalgamation of: (a) SL receptive competence, (b) TL reproduction competence and (c) a supercompetence reflecting the ability to transfer messages between the two languages.

For Neubert (1992: 412), 'translation involves variable tasks that make specific demands on the cognitive system of the translator' and translational competence enables translators to cope with these tasks. He proposes a tripartite structure to this competence: (a) language competence, (b) subject competence and (c) transfer competence—the acquisition of each of these related methodologies and skill components demanding differential methodologies from translation scholars and teachers. While one can see considerable overlap in these two definitions, Neubert points to the mastery of subject matter that a translator needs to have. Pym (1992: 281), in an attempt at transcending the minimalist linguistic bias of the other definitions, offers a more complex picture when he defines translation competence as the union of two skills: (a) 'the ability to generate a target text series of more than one viable term (target text 1, target text 2, ...target text n) for a source text' and (b) 'the ability to select only one target text from this series, quickly and with justified confidence, and to propose this target text as a replacement of source text for a specified purpose and reader.'

A consideration of purpose and reader makes for a more refined articulation of translation competence as it extends the framework to include factors of time, place and politics (for example, who is translating, for whom, which text, why, when and how). These are considerations of history, politics and culture, hitherto largely ignored in TS. Further, it also highlights another quality of the translator—the adaptability to produce different styles for differing purposes, which again forcefully argues for a strong knowledge and skill base for a translator to make appropriate choices, an enterprise at the heart of the translator's profession.

Kiraly (1995: 15) reports on a major controversy about whether translation competence is innate or learned. Scholars such as Harris and Sherwood (1978), Toury (1995) and Lorscher (1991) claim that the ability to translate is innate since, in their view, all second language learners are incipient translators. Therefore they argue that the purpose of a TS programme would be to intervene in the ongoing process of translator competence development and help the native translator move faster and more effectively along a continuum from incipient to active, professional translator. Against this position, Honig and Kubmaul argue that second language learners cannot really translate because they have not acquired an understanding of translation as a unique form of communication. At best, such learners can transcode from one language to another, not translate, which involves the knowledge and skill to incorporate situational factors.

Going by Pym's definition of translation competence, which captures the act of translation in all its complexity, we see that a translator needs to develop multiple styles of translating and then choose from amongst them to suit the intent and audience of the translation. Therefore if a training programme can help a translator evolve modern styles of functioning which would extend his/her repertoire of strategies/styles even while affirming what comes naturally to him/her, then it would constitute a positive intervention. Second, the knowledge component is inevitable for making informed choices. A decision based on reasoning and knowledge will make for a more confident and self-assured translator.

It is for this reason that I wish to argue for the inclusion of the knowledge and the skill components which come together in an effective, holistic manner in a successful translator. There is also scope for a programme that aims to focus on training only scholars who would study TS as a subject rather than become practitioners. Then the knowledge component can be enhanced further and the skills could be underplayed. However, a sound foundation in translation practice and hands-on experience are invaluable even for a scholar/theorist/reviewer/teacher of translation. Further, given the yet-to-be-established status of the discipline in Indian academia, we are well-advised not to get too specialised at the moment.

Methodological Procedures for a Translation Pedagogy

If translation competence is the primary goal of a TS programme, how do we achieve this in actual classroom terms? The first consideration in evolving an effective methodology is related to the fact that acquiring any competence requires the learner to be at the centre of the classroom. Therefore, the learner has to begin by actually translating. This is an obvious but important reminder, for we are still working predominantly with teacher-centred approaches, especially at the graduate level. The lecture may be an appropriate mode for compiling and transmitting information but certainly not for promoting skills such as intensive reading and writing.

Schulte (1996) puts it this way: 'The translator transforms the act of reading into an act of performing the text', and he offers a most graphic picture of this reaching out across languages. Therefore learners have to be trained to read, understand and analyse SL texts thoroughly. As a first step, learners have to be trained in hermeneutics—the science of interpretation. How do we enable learners to focus attention on the reading processes in making sense of the SL texts and on rendering them in the TL?

For any translation pedagogy, there is a further and widely acknowledged problem of linking theory and practice. For these two facets are much more organically related to one another in TS than in any other discipline. Keeping in mind both translational as well as pedagogical considerations, the following approach is suggested for responsive and responsible use by teachers. For every classroom is unique and unpredictable, these general criteria, offered as samples and not as models for teaching, have to be translated into actual classroom terms by the teacher.

Formulating a possible methodology for 'theory revision' in teacher-training, a process in which teacher-trainees relate their intuitions derived from practice to the findings of academic research, Ramani (1987) posits four general processes: articulation, confrontation, examination and reformulation. These processes of theory revision bear an uncanny resemblance to the hermeneutic processes of meaning-making involved in translation. To maximally exploit the sequence of stages suggested below, the teacher should monitor his/her own interventions in a way that 'supports' the occurrence of these processes rather than pre-empt them.

Stage I: Reader Meets Text

It is important that at the very first stage the reader 'meet' the text and interact with it at whatever level s/he can. In trying to grapple with the text unaided and unmediated, s/he will bring to bear on the reading whatever strategies s/he already possesses. It is important that the teacher remain unobtrusive and encourage learners to actively seek out help using standard bilingual dictionaries, thesauri, reverse dictionaries and encyclopaedia. The process of reading thus initiated will now become intrinsically motivating for the reader as s/he will have invested considerable time and effort in coming to terms with the experience that the text presents.

Stage II: Articulation of Response

By way of making their initial grasp of the text explicit, the learners are asked to translate it. These first two stages are best done as homework to save class time.

Stage III: Examination of Different Versions

Having collected the first drafts, the teacher starts a process of examining them more deeply using the text as a 'public court of appeal'. The learners are then encouraged to defend their interpretation of the text, in view of the differing readings offered. By asking a series of general questions on the theme, attitude and structure of the text, the teacher redirects their attention to the intricacies of the text. At this stage, it would be stimulating to bring in extra-textual data such as biographic details, writer's stated intention, prefaces, critical material and period-related aspects into the discussion for a more complex understanding of the text. The students are asked to make any changes they like in their versions in light of the discussion.

Stage IV: Confrontation and Negotiation in Interpretation

We can visualise this happening at three or four further levels in which confrontation of interpretations takes place in small groups, in large groups, with the teacher, with professional translators and with theorists. The learners can be asked to share their versions in small groups. Working with peers provides a non-threatening atmosphere for learning. Also, this collective process of dealing with differences within the group makes for a concerted effort in which learners learn from one another.

Once this kind of total engagement with the text is created, students can then be asked to look at one/multiple versions produced by professional translators. See Schulte (1996) for a very insightful analysis of how multiple translations work. The attempt here is not to lead them all towards one acceptable interpretation but to get them to see how different interpretations become possible.

Each group has to formalise through discussion, the differences between their version and the professional translators'; and in the case of multiple translations, the differences between them. This discussion is bound to generate a working set of criteria to look at any translation. These criteria could then be juxtaposed against established translation norms offered by theorists. For instance, Dryden's concept of paraphrase, metaphrase and imitation could be studied inductively by placing them against the students' criteria. Or, Venuti's (1995) notion of foreignising and domesticating translation strategies can be studied by applying them to the translation of *Shakuntalam* done by orientalist scholars such as William Jones and Moniere Williams, as opposed to the more recent version by Chandra Rajan.

The practice of translation—one's own and others—can thus become a priceless tool to prise open and critically read the theoretical articulations of TS scholars. For an illustration of how case studies can be gainfully used in translation classes, see Gerzymisch-Arbogast and Ursula Schnatmeyer (2001). It is time teachers of translation appropriated translation scholarship to suit their agendas.

Stage V: Reformulation of Revised Interpretations

The last stage in the actual process of translation is crucial in bringing together theory and practice. The students are asked to rewrite their first draft in the light of the various tiers of discussion. This step helps them to consolidate what they have absorbed from the confrontation and use that most concretely and immediately to refine their versions. As a further step towards integration, the students are asked to explain and substantiate their specific choice of style and language in translation. Such an approach breaks the prescriptive, canonical hegemony of theory over practice and reveals the spatial-temporal-ideological biases which inform that theory while simultaneously empowering learners to operate from their individual standpoints: one that has emerged from their full-bodied engagement with the linguistic, literary, cultural and political aspects of the text.

These procedures achieve the two-fold aim of providing a context for analysing the specific factors of the production of the SL text and of encouraging the production of a varied range of versions to suit specific purposes and audiences.

Stage VI: Evaluation

Judging what a good translation is clearly then not a neutral, absolute or universal matter. A translated work is received in a context that is shaped by the canon prevalent in the target language culture. Therefore translations should necessarily be judged by the constituents that make up translation competence: (a) Is the student able to produce different versions of a text? The evaluation of the skills would directly depend on the variety and flexibility in the repertoire of strategies and styles that the student can employ in producing different versions; (b) Is the student aware of the genre, intent, milieu, readership and canonical aspects of the SL and the TL situations? Has there been a match between his/her stated purpose and politics and the strategies used?

Discussing the importance of an appropriate evaluation technique for translator training, Kiraly (1995) mentions the value of translations in which students must justify the translation decisions they have made and display the effective use of resource materials, all of which indicate how responsibly the student has carried out the translation. Kiraly further quotes the work of Holz-Manttari who argues that a valid test requires task specifications (text source, original function-intention, target readership and translation function) which are important not only while testing but throughout a student's training.

Conclusion

If there is consensus then in translation scholarship on any one issue, it centres around the interdisciplinary nature of TS. As suggested by many scholars, only an interdisciplinary approach which takes into account aspects of language, society and culture can provide new principles to guide the teaching of TS. But as Neubert (1992: 418) argues, the crucial question is how an inter-discipline can acquire a sense of identity without losing itself 'in a limbo of competences continually encroaching upon each other'. In response, he points to the integrating power of the act of translation and the role of the translator as the great and only generalist in our age of the unique and self-proclaimed specialist. Acknowledging the central role of synthesis in translation, Schulte (1996) writes,

> *At a time when the world suffers from the nervousness of fragmentation, the paradigm of translation offers an integrating model. Everything in a text and a culture is related to something else. In its final act, translation recreates the wholeness of a work and teaches us to feel comfortable with the complexity of our modern world. The integrating power of translation methodologies also transcends the limitations of disciplinary boundaries and thus opens the path for meaningful interdisciplinary studies.*

Whether one attributes this kind of a harmonising role to translation or one would rather posit a more radical, political agenda of transgression (Niranjana: 1992), what is being underlined here is the fit between intent and strategy that translation demands in a unique chemistry.

References

Ahmed, Aijaz, 1992. *Theory: Classes, Nations, Literatures*. Mumbai: Oxford University Press.

Bassnett-McGuire, Susan, 1991. *Translation Studies*. London: Routledge.

Bhabha, Homi, 1994. *The Location of Culture*. New York and London: Routledge.

Catford, J.C., 1965. *A Linguistic Theory of Translation*. London: Oxford University Press.

Culler, Jonathan, 1975. *Structuralist Poetics*. New York and London: Routledge.

Devy, G.N., 1993. *In Another Tongue: Essays on Indian English Literature*. Mumbai: Macmillan.

Gerzymisch-Arbogast and **U. Schnatmeyer**, 2001. 'Case Studies in Teaching Translation'. In M.L. Larson (ed.), *Translation: Theory and Practice, Tension and Interdependence*. New York: State University of New York Press.

Harris, B. and **B. Sherwood**, 1978. 'Translating as an Innate Skill'. In Gerber and Sinaiko (eds) *Language Interpretation and Communication*. New York and London: Plenum.

Holmes, James S., 1975. *The Name and Nature of Translation Studies*. Amsterdam: University of Amsterdam Press.

Honig, H.G. and **P. Kubmaul**, 1982. *Strategie de Ubersetzung*. Tübingen: Gunter Narr Verlag.

Jakobson, Roman, 1966. 'On Linguistic Aspects of Translation'. In R.A. Brower (ed.), *On Translation*. New York. pp. 232–39.

Kiraly, D.C., 1995. *Pathways to Translation: Pedagogy and Process*. Kent: Kent State University Press.

Lefevre, André, 1992. *Translation, Rewriting and the Manipulation of Literary Fame*. London, New York: Routledge.

Lorscher, W., 1991. *Translation Performance, Translation Process and Translation Strategies: A Psycholinguistic Explanation*. Tübingen: Gunter Narr Verlag.

Mossop, B., 1992. 'Goals and Methods for a Course in Translation Theory'. In Mary Snell-Hornby, Franz Pochhacker and Klans Kaindli (eds) *Translation: An Interdiscipline*. Amsterdam: John Benjamins.

Mukherjee, Sujit, 1994. *Translation as Discovery and Other Essays on Indian Literature in Translation*. Hyderabad: Orient Longman.

Neubert, Albrecht, 1992. 'Translation as Discovery: A Complex Skill, How to Study and Teach It'. In Mary Snell-Hornby, Franz Pochhacker and Klans Kaindli (eds) *Translation: An Interdiscipline*. Amsterdam: John Benjamins.

Newmark, Peter, 1981. *Approaches to Translation*. London: Pergamum Press.

Nida, E.A., 1964. *Towards a Science of Translating With Special Reference to Principles and Procedures Involved in Bible Translation*. Leiden: Brill.

Niranjana, Tejaswini, 1992. *Siting Translation: History, Poststructuralism and the Colonial Context*. Berkeley: University of California Press.

Pym, Anthony, 1992. 'Translation, Error Analysis and the Interface with Language Teaching'. In Cay Dollerup and Anne Loddegaard (eds) *Teaching Translation and Interpretation*. Amsterdam: John Benjamins.

Ramani, E., 1987. 'Theorizing from the Classroom'. *ELT*, vol. 41, no. 1, pp. 3–11.

Schulte, R., 1996. 'Mapping the Geography of Translation for the 1990s'. *Translation Review*, vol. 30, no. 31, pp. 9.

Spivak, Gayatri, 1992. 'The Politics of Translation' in *Outside in the Teaching Machine*. New York: Routledge.

Steiner, George, 1975. *After Babel*. London: Oxford University Press.

Toury, G., 1995. *Descriptive Translation Studies and Beyond*. Amsterdam: John Benjamins.

Trivedi, Harish, 1993. *Colonial Transactions: English Literature and India*. Kolkata: Papyrus.

Venuti, Lawrence, 1995. *The Translator's Invisibility: A History of Translation*. London: Routledge.

Wilss, W., 1982. *The Science of Translation: Problems and Methods*. Tübingen: Gunter Narr Verlag.

Eleven

Horizon of Expectations: Hermeneutics and Translation

C.T. Indra

The central concern of this essay is to examine the subliminal act of interpreting in the act of translating. Hence it may even have been appropriate to give it the title 'Interpreting While Translating'. However, part of my concern is also to locate the interface between critical theory, which has emerged as an all-subsuming academic discipline in recent years, and translation, which has been around for centuries in practice but which has now taken a new avatar in these multicultural, multipolar, postmodern times. One of the key issues in critical theory is to rethink the very idea of the text that is conceived in traditional reading practices as a stable entity flowing continuously from the author to the reader. By now, it is widely acknowledged that meaning is an indeterminate constituent in the pragmatic transaction between the text and the reader. No attempt at interpretation may guarantee a total transmission of meaning. In fact, as I.A. Richards recognised long ago, every attempt at interpreting is a kind of translation. Hence the close relationship between reading and translation.

Subversive developments in critical theory, however, have not completely succeeded in annulling the force of hermeneutical problems. Traditional hermeneutics sacralised the nature of the text because, both in the West and the East, it was concerned with interpreting scripture. In the modern phase of its history, hermeneutics first developed the idea of 'congeniality' as its principal task—that is, 'the re-experiencing by the critic or his reader of the psychical event of meaning undergone by the author in the first place' (Jefferson and Robey 1986: 124). Frederick Schleiermacher (1768–1834) recommended this approach. The reader by a leap completes the 'hermeneutical circle' in his attempts to move from the 'parts' to the 'whole'. The theoretical interest in this model is the Romantic notion of the possibility of achieving an identical reading (in the case of translation, we may use the term 'rendering'). In the history of hermeneutics we next find Wilhelm Dilthey (1833–1911) proposing that hermeneutics may be made to approximate science. Dilthey argued that although every individual is historically situated, it is possible to achieve an intelligible general understanding of human nature.

It is at this point that we find the epistemological turn hermeneutics was taking in the works of phenomenologists such as Edmund Husserl (1859–1938) and his pupil, Martin Heidegger (1889–1976). Husserl claimed that consciousness is always consciousness of something. He used the term 'intentionality' to describe the act of consciousness. The act of consciousness 'completes' the objects of its perception by realising in turn all of their perspectives which are never all 'visible' from one point of view or 'aspect' (Jefferson and Robey 1986: 250). This process is described as 'concretization'. The theoretical interest of this model is its emphasis on the 'intersubjective' nature of the act of perception, i.e., meaning is neither totally in the realm of the objective nor totally in the subjective.

Heidegger went a step further and emphasised the role of historicity in phenomenology. He argued that understanding is not an autonomous, historical human activity. For him understanding is linguistic, historical and ontological. Heidegger thus linked historical, epistemological and ontological aspects of interpretation. This has had a far-reaching impact on poststructuralist theories of text, meaning and interpretation.

Hans-Georg Gadamer, another hermeneutician, goes beyond both Schleiermacher's psychological theory of understanding and Dilthey's privileging of method in interpretation. He starts with

Heidegger's claim of historicism and temporality and acknowledges as productive the temporal distance (*Zeitabstand*: that which separates the interpreter from the subject to be interpreted).

Hermeneutics has been long concerned with the central question: 'How can a text be protected from misunderstanding from the start?'—a concern which translation also shares with regard to the source text. Gadamer proposes the following steps:

(1) *one should bring into consciousness any anticipatory ideas which may affect the act of interpretation;*
(2) *one should be aware of the modern habit of privileging a certain mode of historicism;*
(3) *one should revive and revalue the concept of prejudice (Vorurteil).*

For Gadamer, authority is both a source of prejudice and a source of truth (133). Further, he avers that there is no single object towards which all historical research or all interpretation of a given text is directed, i.e., interpretation is not tending towards some future, perfect, complete recovery of meaning but is rather an act of preservation of the past in our present consciousness. For Gadamer too, then, the act of interpretation is intersubjective.

The insights of phenomenology and hermeneutics have provided part of the basis for a variety of theories focusing on the reception of a work and on the reader. The German school of Reception Aesthetics tries to reconcile the claim of the formal aspects of a work with that of its historical and ideological dimensions. Han's Robert Jauss proposes a new 'aesthetics of reception' on this basis. There is a 'horizon of expectations' which refers to the shared set of expectations among a given generation of readers. This horizon is trans-subjective and can be accessed through textual strategies such as genre, literary allusion, the nature of fiction and poetic language, which confirm, alter or subvert the reader's expectations. We may use them to discern the departure of a work from the horizon of expectations. We can even use them to distinguish between texts which are just passively read and those which offer 'resistance' to the reader.

Although the overall framework of this paper is based on problems in hermeneutical and epistemological practices, it may be relevant at this point to invoke the deconstructive view of a text.

Deconstruction aims at showing that a text deconstructs itself when re-examined rigorously and that meaning is a matter of constant deferral rather than a positive affirmation. Able deconstructionists have demonstrated these radical claims. Even so it would be appropriate to recall the distinction which Roland Barthes once made between 'lisible' and 'scriptible' texts, i.e., 'lisible', or 'readerly', texts are those which don't offer any resistance to the reader but which are simply consumed; whereas 'scriptible', or 'writerly', texts challenge the reader's creativity, even compelling him to remake them. This is true of translation too. The nature of the text may determine the nature of translation.

Metafictionality and Translation

In the reading of literature in our times, it has been widely accepted that one of the marks of modern or new writing is self-consciousness about the act of writing. In post-modern fiction we have a term to describe this feature: *metafiction*. There is also another aspect, namely, self-reflextivity, i.e., where the technique of narration draws attention to itself rather than to any reality which is exclusively objective or external. In fact, much of recent sophisticated writing in English and, we have reason to believe, in many Indian languages, continuously reconstitute the contingent reality and query the very certainty of our quotidian assumptions about reality. This subversive tenor has its echo in ideological fiction too; fiction, that is, which critiques an existing sociocultural order through an oblique technique.

Translation of such *metafictional* and self-reflexive texts should give us an idea of the nature of their textuality. Sometimes good texts in one language read rather drably when translated into another language. Sometimes an ordinary text turns out to be quite impressive in translation. These are features every translator has noticed. Now that translation has staked its claim to being recognised as an academic discipline and that reading practices have changed considerably with radical alterations in the very concept of discourse, it may be worthwhile to draw attention to the nature of the text in dealing with translation. An attempt should be made to closely follow the nature of the discourse in the source text—whether it be an epistemological or an ideological concern.

In dealing with the text in this way, we may gain a refined perception of the problems of translation. The translator may be not only rendering, she may be unconsciously interpreting. Hence translation takes on a hermeneutical dimension. This may lead to a discussion on translation, on varieties of translation of the same literary item for varieties of purposes/readers. In the house of translation, as in the house of fiction, there are many windows, and each one of them offers a different angle of vision. Any translation which combines the virtues of a free-flowing rendition (which attempts to make the reading fluid) and an interpretative type of rendition (which tries to capture the nuances—lexical, syntactic, imagistic, ideological—in the original) is sure to make a happy impact when read. That is where translation and hermeneutics can be shown to share some of their premises.

In translation, we always have a source text and a target language. A professional translator, like a professional critic or theorist, is bound to construct the hermeneutical framework in terms of the author's horizon, his habits of writing, his preoccupations, the type of genre which a chosen text belongs to, or resembles, and the larger social discourse within which the content of the text is embedded, especially while tackling recondite passages or while confronting patches of indeterminacy. This process of 'situating' a text enables a translator to check whether a matching version is emerging or has emerged. In traditional hermeneutics, we have the final task of validating an interpretation. But today the claim of absolute validation has been given up even in hermeneutics. Similarly in translation, there may not be the perfect translation that may be hailed as legitimate. Instead we may have competing versions with varying centres of validity depending, to some extent, on the translator's perception of what is striking about what s/he is working on.

Fiction through Translation

This essay hopes to demonstrate the usefulness of the somewhat abstract points made above by examining two instances of short fiction in Tamil and the interesting points they raise in translation. The first example is Muthusamy's story 'Nadappu'. A Tamil speaker immediately asks herself, shall we render it as 'happening' or 'the way things happen' or 'what is in vogue' or as 'what happens'? It is not merely multiplicity of meaning that is the problem in translating the title of this story from Tamil to English, it is the very undecidability of any rendering that is striking.

The index to this undecidability is the syntax of the story. As a translator I felt at every point how almost every third sentence impeded any straightforward teleological activity such as that of deriving a paired meaning on the basis of a closed syntax. In fact, the syntax of this story is any translator's despair. The switch-over from the past to the present and from the present to the past is common enough in Tamil. But in this story it is deliberately employed to splice different time sequences. This makes it difficult to understand what is going on. For example, the narrator describes in the story a particular event—his falling into a well at the back of the house. But suddenly in the process of describing his confused state of mind as a child while slipping into the well in a bucket, the narrator, without any syntactical marker whatsoever begins to describe an earlier fall he had into a neighbour's well. For a moment the translator is destabilised. That fall resulted in a rather violent descent, bruising the child. At this point, the reader is likely to be confused, thinking that there is a contradiction between the two descriptions. Then the narrator says, 'It was a well with plenty of water into which I had fallen then, it burnt where the water touched the scraped skin'. And then, without the use of any time marker whatsoever, the narrator goes on to say, 'Since I was sitting in the bucket while falling it did not scratch anywhere'.

When this complicated narration is rendered in a free-flowing translation it reads as follows: 'I experienced such a feeling when I fell later into an open well next door, while pushing down with my hands the water scoop of the irrigation shaft'. But in the original there is no word to indicate that it was a later fall. The translation goes on:

Instead of placing my foot on the crossbar, I misjudged my step and my feet encountered emptiness as I fell into the well. I felt the shock then, as my heart gave a jolt. I was bruised all over. Many things happened

> *in rapid succession, each new bruise driving out the memory of the previous one. The crossbar scratched my ribs. The water scoop was jolted out of my hands and hit me squarely in the face. My head hit against one of the steps set inside the well as I fell, leaving pieces of my skin and hair plastered to the stone. This time I had fallen into a well with plenty of water. My body burnt when the bruised portions came into contact with the water. When I had fallen into the well, sitting inside a bucket, there were no bruises.* (Translation A)

Translation A reads smoothly, having sorted out the ambiguities in time sequences by interpolating markers such as 'later' and 'this time'. To another translator, however, the objective of the story might be to stress the primacy of the epistemological process rather than to pose the naïve question: what happened to the boy one night? Or, how did the boy happen to fall into the well? Although the apparent focus is an event which happened to the narrator when he was a three-year-old boy—his falling into a well while playing with a bucket—this focus appears to be deliberately blurred by the mode of narration.

Since the narrative voice itself poses a challenge, a closer approximation to the original syntax may be called for. The reminiscence is that of a grown-up man but the recollections are, curiously, neither those of an adult nor those of a child. Hence the very contorted description of the process of falling into the well is at once reflective of the boy's confusion in the night while slipping down into the well and of the intellectual agility and pleasure of a complex, adult, perceiving mind. The minute, authentic renderings of the sensations felt by the boy, without missing the slightest shades of the experience of falling into the well, are part of the child's sphere. But the register in which they are rendered bears the mark of a highly sophisticated adult mind that takes an impish delight in converting an event into a sheer ontological puzzle. This seems to be at the crux of the abrupt mixing of two different occasions in which the boy fell into two different wells, one with and the other without an apron. The additional hazards that one faces in a well without an apron are suddenly juxtaposed without any transition. The reader is, for a moment, quite confused about his bearings in the story. But the translator might do well to try, at the risk of failure, to capture the ambiguity. Take this extract where the first person pronoun 'my' is not used because, in the original Tamil version, there is an attempt to recall how the child witnessed what happened to him while falling. This is as though he were an extraneous object instead of the subject to which things happened:

> *The plank across scraped the ribs. The bailing bucket that was pressed down slipped from the hand, rose up to hit the face and scraped it. While falling down, on the way the head knocked against one of the rings. A piece of flesh with some hair got stuck there. I had then fallen into a well with plenty of water. The touch of water on the scratched skin gave a burning sensation. Since I was sitting in the bucket while falling it did not cause any scratch.* (Translation B)

In Translation B, one can hardly fail to notice how the last sentence abruptly brings the reader to the present moment of narration.

Indeed, navigating in the tossing waters of this type of narration can be quite a frustrating experience. But therein lies its pleasure and delight too. The opening description in the story of the different types of wells sounds quite professional and makes the reader expect a discursive kind of story. Suddenly the reader is plunged into a verbal maze even as the child-boy in the story plunges into the well. Although every detail about the well's structure is realistic and the minutiae (such as the cobwebs powered over with minced brick) are never missed, it is not certain whether the child is extraordinarily sharp even in the moment of his dizzying fall or whether it is the adult who superimposes his understanding of the event on the narration, in hindsight. On a closer reading, the translator finds that the narration is fascinating not so much because of its ontological quest but because of the epistemological thrust of its rhetoric. Every movement is graphically sketched only to be superimposed on by another movement, blurring its reality:

> *Even so the bucket must have hit hard the bottom of the well, when it fell with such force. The little water that had collected in the spring must have however prevented the full force of the shock from being felt. Notwithstanding, I might have received the shock that was inevitable. I don't know, I might have been frightened by the gathering darkness in such a narrow place. Over me there was the weight of the well rope.*

The water that splashed because of the force of the fall must have made the rope wet. Around me there was water though not deep. In shock I might have been lying unconscious. Or else still conscious, shrinking in sheer fright, I might have been sitting, trembling, holding fast to the bucket. (Translation B)

The syntactical repetition—'I could have felt it', 'I might have done this'—reveals the epistemological emphasis of the narrator. The ambiguity in syntax accounts for the undecidability of meaning encountered, almost from the beginning. A supreme example is the place, a little before the one just cited, where the boy touches the bottom of the well. One first gets the impression that it is the water at the bottom of the well that is referred to. But soon it suggests itself as a simile: that of a pothole which can only hold a handful of water. Compare two versions of the translation:

The heart gives a jolt, even if it is only a small puddle of water one steps into unexpectedly at night, while walking on level ground. When the raised foot encounters an emptiness beyond the pressure exerted to place it on firm ground, it seems to go limp. The brain registers the shock and the nerves under the skin tingle with a raw, bruised feeling. I wonder if one feels all this when one is just three. (Translation A)
In the night even when one sets foot on a pot-hole that can barely hold a handful of water, mistaking it for level ground, the heart experiences a thud. The limb buckles losing even the little energy that went into our walking on level ground. The fall hits the brain. It feels as though the flesh underneath the skin is scraped with something with a rough surface. Who knows if a three-year old can have such a sensation? (Translation B)

While the first version explains the knowledge the boy gets through the experience of falling into the well, the second version tries to lead to this knowledge in and through the experience. The first, thereby, tends to preclude the reader's experiencing the event. The details are there in both the versions, but the ordering either creates or negates the experience.

Another feature of this story is the clever use of hearsay and third person reporting. The central event is the boy's fall into the well. The accretions of the narration are what happens in the village on hearing the news and how people react to it. The camera shifts from within the well to the street and back to the well. Even the ending of the story exploits the ambiguity characteristic of polyphonic narration. The narrator recalls how others recalled his father's reaction on seeing Kannusami come up the well with the child. We are not sure whether the father is sufficiently grateful to Kannusami for rescuing his son:

> *Father had returned for Sembanarkoil. He gathered me in his arms. The blood on my body seemed to have shaken him until somebody shouted, 'that is only Kannusami's blood'.*
>
> *Father looked at Kannusami with blood oozing from his trembling hands and said, 'Kannusami... you saved my son today. Hereafter you shall get a* kalam *of paddy from me every month as long you live.'* (Translation A)

> *Father too arrived from Sembanarkoil. He took me from Kannusami. It seems he was shocked to see the blood running down on me. It's the blood from our Kannusami's hand, Sir, someone in the crowd seems to have said.*
>
> *Looking at Kannusami, his hand dripping with blood and shaking, father is reported to have said, 'Kannuswami, you saved my child. So long as I am alive, I shall give you every month a* kalam *of paddy'.* (Translation B)

When we retain the markers of reporting, the translation captures the original tenor of the narration in the text. It helps to articulate the distinction in the original between the child's consciousness and the adult's recollection of the event.

Yet another feature of the story is its employment of analogies which are at once so certain and yet indefinite. The classic instance is related to the man running at breakneck speed to inform the father about his son's fall into the well. The central figure of the analogy is the rotation of a wheel with its spokes losing shape and its axle whirling. This familiar image is utterly distorted by being used to describe a man running madly. His very human form is lost. He is converted grotesquely from a biped to a quadruped and then to a wheel.

> *How fast can a biped human being run? He isn't a four-legged horse, is he? Or is he a wheel that can move even faster? It has several spokes.*

> *At the most he can become four-legged. He can use his two hands. He should turn them into the spokes of a wheel and not the limbs of an animal. Surely, it is an impossible feat.* (Translation B)

The last sentence as it stands in Tamil can also be rendered as:

> *Only by turning cartwheels can a man run like that.* (Translation A)

But the Tamil phrase 'karanam podudal' (rendered in A as 'turning cartwheels') is an idiomatic expression which suggests 'attempting the impossible'. Since the context here suggests the virtual impossibility of a man actually *turning into* a wheel, the sentence may also be rendered as a comment by a narrator quite astonished at the event.

The interiority of the consciousness of the man running crazy, like a rolling wheel, reconstitutes the reality not just for him but also for the reader, through the eyes of the narrator. The speed and the state of mind of the man are described in terms of his impressions of the visual distortions of the scene around him—trees all swaying in one direction, the scene and sights on both sides of the road whizzing past him and going over behind him. His speed transforms all objects and their reality outside:

> *Even today I have a vision of him running. Like the blades of the table-fan, his arms and legs losing their contours, give the illusion of rotating backwards. The head alone looks like the hub whirling at the centre. The trees on the roadside dash against each other and run like mad towards Punjai.* The groves on the sides of the road revolve trying to change direction. *Banana plants faint falling into one green. With him as the axle all the scenes rotate. On the left and on the right in a semi-circle, swinging in the opposite direction they go behind him and get fixed.*

Supposing we translate the sentence emphasised above as follows: The groves on the sides of the road revolve *as if* trying to change direction. The effect is not the same. 'As if' separates the narrator from the experience. Here the narrator lives the experience.

The ending of the story is an instance of a volte-face. All this seriousness, the terror of the fall, the anxiety of the parents and the devotion of Kannusami, are in one stroke demolished by the simple humorous touch—the boy running away from Kannusami to escape his narration. Given his impish delight in the act of narration, the translation must capture this overtone in rendering the ending:

> *Till he died he was never tired of telling me the tale of his descent into the well. There have been occasions when I had to run away from him to escape his narration.*

Theory and Ideological Practice

My second example is Ambai's short story 'A Deer in the Forest'. The title itself sets up a frame of reference in terms of the narrative category: the subgenre of a children's tale. It contains a tale within a tale inasmuch as we have the story of Aunt Thangam containing the story of the deer in the forest. Any reader interested in subliminal discourse—be he the interpreter or translator—will be able to see that within these stories is embedded an ideological critique of a particular social set-up and its institutionalised values. We learn that Aunt Thangam had a congenital gynaecological problem and therefore never attained puberty. All efforts to treat her failed, leaving young Thangam a terrified woman. However, on her own she arranges for her husband Ekambaram to be married a second time—to a woman called Sengamalam through whom he begets seven children. Aunt Thangam becomes a favourite, particularly with her brother's children, telling them fascinating new stories.

One such story is that of a deer that lives in a herd in a forest familiar to them. The deer strays into another forest and is frightened by its strangeness. After wandering around alone in terror, the deer on a full-moon night comes to see that there is nothing to fear about the new forest—that this place, too, is all right.

A translator may try to enhance the ideological implications of the story since otherwise, to an innocent reader, the story may appear somewhat simplistic. The author herself has loaded the story with feminist issues and even a literal translation cannot overlook the thrust of the syntax and the imagery, and above all the register of the children's tale. But here are some crucial places where a translator might try offering an interpretive translation. Take the opening paragraph, when the narrator recalls the ingenuity of Aunt Thangam in narrating totally new stories and not the usual ones about the crow and the fox or the hare and tortoise. The narrator says, 'they were all stories made up all by herself'. The niece (or it nephew?) recalls in particular her aunt's imaginative power in bringing alive fantasies, transforming those beings such as asuras and demons, who are generally projected as evil characters. 'Even the asuras and the devas would be metamorphosed in our minds.'

The next sentence offers space for the translator to venture an interpretive rendering. The plain rendering of the line would be, 'She would describe Mantarai movingly'. Any Indian knows that unless one means to subvert the traditional estimate of this scheming hunchback of a woman in the Ramayana who is Kaikeyi's undoing, an author will not portray this character with sympathy. At this point, the translator may take some liberty and render the line as: 'Her[1] Mantarai would move us to tears', which highlights Aunt Thangam's defiant sympathy for this proverbially wicked woman. The implication is: perhaps we can never be sure of the truth of anybody's personality. Aligned with Mantarai in the next line are Surpanakai and Thatakai who are transformed into beings with feelings and emotions. Then comes the couple of sentences in the story with most potential for interpretation. The literal rendering could read thus:

> *She would pull out the characters cleaving in the pages of epics. She would draw them in words as if she were stroking comfortingly a bird clipped of its wings.*

But the translator already, by this time, alerted by the vindication of characters like Mantarai and Surpanakai, may take some liberty which will underscore the ideological thrust of the story and hence may render the sentences as follows:

> *She would draw out characters marginalized in the pages of the epics. She would portray them in words (or revive them) as if she were stroking comfortingly a bird which had broken its wings.*

How does the translator justify the use of the word 'marginalised'? On the strength of the preceding references to Mantarai, Surpanakai and Tatakai, and of the ensuring description of the treatment meted out to Aunt Thangam by society because she is incapable of bearing children. The author identifies herself with the cause of such women through the narrator's voice. While the use of an ideologically frontal term like 'marginalized' may appear to be a liberty taken whether warranted or not, the rendering in the printed version of my translation of the story after the editorial changes seems to gain little by translating the line thus: 'the characters hidden in the dark corners of the epics would be drawn out by Athai's...'. The addition of 'dark corners' does not contribute to the understanding of the implication that Aunt Thangam did not view Surpanakai and Thatakai as reprehensible.

A similar lexical item which warrants an interpretative thrust to the translation is the rendering of the Tamil word 'poothal' as 'Aunt never *flowered*'. The biological connotation/charge of the verb 'flower' is not present in colloquial English though, in a formal literary style, the nuance would be easily understood. But here in the context of the story the verb 'flowered' enables the reader to situate the woman in a particular social milieu where attaining puberty mattered most. Hence the failure in the case of Aunt Thangam must be ideologically foregrounded in the translation by a word whose connotation is more powerful than a word which has merely a denotative power—such as, puberty. Very soon afterwards in the story we come across another word to describe the aunt's condition—'hollow', like the withered tree that was felled and sawed.

We have another difficult piece of syntax to translate where the story tells us of the attempt to frighten Aunt Thangam so that in sheer fright she may reach puberty. The Tamil sentence reads rather amorphous and loose, using the active voice but not making clear the real agent of the action. It reads quite neutral:

> *Something might happen to her if suddenly taken by fright, so thinking in the early hours of the night when Athai went to the backyard, a dark shrouded figure jumped on her, it seems.*

This is certainly awkward and unclear. But the translator can foreground the ideological allegation that the literal agent of action may be some individual, but the real agent is society, the people who set the value for others in our communities. Hence the sentence may be made using a mixture of active and passive voices.

> *Hoping that a bout of sudden fright might help, in the late hours of an evening, a dark shrouded figure was set on Aunt Thangam when she went to the backyard.*

The so-called wise people in the community subject the poor woman to such horrible treatment—setting a dark figure on her, administering quack medicines, leaving her at the mercy of healers, and so on—that her humanity is threatened with destruction. And the translation should help readers discern this vein of cultural critique in the story.

Let us compare two more places where the choice of voice may be strategic. In the tale about the deer that the Aunt tells her nephews and nieces, we have at first one forest in which all the animals are at home. In Tamil the sentence roughly reads:

> *They knew on which trees the owl sat and how it would hoot when the forest lay in absolute silence in the night, on which stone the frog, sitting, would suddenly croak gurgle-throated, where the peacock would dance—all was known to them in the forest.*

The translator might render this last phrase here as 'all was familiar to them in the forest', for familiarity is a matter of unconscious knowledge and acceptance of one's surroundings. But very soon when one of the deer strays into a strange new forest, its very unfamiliarity frightens the poor creature. After much roaming about in a disconsolate state, one day the deer perceives the surroundings in the light of the full moon, when every terrifying object is transformed into something glorious and attractive. The deer comes into a new state of knowledge that creates a feeling of acceptance. The Tamil passage reads.

> *It was a full moon light. The light of the moon illumined the forest. The cataract took on a pleasing appearance, gilding itself over with moonlight. A sight that would not strike terror. The moonlight softly touched*

> *everything. All of a sudden, as if touched by a magic wand, the deer lost all fear. It took a liking for the forest. It came to know every nook and cranny of the forest.*

The translator might here highlight the transition from unconscious familiarity to conscious knowledge which comes from a moment of epiphany when the deer is able to view the strange forest under the aspect of the light of the full moon. Hence we may render it thus: 'Suddenly, as if touched by a magic wand, the deer shed all fear'. When we relate the predicament of the poor deer to that of the Aunt, we may read it as an affirmation—of the Aunt not only coming to terms with her world but achieving a knowledge of it which brings peace to her even as the deer is calmed after the new knowledge dawns on it. Hence the last line of the passage may also be rendered as: 'Every nook and cranny of the forest became clear to it'. Earlier it was a mystery, a source of terror born of ignorance. Now there is deliverance leading to clarity of perception.

That takes us to the last of the hermeneutical problems: how does one validate one's reading/rendering?

Conclusion: The Horizon

In the hermeneutical procedure the 'author's horizon' has been considered very important by traditional hermeneuticians. Even radical, subversive authors, when it comes to the interpretation of their works, in general would like their point of view to be respected. In the case of the two stories used for demonstrating the hermeneutical and epistemological dimensions in translation, let us see how far the authors' views are definitive and helpful in determining the translation.

In the case of the first story the author, Na. Muthusamy, listened to my translation, clarified certain expressions that have regional peculiarities and explained certain terms. That is all and nothing more. He had nothing to say about my emphasis on the epistemological thrust of the syntax of the story, even in the Tamil version, leave alone in the English translation. But does that cancel the presence of the feature in the text? Does not the author's horizon still exist despite the author's physical silence on it? Can we not construct it by reading more of his works, fiction and drama, finding that the author challenges our understanding at every point in the way he renders reality?

The second author had a different attitude. She was kind enough to discuss the story with me and she appreciated my ideological thrust. She however thought that the forest in the tale was a metaphor for the Aunt's body. Being a radical feminist—in order to understand Ambai, we construct the author's horizon by reading her other works—she uses the forest to project the Aunt's perception of the acceptability of her own body. My reading is not too divergent except that I might think that the forest also stands for the world which is now trans-valued for the aunt when she rises above its terrors and fears.

My purpose in citing all these instances is to demonstrate that there are still problems in achieving accuracy, if not validation. We have to go over the points again: we have considered whether it is possible to achieve a 'congenial' translation; whether we have achieved a 'method' which is defensible, if not unimpeachable; whether translation is also a process of 'concretization'; and hence essentially 'intersubjective'; whether all reading is bound to be historical and linguistic; and whether a translated text is a new text, a matching text or a passive rendering; and so on. In translation, the horizon is unbounded.

Note

1. This is an effective change the editors of my manuscript version of the translated story have made in the published version. See Indra 1995.

References

Ambai, 1994. 'Kaattil Our Maan'. *Unnatham* Oct. 94. p. 3–5 (Tamil).

Indra, C.T., (n.d.) Manuscript version of the translation of Ambai's story, 'A Deer in the Forest'.

Indra, C.T., 1995. 'A Deer in the Forest'. In Geeta Dharmarajan and Meenakshi Sharma (eds) *Katha Prize Stories*, Volume V. New Delhi: Katha and Rupa and Co.

Jefferson, Ann and **David Robey**, 1986. *Modern Literary Theory: A Comparative Introduction*. London: Batsford.

Na. Muthuswamy, 1984. 'Nadappu'. *Neermai*. Madras: CreA Publishers.

Ramani, Shakuntala, 1994. Manuscript version of her translation of Na. Muthuswamy's story under the title 'Happening', provided for discussion as the British Council—Katha Translation Workshop, New Delhi, 1994.

Seturaman, V.S., 1989. *Introduction to Contemporary Criticism*. Madras: Macmillan India Ltd.

4. Linguistic Descriptions

Twelve

Language Behaviour: Cognition and Translation

R. NARASIMHAN

What then am I? A thinking being. What is a thinking being? It is a being which doubts, which understands, which conceives, which affirms, which desires, which wills, which rejects, which imagines, and which perceives.

René Descartes

No actions but such as are done for an end, and show a choice of means, can be called indubitable expressions of the mind. I shall ... adopt this as the criterion by which to circumscribe the subject matter of this work so far as action enters into it.

William James

The psychologist's most vital challenge is that of uncovering and bringing to light the hidden mechanisms underlying complex human psychology.... The inner mechanisms characteristic of [complex psychological processes] remain hidden....

Lev Vygotsky

Preliminaries: The Computational Paradigm

The characteristic feature of an *agent* (any biological organism) is its ability to engage in *intentional action*. In other words, instead of being merely reactive, it can be proactive. An agent, then, has a set of actions (i.e., it has an action repertoire) which it can deploy to interact with the world in an intentional (goal-directed) manner. An agent has a set of *sensory interfaces* through which information concerning the state of the world and, in particular, the changes caused in the world by its own action, is available to it. An agent, finally, has a set of *internal states* (affects, needs, motivations) which condition the intentions (goals) of the actions the agent engages in or embarks on.

The computational (or information processing) paradigm offers a way of modelling (theorising about, accounting for) agentive behaviour in terms of computational structures and processes. Throughout this text we shall use the terms computational and information processing as interchangeable expressions.

With specific regard to language behaviour, the computational modelling of language behaviour is concerned with the characterisation of language behaviour in terms of information processing activities. We want to understand what kind of information processing systems human beings are that they acquire and use language behaviour in the ways in which they actually do in their normal living.

In normal circumstances, children acquire their first language—their mother tongue—by living and growing up in a language community without any specific tuition or effort. How does this come about? Are there specific cognitive competencies which are prerequisites for language behaviour acquisition?

Language behaviour should not be confused with speech, or with scripts, or with reading/writing. Language behaviour in the sense of social action must be distinguished from its use in formal/logical discourse. What are some of the more important open issues that behaviour studies must come to grips with in order to further our understanding of language behaviour phenomena?

We shall try to address some of these questions in the rest of this paper. The reader must be cautioned that the aspects of language behaviour discussed here form only a very small part of the variety of ways in which language behaviour enters into our daily living. Language behaviour makes human beings what they are. Behaviour in this modality affects, and is affected by, the cultural and social aspects of the world one moves in. Clearly it would not be practical to even attempt to outline all the sociocultural ramifications of language behaviour. In so far as the main theme of this collection of essays is translation, we shall try to focus our attention on language behaviour and cognition in this specific task context.

Language Behaviour: Characterising Features

Medawar (1976) has persuasively argued that it is not tool fabrication know-how that sets human beings apart from other animals, but their ability to *communicate* this know-how from one generation to the next. He points out that it is because of this communicative competence that human beings have come to enjoy a kind of cultural evolution distinct from the Darwinian genetic evolution based on natural selection. Eccles (1979) argues along similar lines by emphasising that human beings are what they are not exclusively because of their genetic endowments and brain mechanisms, but because of the interaction of these with the cultural world that surrounds them.

The communication competence of human beings, which directly underlies the cultural heritage of human kind, is pre-eminently the result of their language behaviour. Although communication competence is something that humans share with other animals, language behaviour seems to be available, in a biological sense, only to human beings. Ordinarily we tend to associate language behaviour with speech. However, speech is not indispensable to language behaviour. The deaf, for example, have evolved a variety of sign (gestural) languages which enable them to interact among themselves and with other sign language users with little, if any, impairment of the richness and complexity of communication.

Two questions immediately arise. First, noting that lack of speech need not be an impediment to the acquisition of language behaviour, why is it that no other animal has evolved language behaviour? Second, noting that the availability of communication competence has not led other animals to evolve a cultural heritage, what are the features that distinguish human communication from other animal communications? These questions have been dealt with at great length in Narasimhan 1998. Here we shall confine ourselves to a brief description of the characterising features of human communication based on language behaviour.

In human beings and other animals, sensori-motor behaviour is underpinned by special-purpose mechanisms, for instance, in the visual, auditory, and other sensory and motor modalities. These peripheral modalities deal with the external world in terms of the signals either directly received or directly generated by the organism. Language behaviour, however, is one step removed from these direct interfaces and deals with the world (outer and inner) essentially through indirection. In this way, language behaviour is based on a 'translated' abstraction of the world available to the peripheral processors. It is for this reason that Pavlov referred to language behaviour as a second signalling system; that is, it is a signal of (primary) signals. Or, more precisely, language behaviour is based on a symbolic level abstraction of the world available to our peripheral processors.

Without the language modality, the sensori-motor behaviour complex can only deal with the now and with what is out there. But with language behaviour one is able to separate the sensory and motor complexes and mediate them via language behaviour. That is, one is able to refer to the sensorily apprehended aspects of the world and to one's own actions *independently*. This is the foundation of semanticity, one of the critical characterising aspects of language behaviour.

With the availability of language behaviour then, instead of merely reacting to, or acting on, the world available via the first signals (which is all that animals, in general, are able to do), humans can talk about this world, decribe it, model it, reason about it, and so on. Clearly, it is this capability that makes it possible to deploy language for strategic purposes (such as planning, problem-solving and elaborate social manoeuvring), as opposed to its mere instrumental usage.

Also, through language behaviour, human beings are able to deal with worlds not necessarily immediately present to the senses, with worlds distanced from them in space and time. Moreover they are able to deal not only with the actual world out there that is given, but with (imagined) possible worlds, and even with counterfactual situations. It is significant to note that precisely these capabilities (made possible through the use of language behaviour) are prerequisites to set up hypotheses, make conjectures, infer the implications of suppositions, and so on, which are indispensable to practising science. And these very capabilities are also essential for engaging in creative uses of language behaviour such as making conversation, narrating stories, playing verbal games (puzzles, riddles), land so on.

In storytelling what one does is use natural language to construct descriptions of an artificial world, i.e., a complex of fictive or imaginary behavioural environments. We 'people' them with agents and objects with fictitious attributes, states and action repertoires.

Offhand, the discourse potentials of natural languages (English, Hindi, etc.) seem to be limitless. It looks, for all practical purposes, as if one can discuss practically anything imaginable in a natural language. How does this come about? To answer this question, first note that it is not true that it is *any* natural language, say English, in some delimited sense, that has this flexibility. What is true is that English, like every other natural language, is extendable in a natural way by embedding into it, fragments of other notational and/or representational schemes. As Wittgenstein (1968: 18) points out: 'Ask yourself whether any language is complete: whether it was so before the symbolism of chemistry and the notation of infinitesimal calculus were incorporated in it: for these are, so to speak, suburbs of our language....'

The important point to note is that every such extension enables the extended language to deal with a specific world of behavioural environments, and this world is pragmatically/semantically analysed along the same lines as the naïvely given world is analysed in the normal use of the concerned natural language. It is readily verified that where the behavioural phenomena encountered in a world do not readily allow these kinds of structures to be imposed on them, we find it hard (if not impossible) to describe them and talk about them coherently or meaningfully. Examples of such phenomena are: completely abstract, formless visual imagery; randomly shaped patches of colour in motion in unpredictable ways; and random noise patterns also in random motion. This is also the reason why one finds great difficulty in devising adequate notations to describe/define complex dance movements, or to script abstract, dynamic visual displays and similar non-standard information events or happenings.

Language Behaviour: Evolutionary History

Looked at in the evolutionary perspective, human language behaviour would seem to pose a fundamental puzzle which can be termed the *continuity puzzle*. At the social level we may share communication competence with other animals although, even here, as we have earlier seen, the availability of language behaviour makes a qualitative difference to what humans can communicate and how they do it. Summarising our earlier discussion about language behaviour, we can identify two features as essentially defining the language modality of behaviour. These are *instructability* and *the capacity to reflect*. It is clear that animal vocalisations and other means of social communication (for instance, chemical) definitely lack these two potentials. The essence of instructability is the capacity to *tell* how to do something rather than merely *show* how to do it. The ability to reflect using language enables one to analyse one's own actions and those of others, or the state of the surrounding world as well as one's own internal states, and thus, to reason about them, draw inferences from them, and so on.

From the perspective of all human languages, having language would seem to be an all-or-nothing affair. At the level of human societies, there is no such gradation as having more or less language. In this sense, all human languages are equal in their potentialities. But language behaviour with all its current potentials cannot have arisen all of a sudden at some specific time in evolution. To account for the appearance of language behaviour as we find it now, we would have to show that its present complexity evolved over a period of time in stages. However, we do not find any evidence for the evolution of language behaviour in such a manner. More importantly, we seem unable to theoretically demonstrate such successive stages through which language behaviour, as we find it now, might have evolved. This is the essence of the continuity puzzle.

During the last thirty years several chimpanzees have been trained in an attempt to determine whether they could be taught language-like behaviour. In the most recent study, a pygmy chimpanzee (a bonobo) was exposed to human speech and the use of a symbol board and was administered a controlled test to assess comprehension of spoken commands. Detailed discussions of these studies may be found in Narasimhan (1981, 1998).

These projects seem to establish that apes (bonobos and chimpanzees, especially) have the necessary cognitive base to acquire the rudiments of symbolic communication behaviour if exposed to appropriate interactive environments. However, apes seem to fall short, in significant respects, of children's capabilities to acquire and use language-like skills even when acquisition is made possible through special environmental exposure. What behavioural mechanisms and processes could be missing in apes, while being present in children, leading to this discrepancy?

It would take us too far outside the scope of this essay to deal with the above question in any reasonable detail. But it can be argued that language behaviour capability is unlikely to develop in the absence of the following non-verbal capabilities: observation learning; imitation and analogising (i.e., example-based learning and its productive use); tool-use (i.e., goal-directed use of objects/agents considered as tools); iconic-gesturing (pantomiming) and onomatopoeic vocalising; role-taking and pretend-play. Human children exhibit all these capabilities from their earliest years. Most of these capabilities are very likely built-in endowments, although we have, at present, no clue about their neural substrates. Significantly, apes seem to lack every one of these capabilities. For a detailed discussion of these missing behavioural links, see Narasimhan (1998).

Language Behaviour: The Oral Literate Context

In the behavioural domain, the ability to 'perform x' is not identical to the ability to 'talk about x'. If x is a speech act, then performing x =

performing that speech act. The ability to do so requires the availability of an appropriate behavioural routine (analogous to a computer program) the execution of which is the performance of that speech act. To talk about a speech act, however, we need: (a) a representation of it to which one can refer independently of the performance of that speech act; and (b) a metalanguage to serve as a basis for the description and analysis of that speech act.

Performing a speech act is behaviour in the oral domain. Talking about it is behaviour in the literate domain. In general, script literacy (the behavioural ability to write—using a script—and read) is a prerequisite to talk about speech acts in a satisfactorily literate manner. However, even without script literacy, one can talk about behaviour in the oral domain to a limited extent by using that very behaviour as its own representation, and by using metalanguage concepts available in the oral domain for describing and analysing the represented oral behaviour. Such a representational technique is feasible because we are able to imitate (in the sense of faithfully reproducing) a given oral domain behaviour. The imitated version serves as a surrogate for the original and, thus, as its representation. However, the representational utility of the imitated version is seriously restricted since it is as transient as the original behaviour and is unavailable for extended contemplation and comparative and contrastive analysis and study.

Script literacy circumvents this problem by making it possible to create a symbolic, hard-copy version of the original behaviour (the speech act) which is then available for extended contemplation, analysis, study and reflection. However, it should be noted that this symbolic hard-copy version is not a replica of the original behaviour in all its particulars. Unlike imitation, symbolisation abstracts away and represents or 'translates' in the copy only certain aspects of the original behaviour.

In general, paralinguistic aspects (prosody, gestures, etc.) and illocutionary aspects of the original behaviour are abstracted away. If there is a need to represent them explicitly, representational conventions have to be suitably augmented. Because of this abstracting away process, an acquisition of expertise is involved in successfully performing the mapping: behaviour → symbolic representation. In other words, literate domain skills (i.e., writing–reading) do not automatically follow from oral domain skills (i.e., performance of speech acts). They have to be explicitly acquired through conscious learning and much drill.

The transition from 'naïve' (or oral) use of language behaviour to a 'learned' (or literate) use of it has been extensively studied during the last two or three decades under the rubric of 'the orality-literacy contrast', giving rise to a rich literature (see, for example, Olson and Torrance 1991 for a compilation of studies and extensive references).

To distinguish oral behaviour (in the oral domain) from its symbolic representation (in the literate domain)—through the use, for example, of script literacy—let us use the contrastive terms:

behaviour (for the original behaviour)
and
text (for its symbolic representation).

Once writing makes possible the creation of texts, it is clear that there is no reason to restrict texts to mimicking oral speech. Extended texts can be produced to stand on their own as autonomous entities, completely dissociated from the *contexts of the situations* they describe, comment on, or otherwise deal with. This possibility, to be successful, requires that the writer make available *within the text* all the contextual clues needed by the reader to assign a proper interpretation of the text (i.e., the interpretation *intended* by the writer of the text). This stage setting plays an essential role in composing texts. Also, problems such as cross-referencing, global coherence, logical sequencing, logical consistency, and a whole variety of compositional techniques play essential roles in constructing a readily understandable text. Superposed on these essential requirements are other stylistic frills which the writer may employ to avoid monotony, hold the interest of the reader and/or manipulate her/his affects.

Lexicalisation and syntax play essential roles in the creation and interpretation of autonomous texts. Most of the structures that are encountered in written texts (or equivalently in *written speech*, that is speech based on written texts) directly relate to the interpretation, stylistics, and to other aspects of written texts. What schooling teaches one are precisely these 'essayist' techniques to write (and speak) in order to communicate coherently and intelligibly one's ideas and thoughts to the reader (and listener) *independently* of the circumstances in which the writing is read (or the written speech heard).

Malinowski (1923) characterised oral speech as social action and differentiated it from prepared texts 'torn out of any context of situation' with which linguists' studies are concerned. According to him oral speech fulfils a social function; in this function it is not an instrument of reflection but a mode of action.

Elsewhere I have argued at length that linguists' grammars relate more closely to autonomous prose texts than to oral speech (see Narasimhan 1998). The orality-literacy studies earlier referred to persuasively argue that one should distinguish between a mother tongue that oral communities use and which children acquire as a first language, and a language specialised to serve the requirements of autonomous formalised texts. This distinction is of direct relevance to analysing the cognitive aspects of language behaviour especially translation, which is a very complex cognitive act.

Language Behaviour: Cognitive Aspects

Recall that earlier we stated that our long-term goal was to work out viable computational models of language behaviour in order to account for its characteristic features and to understand, in general, how human beings are able to make use of it in the ways they actually do. Modelling issues can be conveniently divided into two groups: *representational* issues and *control* issues. Representational issues relate to the kind of structures that underpin behaviour and the manner of internal representation of these structures. Control issues relate to the realisation of some specific behaviour at a given moment of time based on the constraints of the situation eliciting that particular behaviour. With respect to both behaviour representation and behaviour control at the neural level, our present understanding of the real-life situation is practically nil.

Control issues become dominant when we move from modelling the production of isolated utterances to modelling discourse. In ordinary daily living, the following discourse forms would seem to be of central importance:

Conversation (also, as a variant, *monologue*).

Describing an actual situation out there, or a potential/desired situation.

Instructing another through a procedure to successfully perform a task.

Narrating a story, a sample of one's life experience, and so on.

Clearly, children go through well-defined development stages in mastering these discourse forms. We do not, at present, have well-articulated computational models to account for the way these discourse forms are handled in real life.

For modelling language behaviour, a more serious problem is coming to grips with *instructability*. Through instruction we can add knowledge and also regulate control not only in the language modality but across modalities. How is this achieved?

The introduction of computer technology is allowing us to probe the processes involved in language usage along dimensions which would have been difficult to contemplate before the advent of computers. For example, the phenomenology associated with language use differs depending on the mode of use—speaking, writing, translating—apart from its use in the discourse forms we considered earlier. There is no reason to assume that, despite the differences in their outward forms, these modes of language use can all be modelled—or accounted for, or explained—in terms of a unitary framework, for example, in terms of a standard 'grammar', or of a single set of computational processes. It would seem quite plausible to argue that language use is not some one thing but many different things. Hence, a plurality of frameworks may be needed to model the varieties of language use appropriately.

Figure 1 is a schema of the four language actions associated with speaking and writing—speaking, writing, listening and reading. The language objects which are the outputs of expression are explicitly shown in terms of their constituents. If we consider human beings to be computational (i.e., information processing) systems engaging in these language actions, several issues arise for study. We become aware of these issues when we try to program computers to mimic these language actions of humans.

It is not clear, a priori, that speaking a language and writing it are not distinct skills that are served by quite distinct mechanisms at the behavioural level. In other words, distinct subsystems, each incorporating a different representation of the concerned language—say, English or Hindi—at the behavioural level, may be

Figure 1: Language Behaviour Acts: Speaking, Writing, Listening, Reading

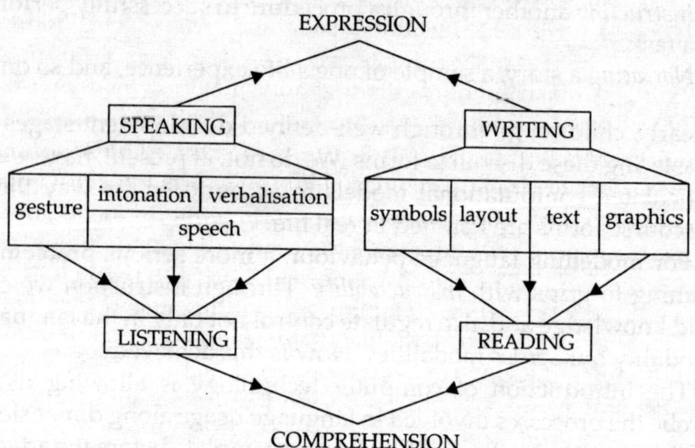

involved in speaking and writing. It is plausible to argue such a thesis because, as we discussed at length earlier, 'oral' speech behaviour is acquired by everyone without any special effort or tuition. On the other hand, 'literate' writing capability requires formal tuition (or self-tuition), much drill and practice.

To sum up, we should not ask 'What is the correct internal representation of a language, say, English?' Rather, we should want to work out effective representations for the tasks at hand: speaking, writing, translating, and so forth. We should experiment with many 'grammars', for example, to determine which one suits each task best.

Consider now the parts of the system in Figure 1 termed 'expression' and 'comprehension'. What is the representational-level characterisation of these? The standard approach is to say, 'First there are thoughts or ideas. These are then expressed in language—in English, Hindi, and so on'. But how are ideas internally represented? To claim that they are represented in the 'language of thought' is not to say very much at all. For, is this language of thought like any other language? What is its vocabulary? What is its grammar? Are these pre-wired into us? Is going from the language of thought to a natural language, say English, a translation process analogous to translating from English to Hindi? Clearly this translation process cannot be pre-wired. How is it acquired, then? What are the relationships between the processes involved in a child's acquiring English, say, and its acquiring this internal translation process from the language of thought to English?

Analogous questions arise in characterising the part of the system labelled 'comprehension'. Are the representational aspects in 'expression' and 'comprehension' the same? If not, we are confronted with yet another translation process! Notice how all the various subsystems are brought into interaction in performing the following tasks:

Task 1: Listen to what I say in Hindi and repeat it in your words in Hindi.
Task 1a: Listen to what I say in Hindi and repeat it in English.
Task 2: Read what I have written in Hindi and rewrite it in Hindi in your own words.
Task 2a: Read what I have written in Hindi and rewrite it in English.

Clearly, the issues we have raised here are genuine and need to be addressed whether we wish to theorise about how people cope with these tasks or program computers to mimic these human capabilities.

Referring to Figure 1 again, usually we assume that the output of the 'writing' action is 'text', and we do not pay much attention to the fact that a text is not a linear string of symbols. Text is laid out spatially according to systematised rules. A little consideration should convince us that the symbol set used in composing the text, and the manner of spatial layout of the text play essential roles in the ease with which we comprehend it. This is especially true of children's comprehension of school texts. Yet, in the preparation of school texts, little or no attention is paid to these expressive details of 'writing' (or 'printing').

Decisions concerning the selection of symbol sets and the layout of text are usually assumed to be primarily matters of aesthetics and so, to belong to the domains of typographers, copy editors and publishers. The design aspects intrinsic to these domains have therefore not been of concern to linguists or writers (authors) in general. However, these design aspects, in so far as they affect comprehension, have psycholinguistic implications and should be of concern to both linguists and writers.

The introduction of computer-based tools for text preparation, text-editing, text-layout and printing has revived interest in the underlying design issues. Although in this context many of these issues have been dealt with at the expressive (i.e., specificational) level with much sophistication, our understanding of the implications of these design issues at the comprehension level is still rudimentary. Much empirical work remains to be done and this requires cooperation between psychologists, linguists and computer scientists.

Conclusion

Our primary emphasis in this paper has been on the need to analyse and study language behaviour at the behavioural level rather than at the level of some theoretical abstraction designated 'language', which is the preoccupation of linguistic studies. The computational or information processing approach was introduced as an underlying framework for studying the behaviour of agents (biological organisms). Agents are distinguished from objects in that the former possess a repertoire of actions which they can deploy in an intentional (goal-directed) manner.

The language modality of behaviour, as far as we know, is available at the biological level only to human beings. The distinguishing features of language behaviour enable human beings to simultaneously live in two worlds—one determined by genes and evolution and the other determined by culture and society.

We have also seen that issues concerned with behaviour modelling fall into two categories: representational and control issues. A priori it would seem to be plausible to argue that oral speech and written texts are the outcomes of two skills that are served by two distinct mechanisms at the behavioural level. Translating from one language to another may be yet another/distinct skill. The thrust of our argument was this: engaging in language behaviour (i.e., language usage) may not be some one thing, but many different things. A plurality of computational frameworks may be needed to model these various usages of language behaviour satisfactorily. We should work out suitable representations and control mechanisms appropriate to each language behaviour-mediated task on hand—speaking, writing, translating, conversing, narrating, etc.—rather than look for a universal scheme of representation and control to cope with all varieties of language behaviour usage.

As we emphasised earlier, the language behaviour phenomena that we have discussed here form only a small part of the language behaviour-mediated actions human beings engage in as part of their normal lives. The acquisition of discourse competence by children, the cognitive consequences of literacy in both children and non-literate adults, enhancing the capacity for reflective thinking in formal and non-formal education—these are some of the issues that have been intensively studied by a variety of scholars. The concerned literature is rich and growing rapidly and may be of great relevance to the area of translation studies.

Acknowledgement: I am much indebted to Ms. S.B. Saraswathi for the computer processing of the manuscript.

References

Bateson, P.P.G., and **Hinde, R.A.** (eds), 1976. *Growing Points in Ethology*. Cambridge: Cambridge University Press.

Eccles, J.C., 1979. *The Human Mystery*. The Gifford Lectures, University of Edinburgh, 1977–78. Heidelberg: Springer.

Medawar, P.B., 1976. 'Does Ethology Throw Any Light on Human Behaviour?' *PPG*.

Malinowski, B., 1923. 'The Problem of Meaning in Primitive Languages'. In C.K. Ogden and I.A. Richards (eds), *The Meaning of Meaning*, 10th ed. (1949). London: Routledge & Kegan Paul.

Narasimhan, R., 1981. *Modelling Language Behaviour*. Heidelberg: Springer-Verlag.

———, 1998. Language Behaviour: vol. 6 in Udaya Narain Singh and Probal Dasgupta (Series eds), *Language and Development. Acquisition and Evolutionary History*, New Delhi: Sage.

Olson, D.R. and **N. Torrance** (eds), 1991. *Literacy and Orality*. Cambridge: Cambridge University Press.

Wittgenstein, L., 1968. *Philosophical Investigations*. Oxford: Blackwell.

Thirteen

Language Patterns: Lexicography and Translation

UDAYA NARAYANA SINGH

In this essay, I will explore the lexicographical bases of translation. The sections that follow are meant to alert both practising and prospective translators to the following range of problems:

(1) The problem of exercising choice of words in the target text as compared to the original.
(2) The problem of storage and retrieval of lexical items which are usually plentiful in literary languages.
(3) The problem of creating neologisms.
(4) The problem of lexical equivalence and difficulties with the related notions of innovation and translatability.
(5) Models of language development and the place of lexical development as a part of this broader scheme.
(6) The common problems a translator faces while trying his/her hand at a technical text, particularly in respect of decisions he/she has to take on the creation or use of technical words, as well as on establishing ground rules for the exchange of technical words—which all technical translators know intuitively but which are not explicitly stated.

The Hierarchies

There are two hierarchies in the field of translation, never explicitly proposed but nevertheless taken for granted. These assumptions have done more harm in the building of bases for a translation theory than any other beliefs. First, a translator and a translating culture were always placed at the lower end of a line of vertical relationship. The paradigm of hierarchy would go like this: Those who failed to be poets became literary critics and those who failed as critics turned into translators. Such paradigms have been the greatest handicaps for translation theoreticians. These unkind remarks have neither helped in creating great poetry nor have they blocked creative translators from coming up with memorable pieces of translation.

The other hierarchy has been this: The speakers of language A translate item X from language B because language A does not have item X, nor have the speakers the means and capabilities to create an X (Singh 1989). A lot of people believe this even now. However, two thousand years of translation practice have changed the situation so much that translation has become a bidirectional activity, both A and B taking turns as donor languages—i.e., A → B as well as B → A. Today, speakers of A translate Xi from language B but at the same time, in terms of acquisition of new knowledge, they also transfer Xj.... Xn from a number of other sources (cultures, languages or sciences). This is possible because the world has become smaller now and scientific/technical communication has become faster. This kind of bidirectional activity then forces the original donor languages to translate this new conceptualisation of X into their languages.

Both hierarchies have had an effect on lexical creativity and lexical transfer. The recipient languages are much less shy in borrowing items now than they once were. The sense of guilt is gone, and the mindless back-formations, classical borrowings and forming of unacceptable neologisms are also almost gone now. It is easier to think of borrowing with naturalisation, loan-translation or borrowing of word formation rules. The end-users are also much more patient now about giving innovations a trial for some time.

Clearly, the status and role of translator having been changed, the time has come to devote more attention to the building of a viable theory of translation. This, of course, is a challenge not too easily met.

The Challenges

One must realise the nature of challenges lying ahead of someone who is trying to discover the bases of translation. There is a general consensus now that translation theory must be conceived of as several things rolled into one:

(1) A paradigm of evaluation to sift out hack works in the name of translation from the work of true interpreters.
(2) A set of language-particular and culture-dependent rules.
(3) A means to understand an alien culture, a distant author or an otherwise unavailable document.
(4) A frame of reference for comparative linguistic and literary studies.
(5) A documentation into contemporary cultural patterns of a speech community waiting to be discovered, introduced or imitated by a target group.
(6) 'A model for the poetic art' as Kenner called it while refering to Ezra Pound's approach to translation in the 1920s (Kenner 1971: 150), and a new method in scholarship.
(7) An evidence of pluralism as a developmental goal.
(8) A test case for semanticists.
(9) A prescription for professionals engaged in accessing texts from other tongues by way of giving them a checklist of techniques or a set of rules of thumb.
(10) An instrument for retaining/eliminating, using/misusing or creating/suppressing ambiguities in a sensitive text or documenting a declared relationship between two nations that may change the face of history.

To regard a contemporary theory of translation as a combination of these ten 'action nominals' listed above brings to mind the Osiris story—which can be compared to the Sati episode in the Saivite mythology—used by Ezra Pound (1911–12) in 'I Gather the Limbs of Osiris' where, by regathering scattered limbs, Osiris not only becomes the God of the Dead, but also the source of new life because of the reunited energetics of the joined limbs (Kenner 1954).

Translation today, not merely discovers and disambiguates the source text, it is also able to produce what Tirumalesh (1990) calls a 'literature three', outside the known worlds of source and target literatures, essentially because there is a lot of scope to create new words and expressions, new patterns of language, in the resultant text. But while new expressions can be used in this manner, we know that literary translation can at best be only an approximation of the original. That is, there is bound to be a considerable degree of meaning alternation, leading to meaning loss or, contributing to meaning gain.

There is also a constant attempt to transpose the lexis of one tradition of art, music, and other expressive phenomena over to another. Besides creative writing, translation, now better called 'transposition' (thanks to Jakobson 1959), has now permeated into painting, sculpture, performing arts, and other art forms, freely drawing from and contributing to the dynamics of different kinds of texts. Truly, all literary translators aim at discovering the 'extra-ordinary' in an 'alien' language, culture and text they have devoted themselves to, but, in the process, realise that they are bound by the lexis, structures and options of the target tongue. However, it is this very bondage that they must try to untangle as they create new structures and lexis—sometimes on the pattern of the source language, and sometimes on their own.

Lexical Innovations

I. Neologisms

Let us start with a possible definition: neologisms are, at the most evident level, new words or expressions not yet regarded as completely naturalised or domesticated elements in the language.

If we consider innovations—both at the lexical/semantic level, which is called neologism and at the sentential/structural level, which we could call 'neotaxis'—we would notice that in the absence of particular form or content, or when one wants to create an entirely novel concept by giving it a new name, innovation is then used as a recourse when one faces problems of lexical choice. A translator is otherwise likely to favour a semantic extension of an existent form. At the outset then, innovations as such have nothing to do with only translation because innovations result from the creative urge of an innovator or from social and intellectual necessity.

Neologisms often spread rapidly and become a part of the common terminological currency of the speech community. But since they are not ordinary words in our languages, they often remain separate and identifiable. A neologism is usually rendered into a target language by a 'neologistic loanword' or by a novel creation within the target language tradition. The main question is how translators can make up their minds as to when to opt for neologisms and when not to (when to 'manage' through semantic extensions, etc.). Further, if one has to use this strategy, what is one to do when direct borrowing of such novel expressions which originated in the source language is not a viable option.

In this context, one might recall the Translation Novelty Paradox, where two forces pull the translator in opposite directions. It is not difficult to understand why there are these contrasting options. Consider the following situation: Any translated document must be new to the target language by definition (or else, why at all translate?). But at the same time this document will have pieces (constructions, words, ideas, etc.) which already exist in the target language, because otherwise the target language readers would neither understand or respond to it, and this would defeat the whole purpose of translation. Now, because there is a need to preserve continuity, we are usually forced to opt for a conventional translation. But the urge to bring in newness also requires us to perform 'a distinct rupture with the tradition and specifically make room for' neologisms.

Particularly in the modern period, much writing takes place under the shadow of what we shall call the technical imperative. This principle demands that all serious statements must (a) express some new and original thinking self-consciously marked in the very form of the text, and (b) link this work to some general impersonal system of expressing thoughts and feelings with objectivity and precision. Both the particular technique of the individual writer and the systematic technology of the collective field of such writing make modern texts especially prone to exact and differentiated modes of expression. This often takes the form of neologisms in original writings as well as in translations. (Dasgupta 1995).

II. Compounding

Let us consider a few examples of compounding and word grouping here where one can see novelty in structures of constructions above word level. If we extend the same lexical strategy of loan creations, we get the following expressions, which are so very common in almost all technical texts in Hindi, particularly in the newspaper variety of Hindi. These instances are mostly from the headlines used in the page for commerce and industry:

1. sarsɔ~ aur uchlii	Mustard jumps up
2. guR cinii majbuutii rahii	Molasses, sugar strong
3. muung camkii	Moong (pulse) shines
4. tel golaa Dhiilaa rahaa	Oil and coconut loose
5. kaalii mirc ko jha Tkaa	Sudden fall in pepper

Under hybrid formations, we get the following examples from the Hindi dailies published from New Delhi:

6. Side winder missile	saaiD winDar prakSepanaastra
7. Iron ore pellets	lauha ayaask pilaiT
8. Atomic reactor	paaramaaNavik riaak Tar
9. Radio active	reDio dharmii

The last four forms are hybrids that include borrowed words. But there can also be forms which are based on several Indian languages but are still meant to be translations of English terms. Here are some examples from Singh 1989 where the words are from S(anskrit), H(indi) and U(rdu):

10. agreement with clause	sasharta qaraar (SU)
11. beneficial fall	dilkhush mandaa (UH)
12. historical fall	aitihaasik giraawaT (SH)
13. capital investment	pu~u~jii nivesh (HS)

14. share market	saajhaa baazaar (HU)
15. fixed deposit	saan vidhika naqad (SU)
16. sick industry	biimaar udyog (US)

Similar examples are found in the CSTT's 1991 glossary (see p. 203):

17. high yielding varieties programme	adhik upaj qism kaaryakram
18. high skilled mechanic	atikuSal maikenik

There can also be multiple hybrid combinations:

19. Export cash subsidy scheme	niryaat naqad madad yojanaa (SUUS)
20. Non-banking financial company	gair bainking vittiiya kampanii (UEHE)
21. Maturable bank deposits	paripakkvataa vaalii baink jamaa raashi (HEUS)

III. Sample Terms

Consider now another set of 'culture words'. These are difficult words from Tamil (cf., Gunasekaran and Singh 1991/1993) which obviously pose problems for translators:

Culture Words	Domain	Approximate Glossing
pu:ppu nanni:ra:t.t.u	Puberty	holy bath on puberty
il.avat.t.akkal	General	stone of young men
munta:nai		the front portion of the house
	Dressing	saree that covers the bosom of a woman
talaippa:kai	Dressing	turban, headdress, headgear
ma:rpukkaccai	Dressing	brassiere
it.uppukkaccai	Dressing	girdle

ta:van.i	Dressing	half-saree worn by adolescent and mature girls
ku:t.am	Housing	a front room in a big house
va:yil	Housing	threshold, doorway, entrance
pantat.ittal	Sports, Games	playing ball
tel terittal	Sports, Games	a game played with the seeds of a particular tree
aiyal kompu	Sports, Games	a rural game played on trees

Now let us take a few concrete instances from this list to go into details of the kinds of problems one faces in translating them:

Word 1: pu:ppu nanni:ra:t.t.u

The term pu:ppu refers to a girl's attaining puberty and the second word refers to the bath given to her as a part of the ritual to get rid of the first menstrual pollution of the girl. The ritual is generally performed on the sixteenth day from the date of the first menstruation. During the period of the fifteen previous days, she is forbidden to go out and is regarded unclean and untouchable. There are two aspects connected with the performance of the rituals: one aspect is that the girl is potential, fertile and holy and the second aspect is that she is polluted, unclean and untouchable. This dichotomy is a significant factor in the celebration of puberty.

Here, the translator has to first of all understand the total meaning of the word in his source language and transfer it to the target language. Different translators who were approached suggested different translations in this case: 'holy bath' or 'holy bath on puberty', etc. Others may even prefer to retain the source cultural term in the target language with a brief explanation either followed by it or provided within brackets to facilitate easy understanding of the word, but the phrase 'holy bath' by itself is inadequate since the key meaning of the term pu:ppu is lost in the transition.

Word 2: il.avat.t.akkal

The term refers to a stone generally found in villages but the purpose of the stone seems to be very special. The young men of the village try to lift the stone to establish their youthfulness. Whoever is able to lift the stone above his head is considered to be very young and healthy. The youngsters join together and tease the one who fails to lift the stone. Sometimes the girl who is in love with the man teases him for his inability to lift the stone and such teasing is encouraged by the friends of the girl. The translations usually suggested are: 'soft round stone', 'tender stone' or just 'stone'. All these equivalents fail to convey the sense or the message in the target language, because of the higher order social ramifications of this particular cultural term.

Word 3: munta:nai

The term refers to that part of a woman's saree that covers the bosom and then goes over her shoulder, to fall over her back, even up to the hip. The belief is that a married woman is supposed to uphold this portion of her saree and spread it out only for her husband, for him to lie down when they are in privacy. (Sometimes mothers do this for their children to sleep on if they happen to meet the contingency of staying outside their residence.) The spread or the use of this part of the saree speaks about the conjugal relationship between husband and wife. Unmarried girls are prohibited from spreading that portion of the saree for a man until they get married to him. Most translators delete the term while they try to transfer the message into English and still somehow manage to maintain the coherence of the given text. Some translators translate it as 'the loose-end of the saree' and one of them has provided the word 'pallu' which originates in Hindi. These are not appropriate English translations. Some may coin a compound word such as 'fore-saree' or 'front-saree', on the analogy of expressions such as forearm, foresight and foreknowledge; this could work in some contexts.

Domains, Styles and Innovations

The problem of novelty shows up differently depending on the domain of language use involved. Fields such as science, technology, business, law, public administration, management and medicine constantly come up with whole sets of new terms and usages.

They all challenge the translator, but not in the same way. It is useful to notice some of the variations.

First, at the most obvious level, business and law are more conservative domains than science and technology. While those in business deal with new merchandise all the time, they treat terms for merchandise description as mere names to be placed on lists. The real business terms which make their discourse tick do not easily change. And the judiciary's tendency to preserve continuity and to resist change is of course well known. In contrast, the spirit of innovation is what keeps science and technology going. Practitioners in these fields have to propose new ideas and invent new methods and machines in order to survive. So they are compelled to use new terms reflecting the constant changes in their thinking.

Second, business, of course, also has to make use of technological innovations all the time. Any successful entrepreneur must exploit new technology to cut costs and beat the competition. Business success also depends on convincing the public that one's rivals are offering less. This job of convincing the public is done through advertising, which is not quite the same as the field of business proper for our purposes. Consider a newspaper. The business pages have an entirely different look to them, in organisation and language, compared to the reader-friendly, graphically attractive advertisements. This shows that the language of advertising and the language of business pose entirely different challenges to the translator. Advertising is a field where linguistic novelty is a constant feature. Business discourse proper is not. Business people discuss technological innovations for reasons external to technology—namely, to focus on. business. This is why people say that business is linguistically a more conservative domain than some others.

Third, this type of classification of domains, however, is only superficial. It focuses on the frequency of use of new terms alone. The translator has to deal with novelty as a whole. Even in terminologically conservative domains such as business, there is a constant process of throwing up new abbreviations for the translator to decipher. Consider, in comparison, the case of legal language. Even if it rests on a firm and slow-changing system of usage, one naturally refers to the whole apparatus of laws and precedents constituting the systemic background presupposed in all legal discussion within a given country. Translators can cope with such material only if they know their way around the legal literature of that country, including even references to specific cases, judgments and legal discussions.

Thus, in practice, even the non-technologically oriented domains have their own technical details which keep changing as the domain evolves, producing novelties for the translator in that field to keep up with new lexical coinages. It is for this reason that translators have to acquire and keep refreshing some specialised disciplinary knowledge in addition to an overall command over the source and target languages. They have to follow the field, keeping up with new developments in both the languages which they are trying to bridge. This is the only way to retain enough familiarity with the scene to make it possible to figure out the meaning of particular abbreviations or learn about the ground realities of specialised translation, where time is a scarce resource and one has to find answers to one's puzzles quickly.

There is a general tendency to seek catchy titles for books, come up with novel names for ideas and products, and opt for other attention-grabbing markers of originality. This is how one ends up getting both abbreviations and 'new names'. Many languages used in the developing countries have properties that make it useful to regard them as 'developing languages'. It is important to notice that in a developing language one expects large amounts of novelty on a routine basis, as most modern diction is supposed to sound new in it. This situation alters the premises of the Translation Novelty Paradox. In a developing language, there is no requirement that new entrants into the set of 'acceptable texts' should exhibit any real continuity with the existing traditions so as to sound natural. Much can be, and is, written in a diction that sounds like 'translationese', without protest from the public. For the public wishes to catch up with the 'developed world', and accepts translationese as one of the costs of this endeavour.

The problem of translating from a developed language into a developing target language, as far as neologisms are concerned, must be viewed in this context. Given the language planning enterprise and the presence of large amounts of routine innovation in such a target language, it becomes appropriate to describe these innovations in terms of a consciously and centrally authorised inventory of neologisms. Thus, neologisms are non-domesticated new expressions, and translators responding to the problem of tackling a generation of new lexis often need to go back to the basics and develop an overall understanding of the issue of newness. The issue is fundamental since a translation must both be new to the target language and keep in touch with old trends in the target language.

Innovation, when used by translators, brings the target and source languages structurally closer to each other. But there is a limit up to which this proximity can be achieved because presumably no two languages or cultures would either like to be the same or tolerate an extreme convergence. There will thus be a kind of compromise brought about by translators who mediate between two languages and communities, and this leads us to the next point, namely, that the translator could also bring about a compromise between overtranslation and undertranslation by innovating. The innovation here may range from a complete novelty to simple transpositions from the source to target language, such as borrowings. Innovation may not thus always mean creation of new lexical items since innovation itself is subject to the constraints of context.

Also, notice that languages vary in terms of the extent to which they can assimilate innovations. There can be languages that resist borrowing on a large scale. The reasons for this hesitation could be many: language pride resulting in a superiority complex; constraints deriving from the way the cultural institutions are organised in the society (i.e., the ratio of indigenousness and borrowing); a false desire to retain the 'purity' of one's language; or even a myth which does not allow one to fill up one's language with words since are, after all, 'divine creations', etc.

Again there may be differences between the degrees of allowance that a society makes for translators. The society at large may allow translators to innovate, because otherwise a transfer of knowledge would be impossible; while it may not encourage its creative writers to do this in a big way. The reverse may also happen, where only authors are free to innovate. Thus, innovation may be either a powerful or a relatively weak tool or technique in a translator's hands.

It should be obvious by this time that some translations could be vastly more successful than others. For instance, for a long time certain texts and authors may be regarded as hopeless cases for translation. At a different point of time, we see that the barrier is broken and a viable translation arrived at. Certain semantic and structural losses are of course expected, and these can be excused up to an extent in non-technical texts, but this cannot be permitted in a technical document, where meaning loss may defeat the very purpose of translation. Newmark (1981: 7–8) has rightly pointed out that the translator is a victim of a constant tension between the acts of overtranslation and undertranslation.

Another possible source of loss may have to do with the source and target language relationship. There are pairs of languages that are different in langue as well as in parole, i.e., in both structure and use. Such differences may occur at any level. For instance, at the lexical level, the differences may be in different dimensions such as: (a) the formality of styles available (from frozen to completely informal); (b) the affectivity that any given text can achieve in the two languages (from no reaction to overreaction); (c) how general or technical these languages can be/become; and (d) how texts are evaluated in the languages concerned (in terms of morality, pleasure, intensity or coverage).

Notice that in the matter of style, it is not only that the writers of literary texts often employ distinct dialects in comparison to hundreds of other texts written and published in the standard variety of the language. These writers may also create a peculiar compound textual style by operating with different styles and dialects within the same text. The result is innovation, in both single words as well as in local word groups or compounds, which becomes very difficult to transfer into any other language.

In the dimension of reactions and feelings towards a given text, and in terms of affectivity, there can be differences of opinion among translators. Similarly, the original writer of a text may attach 'private' meanings to what he says or the way he says what he says. The translator, if different from the author, will naturally write in the style natural to himself. Consequently, there is bound to be a considerable loss of meaning.

This brings us to the next point. Even if we neglect the private meanings, the text writer and the translator may have completely different value systems and different semantic maps with which they operate. Therefore, there are bound to be losses or gains in the domain of the semantics of the text(s) being subjected to any translating activity.

A 'total' replacement of the source language grammar and lexis by an equivalent target language grammar and lexis, with a consequential replacement of source language phonology and graphology by non-equivalent target language phonology/graphology (Catford 1965: 22), may be validated only when differential bilingual dictionaries with careful comparative definitions of all the corresponding units in their intention and extension become handy. It is in this context that bilingual glossaries assume much importance.

Translation presents special problems for languages that are genetically unrelated or typologically different for obvious reasons. The constraints which crop up when one contrasts two such languages are the real problems in the process of translation to be tackled by any comprehensive theory, particularly if one reiterates faith in Jakobson's (1981: 262) dictum that equivalence in difference is the cardinal problem of language and the pivotal concern of linguistics.

In the insightful article entitled 'Translating: Practice Creates Theory', Alokeranjan Dasgupta, a leading poet-translator, raised the important point that cognateness and genetic relatedness do not necessarily make the task of a translator easy. He brings out the genuine difficulty he faced in trying to render Suradasa's Brajabhasa poetry into Bengali. He writes:

> In one of the ambiguous padas I chanced upon the word 'sarang'. On consulting the most reliable dictionary—Brajabhasa Surakosa—I found that fifty-one meanings are given there for this intriguing lexeme. To mention a few here: Siva, sun, swan, horse, lion, lotus, woman, ornament, hair, day, clouds, dove, breasts, collyrium, clothing lighting, flower, melody, etc (Premnarayan Tandon, ed. I. 1320). To my utter dismay, none of these meanings was of any help till, judging the term by its context, I was convinced that it served the sound function of para-rhyme. (Dasgupta, A. 1988)

Like Dasgupta, many now believe that a translator, and particularly a translator of a literary text, is at times forced to opt for some deviations for which one cannot brand translators with the negative credo of *traduttore traditore* ('the translator is a traitor'). And this brings one to the interesting conjecture that any independent translation theory is likely to go against the known theoretical position of modern day linguistics, which is that that a theory of translation has to be inductive. The first and the foremost reason for this is, of course, that 'associations that are self-evident and beyond challenge in one language require a lot of circumlocution in the other' (ibid.: 5).

Rules of Thumb in the Choice of Technical Words

While it is difficult to decide on what could be considered the criteria or principles of terminological translation, we can profitably think of some general guidelines on the kinds of translation techniques adopted by a translator of terms. An outline of these rules of thumb is presented here:

First, unlike the native speaker's unconscious knowledge of his or her language, the most important thing about a term planner's activity is that the creator-translator is fully conscious here. He cannot hide himself behind the curtain of secrecy about the 'mystery' of how one makes use of 'native' intuitions. In fact, he has to be ready to explain, or even defend, his choices and decisions.

Second, the terminological translator cannot choose to be whimsical. He or she cannot merely create a fancy neologism (for instance, 'svaniim' for the well-known English linguistic term 'phoneme') but has to take into consideration all the derivatives of the term that exist in the source language (in this case, the set of terms: phonemic, phonemics, phone, allophone, phonology, phonotactic, phonemicity, morphonological, etc.) so that he is able to give his readers/users a similarly productive family of terms.

Third, the terms must be largely acceptable by the society or that segment of the target language society that is likely to use them. In other words, the terms should not be merely acceptable to their creators. It should also be possible to verify their acceptability through user reaction surveys. For instance, while it is possible that different translators or groups come up with different translations for the same term, each one of them should have some sound reasons for choosing their particular version:

22. atom bomb

a. *Navabharat Times*, Delhi/Bombay:	paaramaaNavika bam
b. *Dainik Navajyoti*, Jaipur:	paramaaNu bam
c. *Janasattaa*, New Delhi:	eTamii bam
d. *Aryavart*, Patna:	aNu bam

Fourth, the above condition does not mean that terms must always be based on commonly known words. There will always be terms that will be completely novel creations or innovations. Let us take certain practical instances of such creations in Hindi:

23. air hostess	vyoma baalaa; vaayu kanyaa; vimaan paricaarikaa
24. executive engineer	adhishaasii abhiyantaa
25. sick industry	biimaar udyog
26. share market	saajhaa baazaar
27. beneficial fall	dilkhush mandaa

It is obvious that while some of these are entirely novel creations (such as 'adhishaasii abhiyantaa'), some others are instances of semantic extensions or establishment of new collocational traditions (such as 'dilkhush mandaa'). Such terms will have to be given a chance to survive because in some cases it is only through continuous use that a term acquires significance in a society. This is comparable to the introduction of traffic signals in a society that did not have any traffic rules other than probably 'one shall not clash head on with another'. It would not be surprising if it took time for traffic rules to gain firm ground in such a society. Thus, none can preclude the possibility of a period of uncertainty before the terminological innovations get stabilised. Meanwhile, there will have to be trial and error. The moral is that terms may initially be floated on an experimental basis and that one should be ready to withdraw a term depending on user reaction surveys.

Fifth, terms are often coined through learned borrowing. Ideally, these should not have an elitist bias. They must be easily comprehensible and easily pronounceable. It also means that the translator has to ethnologise his technical terms, i.e., he should modify them in such a manner that they are culturally acceptable and naturalised too. Some well-known instances of such naturalisation are the following:

28. registered	rajis Triikr.t
29. classical	klasikii
30. academy	akaadamii
31. hospital	aspataal
32. tragedy	traasadii

Wherever care has not been taken to ethnologise, the result is a peculiar construction, although in course of time, some such terms gain acceptability. One of the best examples here is the loan translation of Union Public Service Commission as '*sangh lok sevaa aayog*' instead of a more natural '*kendriiya*' or '*sanghiiya* lok sevaa aayog'.

Sixth, depending on whether one is creating these terms with an official directive, as a part of the language planning activity of the administration, or whether one is translating as a purely academic exercise without any official sanction but with an aim, say, to contribute towards the 'modernisation' of a language, one may be more bound or free as a translator.

Finally, time may be another binding factor. It is possible that the job has to be completed within a definite time frame. This time constraint may arise out of a commitment the administration may have given to the masses or to any segment of the population such as academics, legal practitioners, businessmen, industrialists, etc. A lot will depend, therefore, on the urgency and the time frame for the implementation of the terms one has translated.

The Official Guidelines

Let us now consider the principles for the evolution of technical terms that have been approved by the Government of India's

Commission for Scientific and Technical Terminology (CSTT). The CSTT has given us a set of guidelines which can be explained and restated as follows:

First, 'international' terms, which have been accepted the world over without any major change, should be adopted in their current forms as far as possible. For us, the window to the world being through English, the chances are that these terms will enter into Hindi via English, even if they may have different origins in languages such as Portuguese or French (as with the words restaurant, ticket, signal, bureau, police or deluxe). These will also include proper names and terms based on proper names from English, such as boycott (from Capt. Boycott) or marxism-leninism (from Karl Marx and V.I. Lenin), and the frequent expressions such as licence, permit, royalty or tariff. Such terms are then transliterated into Hindi (as well as in other official languages of the Indian Union) without disturbing the phonological and graphemic pattern of our languages. In fact, it has been clearly stated by the CSTT that:

> the transliteration of English terms should not be made so complex as to necessitate the introduction of new signs and symbols in the present Devanagari characters. The Devanagari rendering of English terms should aim at maximum approximation to the standard English pronunciation with such modifications as prevalent amongst the educated circles of India (Comprehensive Glossary of Administrative Terms 1991: xiii–xiv).

Second, all conceptual terms will be attempted to be translated, unless they have somehow already entered into our vocabulary by naturalised borrowing.

Third, indigeneous terms, which have come into vogue in our languages for certain technical words of common use (such as 'taar' for 'telegram/telegraph' or 'daak' for 'post') should be retained.

Fourth, the aim of vocabulary coinage should be that one is able to achieve maximum possible identity in all Indian languages by opting for either terms based on Sanskritic roots or terms common to a number of other regional languages so as to eliminate undue taxation on official language learners from a background of other Indian languages.

Fifth, the choice of Hindi technical terms must be such that the Hindi equivalents appear simple, semantically precise and easily intelligible. Obscurantism and purism should be avoided.

Sixth, hybrid forms are normal and natural linguistic phenomena in technical terminology and, therefore, such forms may be adopted, keeping in view the contexts and requirements. Examples of such forms are 'gaaraNTit' for 'Guaranteed', 'klasikii' for 'Classical' and 'koDkaar' for 'Codifier'.

Seventh, as far as possible, complex forms generated by the sandhi rule should be avoided. In the case of compound words, the hyphen may be placed in between two terms for a quicker and easier grasp of the word structure of the new terms.

Problems of Lexical Equivalence

I. In Other Words: Paraphrasing, or the Search for Terminological Equivalents

Looking for another word or expression from within the same language can be called intralingual paraphrase or translation, which is very different from translation as interlingual transfer. While interlingual rendering is a product of history, intralingual paraphrasing is a response to necessity at a particular point of time. At a given moment, when your interlocutor is unable to follow you or unable to get the full import of your statement, you cannot but try to say the same thing 'in other words'—which is what 'paraphrasing' is. But one may ask at this point what the problem with paraphrasing could be.

Consider the following example. It is often observed that an author, especially a fiction writer or a playwright, or sometimes a legal luminary, restates the same point by using a different set of terms or a modified syntax. This is a intralanguage skill that an interlanguage interpreter must learn to master, because quite often, in the course of quick-speed translation, the target language renderings of dialogue carry over the same source language lexis, word-formation devices or even syntactic structures, making it difficult for the person employing/using the interpreter to grasp what was said by the original speaker-interlocutor.

In fact, while listing a few psychological problems in teaching the theory and practice of interpretation, Pegacheva (1959: 138) describes translation as a 'peculiar instance of speech activity in course of which a number of psychological difficulties have to be overcome'. The most important of these is the problem of retrieving the right word or expression, or the problem of equivalence.

This brings us to the question: how natural is translation as a linguistic activity? It appears to some theoreticians that translation is like any other speech activity natural to us. Zimnyaya contends that:

> Translation is essentially [an] activity. My aim is to show that translation is a complex, specific, secondary type of speech activity. This statement holds good for all forms of translation.... Translation is a type of speech activity that can be studied alongside other types, such as listening, speaking, reading and thinking. (Zimnyaya, 1993: 88–89)

Now, viewing translation as an extension of speech activity has many interesting consequences. With this view, we take it for granted that every native speaker of a language has an intrinsic competence in translating just as he has been claimed to have linguistic competence as a speaker-hearer of his language. Reading and writing, on the other hand, are acquired secondary skills, which one can only 'know' as applications of speech through conscious training or through other non-formal methods, including self-learning.

The question then is the following: is translation comparable to secondary speech activities or is it one of the primary speech activities? If translating is like reading and writing, it must be an acquired craft. If it is not, it must be something that one learns unconsciously. In fact, one could claim that all native speakers constantly paraphrase themselves or redraft their statements—potentially all statements but, practically, at least some. Therefore everybody takes recourse to intralingual translation or paraphrasing. At the same time, when we learn even our mother tongue as a school subject, we have to master various extensions of both written and spoken skills in it—such as summarising or writing a precis or a paragraph or an essay—all of which require us to learn to formally paraphrase while working on a given text. Here we are learning to 'translate' intralingually through a formal method.

Now we can return to the question of whether translation could be a secondary speech activity or whether it must be regarded as a kind of primary speech activity. Our answer is that it can be both. Even if we consider paraphrasing as a natural instinct which all native speakers possess, it is nevertheless a skill which needs polishing when it comes to looking for the right word. It is this greater degree of perfection that any formal education system helps us in achieving. In this sense too, translation is comparable to 'speaking' which everyone knows how to do. But one has to learn many extensions of it, for example, to speak on a topic for which no planning is done (extempore speech), to present, through structured speech, arguments for or against a motion (public debate), to speak on solemn occasions (condolence speech) or in formal meetings (introductions, presidential remarks, votes of thanks), etc.

The second consequence of viewing translation as a speech activity is that when someone is born into a bilingual context, or when one acquires a language other than one's mother tongue, one naturally knows how to say the same thing in different languages. There are exceptional bilinguals, however, who know how to use the other tongue only in limited domains, or who use two or more languages mostly in mutually exclusive complementary situations, i.e., where language A is used, language B is never used, and vice versa. Except in such instances, a bilingual person is a 'natural' translator—all the time employing the natural search techniques at his or her disposal to hunt for the right word. Once again, he just has to sharpen his retrieving abilities if he has to qualify as a 'professional' translator. Thus, even in this respect, translation is a kind of natural ability.

The third consequence is that a large number of native speakers in each community first learn to speak a particular speech variety which in later life may be used mostly in, say, home and family domains, i.e., in a limited circle, whereas what is used in most other spoken contexts is the standard speech variety. The nature and quality of this standard will differ from person to person, although ideally it should not. The fluctuation or variation also depends on one's dialectal or sociolectal background. Sometimes, people think and dream in a non-standard speech variety and give their thoughts and dreams shape in words from the spoken standard, thus adopting a strategy of intralingual paraphrasing.

II. More Problems with Interlingual Transference

Wittgenstein (1958) states that 'the meaning of a word is its use in the language'. This is a very important statement that generalises translation activities. So, the translator should note the words which express the leading ideas, and hunt up their nearest, if not the exact, equivalents in the target language and should choose from many available lexical choices while translating. To search for an equivalent while paraphrasing is extremely difficult. Hartmann (1990: 47) argues that 'the notion of equivalence has been tied to the description of, and giving training in, various replacement processes....' This idea of equivalence as 'replacement' lays an emphasis on lexis because of the inevitable semantic differences between two languages or texts.

Let us take some concrete examples of lexical equivalence between two Indian languages where paraphrasing as a translation strategy is involved. The source language here is Marathi:

33.	ga:Dhava:la:	gula:ci	cava ka:ya?	(Marathi)
	donkey-to	jaggery-of	taste what	

In Hindi, this is literally

33a	gadhe-ko	guRa kaa	swad	kyaa?	(Hindi)
	to donkey	jaggery of	taste	what	

(What is the taste of jaggery to a donkey?)

But, obviously, a more 'natural' translation would be:

33b	gadhaa	kyaa	jaane	guRa kaa	swad?	(Hindi)
	donkey	what	knows	jaggery of	taste	

(What does a donkey know of the taste of jaggery?)

There could be two Oriya equivalents of this statement, where both options are close to 33b but the lexical choice in 34b seems more interesting. They are as follows (cf., Dash 1994):

34a	gadha ki	ja:Niba	guDara	sva:da?	(Oriya)
	donkey how	know	jaggery of	taste	

34b	ghuSuri ki	ja:Niba	kadaLira	sva:da?	(Oriya)
	pig	how	know	banana-of	taste

(How does a pig know the taste of banana?)

Obviously, even though 34b is lexically far removed from the source text (33), it could be considered to be a total translation. In word-for-word translation, sometimes one does not get the sense of the original, though the overall meaning is present in the rendering. Whenever there is a story or an event behind a proverb, the word-for-word translation strategy accompanied by a footnote about the story or the event can help to convey the sense. As an example, consider the following Marathi saying:

35.	ga:ya	ghore	goTha:	bhare	bEla	ghore	dhani:	mare.
	cow	snores	animal-house	full	bullock	snores	master	dies

The literal meaning of the proverb is: 'If the cow snores, the animal house will be full; but if the bullock snores, the master will die'. This proverb denotes a superstition in the source language culture. To retain the sense of the above Marathi proverb one can adopt a word-for-word translation approach and thus retain the rhythmical form also. As there is no such superstition in the Oriya culture there is no Oriya proverb available which could convey the sense of the original. Here is the possible Oriya equivalent where very little change has been made:

36.	ga:i	ghuN'guDire	guha:La	bhare,	(Oriya)
	cow	snores-by	animal-house	full	

baLada	ghuN'guDire	ma:lika	mare.
bullock	snores-by	master	dies

There is always the possibility of a translator getting carried away in the process of retaining the rhythm of the original when he is trying to achieve a word-to-word translation. It is therefore important to appreciate that translation is a semantic endeavour rather than an attempt to preserve or transmit mere forms or structures when we are referring to the transfer of texts from one language to another. It also has a complex pragmatics and is an attempt at cross-cultural communication. As Wilss suggests:

> Translators do not work independently, nor are their actions directly attributed to themselves, which makes the definition of their role in the interlingual/intercultural communicative process so difficult; they work within the context of a mediating situation rather than a direct actional situation. (Wilss 1990: 21)

Being Communicative versus being Semantic

At this point one could very well raise the methodological issue of precisely how 'semantic' one needs to be in the search for patterns of lexical equivalence. Newmark (1981 and 1988) has come up with an important distinction between communicative translation methods and semantic translation methods which could be profitably discussed here. The basic differences between the two approaches are given here in brief:

(1) While communicative translation lays more importance on performance factors such as message, receiver or utterance, semantic translation stresses meaning, sender, author and thought processes. In strictly lexicographical terms, it is the latter which is more important as a method. But if we move beyond lexis and wish to do either interlingual or intralingual paraphrasing, we will have to draw on both strategies because they both emphasise the message as well as meaning on the one hand and, on the other, the complemetary roles of addresser and addressee.

(2) Where there is a conflict between the two methods, communicative translation in the context of interlingual transfer must dwell on the 'force' rather than on the 'content' of the text. It also addresses itself completely to the second reader, who does not anticipate difficult words or expressions or obscurities in his own language, and would rather expect a generous transfer of foreign elements into his language. Intralingual paraphrasing is more like a semantic translation device which remains within a given culture and assists readers or users of this method in decoding the necessary connotations and import of words which constitute the essential human, non-ethnic message of the text.

(3) Generally, when one applies communicative translation methods, paraphrasing is in all cases likely to be smoother, simpler, clearer, more direct and conforming to particular conventions of the concerned language, tending towards undertranslation. In contrast, semantic translation tends to produce a more complex, more awkward, more detailed and probably a more faithful text, resulting in the resurrection of many words and expressions that are not in general currency, and even creating new forms. Instead of discovering the intention of the original author, semantic translation pursues the thought processes that lie behind the lexical coinages in the source text.

(4) These different strategies are to be taken as general guidelines. A translation can be more semantic, even while a particular expression or sentence is treated more communicatively in the same translation. This means that if a translator approaches the problem of looking for equivalences as a whole semantically, and yet if some portion of a sentence or paragraph needs communicative translation, there should be no strong objections. The reverse is also true.

(5) In interlingual paraphrasing and communicative translation the translator has the freedom to improve the flavour of the original in the target language, where he can recreate, modify and adopt words and expressions to enhance the tone of the original. But this freedom is totally absent in semantic translation, as the words become 'sacred' due to the importance given to the form and content of the source text. In the case of intralingual paraphrasing, it is not the sacred nature of the lexis which is at play, but freedom too is missing here, because in case of intralingual transfer, there are the inherent cognitive limitations of being confined within the same language community.

The Problem of Creativity: Negotiating Poetic Metaphor and Imagery

In terms of what has been called the 'de-leeching' of texts (Barthes 1986: 352–53) in the contemporary critical idiom, there is a crisis of cognition in today's literature. The metaphors that describe the human experience seem to have undergone a radical change. In modern and postmodern poetry, for instance, the earlier trend of using the metaphors of mother, father, or other human icons to describe the locus or the land we live in is being replaced with 'language', which is itself perceived as a living organism. This emphasis on metaphors is important in translation because the semantics of equivalence (for example, life = playground whereas noises = language) heavily depends on our identification of images in terms of lexical categories such as nouns, pronouns, adjectives and adverbs derivable from our legacy of grammar.

To analyse some concrete examples of nominal imagery, let us examine a text or two in both the original and in translation. How can we explain the use of language-based images in the following text?

37. Text A
kɔthara chinnobhinno hoye ache
ki ar bolbe
haway dushɔn onugɔndho
bakke dushɔn
bakko bhishon jɔRo hoye jay
jɔRojoibo hoye mɔre
Ekhon mɔRok kɔthar mɔRok colche Ekhon
ebɔng pɔcon jEmon dharer shɔngskriti
ki ar bolbe
kɔtha shɔb jEno kɔto kal age bɔla hoye gEche
khin kɔtha pran
phu Te oTho bak
bishal spho Ton bhabchi ami ('Katha' in Sen 1988: 16)

38. Translation A
Discourses tear asunder
What shall they speak
Air pollutes
Smell of atoms
Sentences infected
Sentences get terribly stiffened
Die stillborn grisly
Now is a drought-epidemic of words now

And putrid becomes the borrowed culture
What will they speak
Words galore have already been said long ago
Slender life and words
Ascend O Vak
I cerebrate a large plosion
(Translation: U.N. Singh, forthcoming)

In this poem, the poet finds his space, his private world polluted, so much so that his sentences are now born crippled. The existing ones get stifled and the forthcoming ones die a repulsive death. This piece is a part of a larger text and has to be read closely with 'Akor0n' ('The Structure') which follows:

39. Text B	40. Translation B
bheshe uThche shomosto kal	Time Eternal emanates
shɔkol ebɔng shɔrbo	All and entire Time
bheshe uThche adim ɔstro	The ancient arms too appear
jibɔssho~ ar protno	Fossils and ántiquaria
akar nicche bɔrnoguli	The letters are taking shape
shɔbdomalar pak	In the cauldron of lexis
akar nicche ognikɔna	The fireballs are shaping up
ebɔng tahar jala	And their blaze
jɔnmo nicche rupokɔlpo	Metaphors in the making
ek Ti shishu akar nicche	A child is taking shape
shomosto kal khola	All times are open
mɔra gaNge mriter bhashan	Immersion of the corpse in the dead river
khin Taner bhasha	Drifting through sluggishly
jɔnmo ebɔng mrittumala	The alphabet of Birth and Death
('Akorɔn' in Sen 1988: 15)	(Translation: U.N. Singh, forthcoming)

The text 'Akorɔn' is a history of sentential construction and creation of the 'sign'. The earlier text, 'K0tha' seems to be showing the degeneration and decadence of the 'sentence'. Let me borrow the words of Malcom Bradbury (1983: 151–52) to describe the degeneration that the poet talks about, in which it appears that the 'conditions of crisis are evident: language awry, cultural cohesion lost, perception pluralized'.

Language can, of course, also act as a pronominal in the vernacular of imagery and be viewed as *pomme frite* (French fries) on a frying pan (Barthes 1978) where 'on any object, a good language-system functions, attacks, surrounds, sizzles, hardens, and browns' (Barthes 1986: 355). I would like to call this Barthsian imagery pronominal because here 'language' stands only as an object which is not the real thing but without which nothing real or substantial can be stated.

Let us begin using qualifying words or adjectivals in characterising 'language'. Like the duality of patterning that characterises human language, the 'image' is also subjected to another kind of duality which has been called the dynamics of 'reverberation' as against the energetics of 'causality' (Minkowski as in Bachelard 1958: xii).

The poetic image has the quality of 'trans-subjectivity', even when it shows variations as against other concepts that are constitutive and which are, therefore, open to causal relationships. A poet creates his own world of words, and even when 'the poet does not confer the past of his image upon…[us], yet his image immediately takes root in…[us]' (Bachelard 1958, 1964: xii). At the level of 'reverberations' then, a poem can possess us entirely. Knowing that the image in the text has been produced by another man, the image that we as readers derive makes us feel so involved with the text that we begin to feel that we ourselves could have created it. The twists and turns that we enact in speaking, repeating, singing poetic words derive precisely from this confidence that they have become 'really our own'.

The question is: what does the creative writer do with language in order to actuate such images or such qualities? One idea seems to be that he distorts the world of words, corrupts vocabularies, cripples the syntactic norms of the canonical language and introduces an unprecedented grammatical violence. He bends and mends expressions to accommodate his images. And the task of the translator is to transfer all this violence into another tongue. To the extent that this is true, the literary interpreter as well as the translator as the 'subjects' of the given texts begin to qualify and quantify their dual 'objects'—the direct (text) as well as the indirect (the source or target reader).

In order to contextualise our translator/interpreter, or to take an adverbial approach, one must appreciate that source and target texts quite often refer to a completely or substantially different space and time, or that the encoder 'manipulates' a message to achieve a certain 'unreadability/incomprehensibility'. In such cases, it becomes crucial for us to know the answers to the questions why, how, when, where and for whom, vis-á-vis a given text. Particularly, we need to know whether manipulation occurs because an author wants to use private words for certain personal feelings and wishes himself to be unreadable or because the cultural differences between the two times, two cultures or communities is such that the words of the text seem to have acquired an intrinsic unreadability. As I have shown elsewhere (Singh 1990/1992), the translator requires answers to such questions if he has to chalk out his strategy of deciding whether to opt for neologisms or deal with a particular text in some other manner.

Crisis Today: The Devaluation of Words

The questions that can legitimately be asked today are: what is the nature of crisis in our language of literature? Do our words today—battered, bruised and overused as they may have been—render our languages unfit for great poetry? And is this crisis one of atrophy or devaluation? Is there any correlation between this debasing and the changes that came in due to the democratisation and commercialisation of language? Before the critics of today sign a decree declaring a given language unfit for creativity (that is, decreeing a language 'not for sale'), shouldn't we decide what our standard of comparison and our measures are? Even if one grants for the sake of argument that our languages are diseased, would or would it not be the case that our other creative forms are also debased?

There is another important worry that is slowly assuming the shape of a question from a mere dubiety and it has to do with the way the poets of today perceive language. In contemporary verse, we notice that either the word 'language' or its various synonyms reverberate everywhere in the poems of all major poets. It is, therefore, no exaggeration when a post-structuralist such as Barthes declares that "Language", for the man of the present age, is what

"Nature" was for the ancient Greeks'. Consider what Barthes had to say about language having taken the centre stage in our literary performance.

> I imagine myself today something like the ancient Greek as Hegel describes him: he interrogated, Hegel says, passionately, uninterruptedly, the rustle of branches, of springs, of winds, in short, the shudder of Nature, in order to perceive in it the design of intelligence. And now it is the shudder of meaning I interrogate, listening to the rustle of language, that language which for me, modern man, is my nature (Barthes 1975: 79).

To understand lexis and neologos in today's texts, we will have to consider the images in terms of different dimensions. Images in today's literature are so variegated that this makes the task of a translator very difficult. It is thus important for us to understand that:

> in our time, space is conceived not as one-sided or linear—as in the Renaissance idea of perspective—but as many-sided and virtually inexhaustible in its potentiality for relationships, none of which are mutually exclusive. Consequently, absolute description of any object or area is impossible from a single point of reference. (Spencer 1971: xvi–xvii).

Hence the perspective of the plural word.

Developing a Programme in Transculturation

The development in the application of linguistic theories to various fields opens up the possibilities of using modern techniques to analyse the problems of translation. This requires a more realistic, process-oriented framework drawing on data from case studies. The traditional way of looking for various lexical replacement processes without using a theoretical model that makes the analysis explanatorily adequate loses ground since translators' intuitions are not always correct. To identify and explain the mechanism of languages involved in translation, the issues of how texts get transferred and how contexts and goals influence the search for the right lexis are considered most relevant in the present paradigm of translation studies. In this connection, one has to agree with Hartmann's remarks:

> The trouble is that translation theorists have not managed so far to explain what motivates the choice and appropriateness of particular interlingual equivalence, and whether (and how) the directionality of the process might be crucial to its success. In any case, translator and interpreter training practice seems to proceed without much reference to an explicit set of principles derived either from an adequate theory or from empirical data (Hartmann 1990: 47).

Also recall the profound statement made by the Russian stylistician Juri Lotman (1972), echoing the linguistic relativity hypothesis of Sapir and Whorf: 'No language can exist unless it is steeped in the context of culture; and no culture can exist which does not have at its centre, the structure of a natural language'.

Today's translation specialists do not believe, quite rightly, that any artist—and I include here both creative writer and translator—can meditate in a realm that precedes language. This is because language is the primary modelling system—literature, art and culture being secondary modelling systems. Bearing in mind the fact that language is the system that imprints us with our primary cognitive patterns, I shall, in the final section, attempt to identify how and where translators adopt different translation strategies to meet the challenge of the job at hand, namely, the successful transference of lexis (being the minimum level of accomplishment) as well as the text (being the maximum possible accomplishment).

Conclusion: The Imperatives

After the advent of descriptive-structural linguistics, some structural linguists adopted simple correspondence models of translation in the 1960s. These contrastive linguistics models failed to help in building a translation theory because they relied on the overly simplistic assumption that similarities and differences between the source and target languages would account for ease or difficulty in translating from one language to another. This position did not go beyond the level of identification of areas of difficulty, although for a practising translator its contribution to translation application was, and is, still great. J.C. Catford's 1965 claim of discovering the appropriate target language unit at the corresponding 'structural rank' and his suggestion of using it as a substitute for the source language unit, Eugene Nida's 1964 notion of 'deep structure conversion' and Michael Sharwood-Smith's 1976 concept of a 'congruence machine'—none of these managed to describe the competence needed to actually achieve congruent conversion, nor did they account for the acceptability of a particular rendering produced as a result of such conversions.

It is understood today that translation demands not just linguistic 'congruence' but involves a complex 'cognitive process', which requires a mental operation to be performed each time the process of 'decoding' the message of one text and 'encoding' the same content into another text is undertaken. Hence the emphasis on the claim that 'translation is an action', and hence the importance of the cognitive aspect of translation. The complex nature of the cognitive process we are talking about could be better understood if the following question is answered: what happens in the translator's mind starting from his reception of the original or source text to the translator's understanding of the text's message and until its reproduction? Wilss (1990) says that:

> the effort toward cognitive embedding of the translation process finds justification in the fact that translation, like any other usage, is a goal-directed action. Any activity, either physical or cognitive, is naturally controlled, stimulated and obstructed by certain factors.

Modern translation theoreticians seek to understand these various factors or parameters that influence the translation process. They derive ideas from sociolinguistics, psycholinguistics, anthropology and other allied disciplines in order to move towards a more flexible and testable theory of translation from a rigid rank-scale type comparison model bound by one or another design of grammar. It is now increasingly recognised that more accurate diagnostic testing can be introduced based on authentic materials drawn from persons involved in the process of translation. Such recent research techniques involve the following steps:

(1) Usually, the first step is that observations are recorded through a well-designed survey and raw data collected from respondents. These practical observations are then compared with the existing knowledge in the field. One can also compare the existing and possible translations of the same texts.
(2) As a second step, depending upon the set of postulates with which one is working, a set of grammatical statements or a comparative description can be prepared from these comparisons.
(3) Certain hypotheses can then be derived from such a description.
(4) The next step consists of the execution of empirical tests which can be designed in such a way as to examine the postulates as well as the hypotheses.
(5) From the results of these tests, the existing knowledge or theory will have to be approved, appended, modified or even refuted, in which case a new theoretical position will have to be taken.
(6) Finally, one could always think of possible extensions of the findings to another language for application.

The most important aspect in creating the methodological designs in any experiment on translation is to have the right idea and to determine the extent to which the research stems from observation and experience gained from the actual process of translation. Hence the new methodology has to be out and out 'process-based'. Modern linguistics admits this type of empirical investigation into the theoretical fold which seeks the underlying facts that remain hidden beneath the surface.

To conclude, translation has become a very significant instrument of international communication in all branches of human knowledge and experience in recent years. As a result there has been an increased impetus and commitment to scientific research in the area of translation theory and practice. Although the history of translation practice is quite old not only in the West but also in India, the study of translation has only recently emerged as a discipline with renewed vigour. The theories proposed so far are descriptive in nature and speak about the general properties of the translation phenomena. These attempts are inadequate as they do not clarify the principles, structures and categories of the process of practical translation. An exploration of problem areas and strategies in practical translation would therefore be the first step towards a systematic and scientific study of translation. It is for these reasons that a detailed discussion of patterns of lexical transference in general and the problem of lexical coinages or 'neologisms' in particular has been undertaken here.

References

Bachelard, Gaston. 1958. *La poetique de l'espace*. Presses Universitaires de France. [Tr. into English by Maria Jolas]. 1964. *The Poetics of Space*. New York: The Orion Press.

Barthes, Roland. 1975. Vers une esthe/tique sans entraves. U.G.E. See also Barthes, Roland. 1993. 'Steak and Chips' in *Mythologies*. (Tr. by Annete Lavers) London: Vintage Books.

———. 1978. 'The Image' Paper given at the Colloquium at Cerisy-la-Salle.

———. 1986. *The Rustle of Language*. [Tr. by Richard Howard]. Oxford: Basil Blackwell.

Bradbury, Malcom. 1983. *A Dictionary of Modern Critical Terms*.

Catford, J.C. 1965. *A Linguistic Theory of Translation*. Oxford: Oxford University Press.

Commission for Scientific & Technical Terminology (CSTT), Government of India. 1991. *Comprehensive Glossary of Administrative Terms*: English-Hindi (Computer Database). New Delhi: CSTT, Ministry of HRD.

Crystal, David. 1987. *Clinical Linguistics*, London, Edward Arnold.

Dasgupta, Alokeranjan. 1988. 'Translating: practice creates theory'. Paper given at the Regional Workshop on Literary Translation, Sahitya Akademi, Calcutta. 5–25 January.

Dasgupta, Probal. 1995. 'Types of neologism'. DTS (Theories of Translation) 411: 10. 156–76.

Dash, B.N. 1994. 'Problems of Translation of Proverbs from Marathi to Oriya'. M.Phil. Dissertation, University of Hyderabad.

Gunasekaran, D. & Udaya Narayana Singh. 1991/1993. 'The problems of transculturation; or, does it make sense when one translates cultural texts?' *CALTS*

Working Papers, Vol. 3 (1991; issued 1993), eds. by P. Mohanty & S. Padikkal. Paper given at the Suniti Kumar Chatterji Centenary Seminar, University of Calcutta, Calcutta. 30 Nov–2 Dec, 1990.

Hartmann, R.R.K. 1990. 'The not so harmless drugery in finding translation equivalents'. *Language and Communication* 10:1, 47–55.

Jakobson, Roman. 1959. 'On Linguistic Aspects of Translation'. In R.A. Brower, ed. *On Translation*. Cambridge, MA: Harvard University Press.

———. 1981. 'On Linguistic Aspects of Translation'. In: *Selected Writings*, Vol II, ed. Stephen Rudy. The Hague: Mouton. 261–266.

Kenner, Hugh. 1954. Introduction to Ezra Pound's *Translations*. New York: New Directions.

Lotman, Juri. 1972. 'Die struktur literarischer texte'. *Uni Taschenbucher 103*, Munchen: Wilhelm Fink Verlag.

Newmark, Peter. 1981. *Approaches to Translation*. Oxford: Pergamon Press.

———. 1988. *A Textbook of Translation*. New York: Prentice-Hall.

Nida, E.A. 1964. *Toward a Science of Translating*. Leiden: Brill.

Pegacheva, Z. 1959. 'Nekotorye pshihologischeskye voprosy obucheniya ustnomu perevodu'. In *Bulletin' kolokviuma po eksperimental'noj fonetike i psihologii rechii*, Vol. 2: 130–48. (Moscow: MGPIIJ).

Pound, Ezra. 1911–12. 'I gather the limbs of Osiris'. *The New Age*, 10 (November-February issue).

Sen, Anjan. 1988. *tin bisshe din ratri*. Calcutta: Hardya.

Sharwood-Smith, M. 1976. 'Interlanguage and intralanguage paraphrase'. *Papers and Studies in Contrastive Linguistics* 4: 297–301.

Singh, Udaya Narayana. 1989a. 'Introduction' to *CALTS Working Papers*, 1, eds. by P.R. Dadegaonkar & G. Umamaheswara Rao. Hyderabad: University of Hyderabad. 5–22.

———. 1989b. 'Language of literature and fine arts'. Paper given at the S.K. Chatterji Centenary Seminar, Sahitya Akademi & Centre for Applied Linguistics & Translation Studies, University of Hyderabad. November 2–4. To appear in 1997 in Singh, U.N. & S. Padikkal, eds. *Suniti Kumar Chatterji: A Centenary Tribute*. New Delhi: Sahitya Akademi.

———. 1992. 'Dynamics of textuality and configuration of space'. *International Journal of Translation*, 2.2:25–48. A revised version of the paper presented at the International Seminar on Oral Tradition, Written Word and Communication Systems, Sahitya Akademi, New Delhi. 16–29 February, 1992.

———. 1992a. *Language Development and Planning: A Pluralistic Paradigm*. Shimla: IIAS and New Delhi: Munshiram Manoharlal.

———. 1992b. 'On aesthetics of neologism and neotaxis, or when do we create when we translate?' In Amiya Dev, ed. *Papers in Comparative Literature*, Vol. 2. The Aesthetics of Translation. Calcutta: Jadavpur University. 21–35.

———. 1994. 'Translation as a way of growing'. *Meta: Canadian Journal of Translation* 39: 2. 401–403.

———. 1996. 'Reading of literary texts in translation'. *PICL Journal of Dravidian Studies* 6.1: 39–62.

Spencer, Sharon. 1971. *Space, Time and Structure in the Modern Novel*. New York: New York University Press.

Tirumalesh, K.V. 1990. 'Translation as literature three'. *International Journal of Translation*, 1.2: 1–11.

Yule, George. 1985. *Study of Language*. Cambridge: Cambridge University Press.

Wilss, W. 1990. 'Cognitive aspects of translation' *Language and Communication*, 10, 19–36.

Wittgenstein, L. 1959. *Philosophical Investigations*. (Tr. by G.E.M. Anscombe) Oxford: Blackwell.

Zimnyaya, Irina. 1993. 'A psychological analysis of translation as a type of speech activity'. In Zlateva, ed. ibid., 87–100.

Fourteen

Language Barriers: Machine Translation

AKSHAR BHARATI: VINEET CHAITANYA, AMBA P. KULKARNI, RAJEEV SANGAL and G. UMAMAHESHWAR RAO

The *anusaaraka* system makes text in one Indian language accessible in another Indian language. In the *anusaaraka* approach, the load is so divided between man and computer that the language load is taken by the machine and the interpretation of the text is left to the man. The machine presents an image of the source text in a language close to the target language. In the image, some constructions of the source language, which do not have equivalents, spill over to the output. Some special notation is also devised. The user learns to read and understand the output after some training. Because the Indian languages are close, the learning time of the output language is short, expected to be around two weeks.

The output can also be post-edited by a trained user to make it grammatically correct in the target language. Style can also be changed, if necessary. Thus, in this scenario, the computer can function as a human assisted translation system. *Anusaarakas* have been built from Telugu, Kannada, Marathi, Bengali and Punjabi to Hindi and are available for use over the Internet (http\\:www. iiit.net). They can be built for all Indian languages in the near future. Anybody can build such systems connecting Indian languages, using the free software model.

The Coding of Information in Language

Fully automatic general purpose high quality machine translation systems (FGH-MT) are extremely difficult to build. In fact, there is no system in the world for any pair of languages which qualifies to be called FGH-MT. The reasons are not far to seek. Translation is a creative process which involves interpretation of the given text by the translator. Translations also vary depending on the audience and the purpose for which they are meant. This would explain the difficulty of building a machine translation system. Since, at present, the machine is not capable of automatically interpreting a general text with sufficient accuracy, let alone re-expressing it for a given audience, it fails to perform as an FGH-MT.

Most researchers in the field would agree that the major difficulty that a machine currently faces in interpreting a given text is its lack of general world knowledge or common sense knowledge, subject-specific knowledge, knowledge of the context, etc., which can collectively be called 'background knowledge'.

The first difficulty faced by the machine occurs at a level which we normally do not even recognise as a problem. It pertains to information coded in a text. To understand the idea of information and its coding, let us consider an example. In Indian languages, which have a relatively free word order, information that relates an action (verb) to its participants (nouns) is primarily expressed by means of post-positions or case endings of nouns (collectively called *vibhaktis* of the noun). Such a relation between the action and its participants is called a *karaka* relation. For example, take the following sentence[1]:

Example 1
H:/ rAma ne roTI khAI
!E:/ Ram-erg. bread ate
E:/ Ram ate the bread.

The ergative (erg.) marker ('ne') after 'rAma' indicates that Ram is the *karta* of 'eat', which here means that Ram is the 'agent' of eating. Note that, in English, the primary device for expressing the same information is by means of word order.

Noun–verb agreement also helps in identifying the *karta* or agent. For example:

Example 2
H:/ rAma roTI khAtA hE
!E:/ Ram (m.) bread (f.) eats (m.)
E:/ Ram eats bread.

The masculine ending of the verb indicates that the *karta* is masculine, which in this sentence is unambiguously Ram. However, the identity of the *karta* is not always unambiguous. Consider the following sentence:

Example 3
H:/ cAvala rAma khAtA hE
!E:/ rice (m.) Ram (m.) eats (m.)
E:/ Ram eats rice.

Here, the agreement does not help in identifying the *karta* unambiguously. There are two masculine nouns ('Ram' and 'rice'), one of which is the *karta*. Translation into English, say, would therefore be quite different depending on which one is the *karta*.

This example raises an important point. A language text actually 'codes', or contains only partial information. When a reader (or listener) interprets the text by suitably supplying the missing information, he gets the intended meaning. A text is akin to a picture made up of strokes as well as gaps. A viewer fills in the missing parts appropriately and views them as part of the picture. If done properly, the reader gets the message intended by the writer. In any language, there is a continual tension between brevity and ambiguity. If everything was explicitly stated, the text would be less ambiguous but would be long. Brevity also helps in focusing attention to the relevant parts. Ambiguity thus seems to be a necessary price to be paid for informational conciseness and focus.

What the Machine Can and Cannot Do

Weaknesses

To understand the nature of the difficulty the machine faces, let us return to the sentence in example 3. It seems trivial for us to assume that a person—Ram, in this particular sentence—would be the agent of eating, and rice, the thing which is eaten. But the machine does not 'know' that. This knowledge is said to be world knowledge, as it pertains to the world as it exists.

It turns out that, if we try to put this kind of information into a machine, there would be a very large number of such facts. For all the nouns, we will have to say who can eat whom. How should such facts be organised? That is the first problem, but there is a still harder problem that turns up. Such knowledge is quite easily overridden in language to convey a metaphorical sense, irony, etc. Consider the following sentence:

Example 4
H:/ SharAba Apa nahiM pIte, SharAba Apako pItI hE
!E:/ Alcohol you not drink, alcohol you (accus.) drinks.
E:/ You do not drink alcohol, alcohol drinks you.

Here, the meaning of the sentence is that alcohol drinks a person! And it is a perfectly good sentence. Thus, it is not enough to put such a large number of facts about the world in the machine, we must also put conditions regarding when they can be overridden while processing text. This turns out to be an incredibly hard task. This is the major problem, which the discipline of Artificial Intelligence is currently addressing, but with only limited success. There are no known methods by which the machine can satisfactorily handle and use world knowledge today while processing unrestricted language text.

The examples we have considered are rather easy because the world knowledge that needs to be referred to is fairly well pinpointed. Quite frequently, though, there are ellipses in sentences (i.e., parts of sentences are dropped). The missing part(s) may have to be inferred (possibly using world knowledge) before the processing can be carried out further.

Strengths

We have just witnessed a major weakness of the computer as an information processing machine. It has little or no common sense or world knowledge. Therefore, it cannot interpret or use judgment well. But there are two aspects in which it is strong; (a) it has a large memory: and (b) it can perform arithmetic and logical operations very fast. For example, it can easily store a large dictionary of a few hundred thousand words, and it can search for, and find, a given word very quickly. Similarly, if the machine is given a grammar rule, it can apply it faithfully and with great speed. Language related data and rules can therefore be fed into the machine much more easily than background knowledge.

Sharing the Load

Does it mean that since the machine cannot interpret text with a fair degree of accuracy, machine translation must be abandoned as a distant dream? The answer lies in sharing the load between the reader and the machine so that the tasks which are hard for the human being are done by the machine, and vice versa. A clean way to share the load is for the machine to take up the task of language related processing, and to leave the processing related to background knowledge *to the reader*.

Language related processing consists of analysis of the input source language text, such as morphological processing, the use of a bilingual dictionary, and any other language related analysis or generation. These are the primary sources of difficulty for the reader. These are also the tasks which are relatively easy for the machine. On the other hand, aspects related to world knowledge are left to the reader, who is naturally adept at it.

In translation, two opposing forces are at work—faithfulness and naturalness. The translator must choose between faithfulness to the original text and naturalness to the reader. If the translation is to be made easy and natural for the reader, the translator may have to depart from the original text and put it in a style and setting familiar to the reader. But then the flavour and subtlety of the original gets lost. For a reader who wants to read and study what the original writer wrote, such a translation is not satisfactory. This also means that there is no unique 'correct' translation—in fact, the appropriateness of a translation depends on the audience and the purpose it is meant for.

Most translators that we have come across are inclined towards achieving naturalness to the reader. *Anusaaraka* is at the other extreme; it tries to be as faithful to the original text as possible. In fact, its output must contain all the information in the source language text and no other new information, although it can, if called upon, present the information in stages. But of course there is a problem in 'exactly' coding the same information with 100 per cent fidelity, whether in stages or not, from one language to another, particularly if we want to generate sentences of about equal length, paralleling the sentence constructions wherever possible.

In this sense, translation is sometimes said to be an impossible task. This context also suggests the incommensurability of information. When some information is transferred from one language to another, there is no way to express it exactly. If one tries to move from one construction to another, some part of the information is perforce missed. To take a mathematics example, there is no way to express the cube root of 3 in rational numbers; real numbers are needed for this. However, it *can* be approximated to a given degree of precision.

The *anusaaraka* answer lies in deviating from the target language in *a systematic* manner whenever necessary. This new language is something like a dialect of the target language. For example, Kannada to Hindi *anusaaraka* is likely to produce the following Hindi from a normal Kannada text:

Example 5

@H:	mohana	kala	AyegA	ESA	rAma	kahA
!E:	Mohan	tomorrow	will come	this	Ram	said.

Example 6

H:	rAma	ne	kahA	ki	mohana	kala	AyegA
!E:	Ram-erg.		said	that	Mohan	tomorrow	will-come.

The *anusaaraka* output can be said to be the image of the source text, much like that produced by a camera. Reading the image of the source text is like reading the original text. It has the same flavour. Translation, on the other hand, is like a painting. The translator interprets the original in the source language, and 'paints' a text in the target language with the same meaning. In the *anusaaraka* system, readers usually require some learning of the dialect of the target language, a matter we discuss in detail in a later section of this essay. However, this learning time is negligible compared to the learning time of the source language.

Some Standard Components of an MT System

In this section, we take a look at some of the components needed to perform some standard tasks in any machine translation system. We also discuss how they can be put together. In the following system, we return to a discussion of issues regarding the relatedness of Indian languages, language bridges, etc., and how *anusaaraka* makes use of them.

A basic MT system consists of an analyser of the source language whose output is fed into the generator of the target language. Between the analyser and the generator is a mapper which uses bilingual dictionaries to map the source language elements to target language elements. The important components are described here.

Word Analyser

Words in the input text are first processed by the morphological analyser. Its tasks are to identify the root, lexical category, and other features of the given word. For example, for the Telugu word 'mAnavA', a morphological analysis yields two possibilities—noun and verb.

1. mAnavuDu {category = noun, number = sg., case = address}
   The above Telugu root 'mAnavuDu' means: mAnava or 'man'
2. mAnu {category = verb, TAM = non-past-neg., GNP = 2sg.}
   The above Telugu root 'mAnu' means ghAva_bharanA or 'heal'

(GNP stands for gender-number-person, TAM for tense-aspect-modality).

In the case of the noun, number and case are shown, and in the case of the verb, TAM label and GNP are shown. Some more examples:

smRti
(1) smRti {category = noun, number = sg., case = 0}
(2) smRti {category = noun, number = sg., case = oblique}

vyAdhulaku vyAdhi {category = noun, number = pl. case = ki}

ayiuna Tlu avvu {category = verb, TAM = jEsA, GNP = any}

jAta
(1) jAta {category = noun, *adj_0*}/jAta_adj_n{n sg *obl*}/
(2) jAta_adj_m {cat = n, num = sg *obl*}

telipiri telupu {category = verb, TAM = *iti*, GNP = non-neuter_pl_3}

The morphological analyser we describe is designed to handle inflectional morphology. A separate module would be needed for derivational morphology. The analyser checks whether a given word is in the dictionary. If found, it shows its lexical category, such as pronoun, post-position, noun, verb, etc., and other grammatical features.

Another task that the analyser attempts is to check whether the word can be broken up into a root and a suffix. At the break-up point, some characters such as vowels may be added or deleted. It may have to try several times, proposing to break the word at different points. For each proposed break-up, it looks up the proposed root in a dictionary and the proposed suffix in a suffix-table. When both look-ups are successful, it is a valid root and suffix (provided that they are compatible with each other, information about which is also stored in the dictionary). From this exercise, information is returned regarding the root, its lexical category and its grammatical features.

If morphological analysis does not yield an answer, compounding or *sandhi*-breaking is tried. The given word is broken up into two parts, and each part is analysed as a proposed word. Thus, for each of the two parts, the morphological analysis is repeated, which might again result in a proposing of roots and suffixes, etc., for each proposed word. This method we call the 'propose and test' method.

A large number of steps may have to be tried in this procedure. There are ways of speeding up or eliminating some of the steps. But since each step is mechanical and small, the machine can carry it out precisely and fast.

Local Word Grouper

Indian languages have a relatively free word order. Still, there are units which occur in fixed order. In Hindi, the most important examples of these are the nouns followed by post-positions, the main verb followed by auxiliaries, or compound nouns. In general, whenever there is a sequence of words that has a meaning which cannot be composed out of the meanings of the individual words, they must be grouped together and the group as a whole will have a meaning. The group as a whole, together with its meaning, will have to be stored in a dictionary or a table. Some examples are given here:

H: khAtA calA jA rahA hE
!E: eat walk go live is
E: going on eating (without stopping)

H: kAlA pAnI
!E: black water
E: rigorous imprisonment

Local word grouping is more extensive in Hindi and other north Indian languages compared to the south Indian languages, while their morphology is simpler. Thus, the two taken together (morphology and local word grouping) are likely to have the same level of difficulty across the north and south Indian languages.

Mapper Using Bilingual Dictionaries

This process involves looking up the elements of the source language and substituting them by equivalent elements belonging to the target language. For example, the root of a source language word obtained using a word analyser is substituted by its equivalent root in the target language. For example, 'Apa' would be produced in Hindi for the Telugu word 'mIru' (you). The grammatical features also need to be suitably mapped. For example, a pronoun and a noun in the source language ('mIru' and 'pustakaM' respectively) are mapped to an appropriate pronoun and noun in the target language with the same number, person, etc.

Example 7
T: mIru pustakaM caduvutunnArA?
@H: Apa pustaka paDha_rahA_[hE | thA]_kyA{23_ba.}?
!E: You book read_ing_[is | was]_Q.?
E: Are/were you reading a book?

In example 7, the last word in the sentence is a verb and illustrates the mapping from Telugu to Hindi, morpheme by morpheme: the root is mapped to 'paDha' (read), and similarly the tense-aspect-modality label is mapped to 'rahA_[hE | thA] (is_*ing or was_*ing), which is followed by the 'A' suffix which gets mapped to 'kyA' (what?) as a question marker in Hindi. Telugu leaves the tense open as: present or past, which is reflected in the output. GNP information is also separately shown in curly brackets—'{23_ba.}' for second or third person and *bahu-vachana* (plural).

Word Synthesiser

A word synthesiser is the reverse of the word analyser. It takes a root, its lexical category and grammatical features, and generates a word. Two examples in Hindi are given here:

rAjA {category = noun, number = pl., case = obliq} → rAjAoM
king

khA{category = verb, number = sg., TAM = tA, GNP = fs3} → khAtI
eat

Word synthesis is a much simpler task compared to word analysis. This can usually be done directly by the given rules, without having to try various alternatives by proposing and testing.

Putting the Components Together

The components just described can be put together, resulting in an MT system. A sample system is described here, but there can be variations on this theme.

First, the input text in a source language is passed through the word analyser in an MT system which analyses each word and produces its root and grammatical features. These are then fed into a local word grouper which combines the words and produces local word groups.

Second, the mapper takes the output produced so far, to replace the elements of the source language with elements of the target language. Thus, at this stage, the source language root will be changed to the target language root.

Third, the output of the mapper is fed into the generator of the target language, which itself might consist of a local word splitter and morphological synthesiser. The output produced is the MT system output. Interfaces are also provided for human pre-editing of the input and post-editing of the output. These are also a part of the overall system, but a discussion on them is postponed to the section following the next one.

The *Anusaaraka* Approach

As explained earlier, *anusaaraka* takes information in the source language text and presents it in the target language, or in a language close it. Thus, at the suffix level, a suffix in the source language is replaced by a suitable element in the target language; and at the word level, source words are replaced by equivalent words in the target language. Similarly, word groups are also replaced by equivalent groups in the target language. The reason this approach works even without a parser is that Indian languages are syntactically similar.

Indian languages are relatively free word order languages where the noun groups can come in any order generally followed by the verb group. The order conveys aspects such as emphasis but not information about *karaka* relationships. If we take a sentence in a source language and substitute the word groups in it by appropriate word groups in the target language, it works well because the languages make similar use of order to convey emphasis, etc. The *vibhaktis* for the word groups (that is, case endings and post-position markers for nouns, and TAM for the verb groups) must be mapped from the source language to the target language carefully, as they contain important *karaka* information regarding the verb and the nouns. Again the languages behave in a similar way.

Besides the ones just mentioned, there are also similarities in the meanings of words. Many words in the Indian languages have a shared origin deriving from Sanskrit, and because of shared culture, they usually also share meanings. This implies that for a source language word, the bilingual dictionary provides a unique answer in the target language. Thus, the reason why the method outlined in the last section works well is the similarity among Indian languages. Even if the languages have different origins, but are in close contact, they acquire each others' features. This is called the 'areal hypothesis'. Scholars further agree on calling the Indian subcontinent 'a linguistic area'.

Now we will discuss some of the problems that arise because two languages differ, and see how these problems can be handled. We will take examples from Hindi, Telugu and Kannada. Apart from agreement, there are only three major syntactic differences between Hindi and Kannada. Surprisingly, all of these can be taken care of by enriching Hindi with a few additional functional particles or suffixes as shown here. Thus, they can be viewed as lexical gaps or function-word gaps. But first we will discuss issues related to agreement.

Agreement

Let us consider the case of noun–verb agreement. There is a lack of agreement (of gender, number and person, or GNP) as per the rules of the target language in the *anusaaraka* output. The information displayed about GNP corresponds to the source language. For example, in the following *anusaaraka* output, the masculine and feminine genders are marked against the personal pronoun 'vaha' by {m.} and {f.} respectively ({~m.} stands for non-masculine). Note that in Hindi, the personal pronoun 'vaha' is the same for both masculine and feminine gender.

Example 8
T: Ame vADito mATIADiMdi kAnI
@H: vaha{f.} usa{m.}_se bAta_kiyA_{hE | thA}{3_~m._e.} lekina {hone_do}
!E: she he (instr.) talked (non-masc.) but,

Example 9
T: vADu Ameto mATIADaledu.
@H: vaha{m.} usa{f.}_se bAta_kiyA_nahIM[nahIM_bAta_kara_sakatA_hE{3_~m.e.}]
!E: he she (instr.) did[could] not talk (non-masc.)
E: She talked to him, but he did not talk to her.

If the gender information was not shown, the sentence would have been rendered as:

Example 10
H: usane usase bAta kI, lekina usane usase bAta nahIM kI
!E: s/he s/he (instr.) talked, but s/he s/he (instr.) talk not do

In short, without the gender information in *anusaaraka* Hindi, the meaning of the sentence is not clear. To produce good Hindi from such a sentence requires different strategies. One solution would be to explicitly add 'laDakA' (boy) or some morpheme indicating the sex:

Example 11
H: usa laDakI ne usase bAta kI, lekina
usa laDake ne usase bAta nahIM kI
!E: that girl-erg. her/him talked, but that boy-erg.
her/him talked not

But whether it should be 'boy' or 'man' or something else would depend on the context, and is quite beyond the capability of the machine to correctly infer in all possible situations. Another solution would be to change the tense-aspect label slightly, so that it becomes different from past-completive (at the cost of faithfulness to the original). By doing this, *karta*–verb agreement would no longer be blocked by the post-position marker, and would show the gender in the verb. Yet another solution would be to use 'bolatA hE' (speaking), a construction in which agreement between noun–verb specifies the gender of the *karta*, or the speaker.

Example 12
H: vaha usase bolI, para vaha usase nahIM bolA.
!E: spoke(f.) spoke(m.)

Appropriate selection and use of such strategies is left to the post-editor in the *anusaaraka* approach. This post-editor is actually a reader who is editing the output to make it grammatically correct and suitable for wider use. This issue is discussed in the next section. Some interfaces are provided so that such a user can make changes with ease.

The 'ki' Construction

In the case of embedded sentences in Hindi, the subordinate sentence is put after the main verb, unlike in Kannada. For example:

Example 13
H: rAma ne kahA ki mEM ghara ko jAUMgA.
!E: Ram-erg. said that I home_dat. will_go
E: Ram said that he will go home

There is a construction in Kannada which is similar ('K' stands for Kannada):

Example 13a
K: rAma heLidanu eneMdare nAnu manege hoguttene.
@H: rAma kahA ki mEM ghara_ko jAUMgA.

!E: Ram said that I home_acc. will_go
E: Ram said that he will go home

However, it is seldom used. Kannada normally uses another construction for which the *anusaaraka* Hindi is given next (repeated from example 5).

K: mohana nALe baruvanu eMdu rAma heLidanu.
@H: mohana kala AyegA EsA rAma kahA.
!E: Mohana tomorrow come-fut that Rama said.

The 'EsA' construction is a proper construction in Hindi; only it is used less frequently. In the dialect of Hindi produced by *anusaaraka* from south Indian languages however, this is the normal construction used.

The 'jo' Construction

In this section, we will discuss how *anusaaraka* handles participle verbs (verbs behaving as adjectives) in Kannada to produce the same information in Hindi. The solution works for all south Indian languages which display this phenomenon.

We first try to derive the meaning of TAM labels which stand for adjectival participle, in a mathematically precise way. Let us take the following sentence in Telugu:

Example 14
T: rAmuDu tinina camac A veVMDidi
——— ——— ——— — ———— T_1
1 2a 2b 3 4
!E: Ram *eaten spoon silver-of
E: The spoon with which Ram ate is of silver.
(* 'eaten' is only an approximation, 'tinina' is a past-participle form of 'tina' or 'eat')

We are interested in finding the meaning of the TAM label, or the 'ina' suffix, in 'tinina'. Let us name it 2b, and the rest of the words are also named for easy reference. If a Telugu–Hindi bilingual person is asked to translate the sentence into Hindi, he is likely to write down the following:

```
H: rAma ne  jisa  cammaca se   khAyA, vaHa cAMdI kA HE.
   ----  ++       ---------    -----       ---------  ++
    1                 3          2a            4
!E: Ram  erg. which spoon instr. ate,  that  silver_of  is
```

Here the Hindi words are marked corresponding to the Telugu words (other than 2b whose value we want to find out). '++' is used to denote words that have been put by the translator but which are not there in the original Telugu sentence. 'ne' corresponds to the ergative marker which is an idiosyncracy of Hindi. Also it is known that 'HE' at the end (copula) is mandatory in the Hindi sentence but is absent in the given Telugu sentence.

We can rephrase the sentence in Hindi to get the words in the same order:

```
H: rAma ne jisa se khAyA HE vaHa cammaca cAMdI kA HE.
   ----  ++        -----         -------  --------  ++
    1               2a              3        4
```

or better still, we may rewrite the above as:

Example 15

```
H: rAma ne  khAyA HE jisa   se   vaHa cammaca cAMdI kA
   ----  ++ -----                     -------  --------
    1       2a                           3        4
                                                     HE.
                                                     ++
!E: Ram erg. eaten has which instr. that spoon  silver_of is
```

wherein the order of the words including the parts of words (2a and 2b) is exactly the same as the order in the original sentence. Now the part which remains unassigned, stands for 2b. Therefore, we get the equation:

ina = yA_HE_jisa_se_vaHa

But a closer scrutiny reveals an assumption, 'se' or instrumental marker is not there in the Telugu sentence. For example, consider the following sentence:

Example 16

T: rAmuDu win ina PleTu veVMdixi

1 2a 2b 3 4

E: The plate in which Ram ate is of silver.

Its equivalent Hindi sentence is:

Example 17

H: rAma ne khAyA HE jisa meM vaHa pleTa cAMdI kI HE

++ ++

1 2a 3 4

The above sentence yields the following equality:

ina = yA_HE_jisa_meM_vaHa

The two different equalities for 'ina', and similar other examples lead us to conclude that the 'se' or 'meM' markers are not present in the 'ina' but are supplied by the reader based on the world knowledge. Therefore, the equality becomes:

ina – yA_HE_jo_*_vaHa

where '*' stands for an unspecified post-position to be supplied based on context. The claim is that this is a mathematically precise equivalence between the 'ina' Telugu TAM and *anusaaraka* Hindi.

This claim can be restated as follows: It shows the equivalence between the adjectival participle in Telugu and the relative clause in Hindi, which has been known, but which the above equation makes precise. Although, Hindi also has participial phrases it has only two TAMS: yA and tA_HuA (with perfective and continuous aspects, respectively).

Example 18

H: khAyA HuA phala

eaten fruit

Example 19
H: khAtA HuA hiraNa
eating deer

As a result, these are not sufficient to capture other TAMs which might occur in Telugu. There is a gap significant in Hindi.

There is another problem, too, as we have seen. The two participial phrases in Hindi have codings for *karaka* relations which are absent in Telugu. TAM tA_huA codes *karta karaka* (roughly, agent), and example 19 reads, 'the deer who is eating' (and not the one who is being eaten). Similarly, 'yA' codes *karma* as in example 18 (the fruit being eaten, and not the fruit who is eating). Or, more correctly, 'yA' codes *karma* in case of *sakarmaka*, or transitive verbs, and *karta* in the case of intransitive verbs.

Thus, Hindi is poorer than Telugu in coding tense, aspect, modality information, while richer in coding *karaka* information. This creates another difficulty for *anusaaraka*. Using these constructions in Hindi would mean putting in something that is not contained in the source language sentence, and the information equivalence would be lost.

To take care of the limitation of the TAMs, we select relative clause constructions in Hindi. This, however, also requires the *karaka* information to be specified. To express the same information as in the Telugu in examples 14 and 16, we have invented a notation along with the *jo* construction as described earlier.

'jo_*_vaha' could even be replaced by *so* to produce a kind of colloquial Hindi in south India (*dakkhini* Hindi).

khAyA hE so cammaca

Unlike the 'ki' construction this idea takes some time and effort for the Hindi reader to get used to.

The 'ne' construction

The 'ne' construction, or ergative marker, is a peculiarity of only the western-belt languages in India. In case of the present or past perfective aspect of the main verb in Hindi sentence, 'ne' is used with the *karta*:

Example 20
H: rAma ne phala khAyA
!E: Ram-erg. fruit ate
(Ram ate the fruit.)

In *anusaaraka* output from Kannada to Hindi, the 'ne' post-position would never be produced. It would not be produced even with the TAM label yA in Hindi (wherein it is mandatory barring a few verbs). For example:

Example 21
@H: rAma phala khAyA

Therefore, we can postulate a new TAM '(yA)' with the same semantics as 'yA', but which does not use the 'ne' construction in *anusaaraka* Hindi. With this TAM, we can express the corresponding Kannada sentence more faithfully as:

!H: rAma phala khAy

It may be of interest to note that the 'yA' *pratyaya* in Hindi correspond to 'kta' *pratyaya* in Panini's grammar and so the new proposed *pratyaya* '(yA)' will be a natural counterpart of the *'ktavatu' pratyaya* in the Sanskrit grammar.

Thus, in this section we have tried to show how differences among the languages are bridged and information carried across. The reader might need some training to read the *anusaaraka* output.

Pre-editing, Post-editing and the Issue of Training

The *anusaaraka* system has been designed so that the combination of man and machine together can perform translations. We have earlier said that the tasks which are routine can be handed over to the machine, and those difficult for the machine can be left for the user. In this section, we will briefly discuss user-intervention in the task.

We have indicated earlier in this essay that all the information in the source text is preserved in the output. Also, although it preserves information in the output, the machine can present this information in stages. The raw output, which is the first output that a user sees, might not show all the details. Only when the user requests for details are they shown. The raw output could also be fine-tuned to the requirements of a user, and thus could be made different for different classes of users.

There are two principal points in this whole process at which the user can help—pre-editing the input and post-editing the output.

Pre-editing and Language Variation

In pre-editing, the input text is corrected and edited by the user. Words spelt with non-standard spellings are changed to conform to standard spelling, external *sandhi* between words is broken (unless it changes meaning), and so on.

This is an important task for Indian languages because of the lack of standardisation and consequent variation. It is particularly serious in Telugu, where spelling variation is very large. On an average, a word can be written in three alternate ways. The reason for this is partly that written materials have been influenced by local dialects in the last forty years. In fact, the use of local dialects of Telugu in written texts was actively promoted by the young and influential writers in this period. There has also been no major effort at standardisation.

Similarly, there is a lack of standards in the use of space. Sometimes *sandhi* between words is performed, sometimes not. Worse still for the machine, when *sandhi* results in a long word, it is broken up at a point different from where the *sandhi* has been done. The machine will thus have difficulty with both the resulting words.

Spelling variation might be severe in written Telugu, but is present in all Indian languages. Much more so than, say, in English. One will have to live with this reality while designing MT systems.

It might be argued by some that a machine must handle all the variations. For the phenomena just mentioned, it does not, in principle, seem to be a problem. However, in practice, it requires a much bigger effort. Instead of three years, it might take twenty years to develop a working system. Therefore, for the machine to start doing something useful, it becomes important to handle a sub-language first, say, the standard language (to the extent defined already or by extending the definition). However, the sub-language should be so chosen that a sufficient amount of written material exists, which is needed by other language groups or persons for the system to be useful.

A pre-editing interface, which points out the non-standard forms and seeks corrections, can help the human pre-editor. It can also present alternatives out of which the human pre-editor can then choose.

Post-editing the *Anusaaraka* Output

It has already been suggested that the *ansuaaraka* output is close to the target language, and in general is not grammatical from the viewpoint of the target language. When an output is created only for personal use by someone, he might choose not to bother to produce a grammatically correct and stylistically suitable output. However, when a document is going to be distributed in large numbers, it would normally have to be post-edited before distribution or publication.

There are three levels of post-editing, the first of which attempts to make the output grammatically correct. The emphasis here is on speed and low cost. The post-editor might drop phrases, change constructions in the interest of speed, as long as it does not alter the gross meaning. At this level of post-editing, corrections are made regarding agreement, putting in 'ne' (the ergative marker) where necessary, inserting the correct *vibhakti* in the 'jo' construction, etc.

In the second level of post-editing, the raw output is corrected not only grammatically but also stylistically. There can be many different types and qualities of output at this level, depending on the audience. One audience might be willing to accept some constructions in the raw output which are grammatically correct in Hindi but not used often. Another audience might not be willing to accept these constructions. For example, the 'EsA' construction can be changed to a 'ki' construction for such an audience.

In the third level of post-editing, the post-editor might change the setting and the events in the story to convey the same meaning to a reader who has a different cultural and social milieu. This is really transcreation, and a creative post-editor can go all the way up to this level.

What a post-editing interface would do is allow a post-editor to work rapidly. Rather than making corrections character by character, he can supply the missing information and the computer can carry out the corrections. For example, to make a verb form into a feminine plural, he need not manually change the individual verb and its auxiliaries to the correct forms. Instead, he can place the cursor on the verb sequence and give a command, and the computer would accordingly change the forms of the verb and its auxiliaries.

Training

The reader of the *anusaaraka* output would need to undergo some training. Besides covering the special symbols used in the output, the training would also familiarise him with the differences between the source and target language. This is important because he is likely to encounter constructions of the source language in the output, the output being an image of the source text. Where constructions in the two languages are similar, the output will be transparent, but when they are different, he would need to know the construction in the source language. It is hoped that such training would take about two weeks.

Additional training for post-editors would teach them about the different levels of post-editing and how to choose among them based on the requirements. It would also familiarise them with the computer interface which speeds up post-editing.

The Current Status of the *Anusaaraka* Project

To summarise, we have discussed the *anusaaraka* approach to building computer software so that text in one Indian language becomes available in another Indian language. In this approach, the load is so divided between man and machine that the language load is taken by the machine and the interpretation of the text is left to the man. The machine presents an image of the source text in a language close to the target language. The user, after some training, learns to read and understand the text in this language. The output can also be post-edited by a trained user to make it grammatically correct. Style can also be changed, if necessary.

Anusaarakas can be built for all Indian languages in the near future. Currently, *anusaarakas* are being built from Telugu, Kannada, Marathi, Bengali and Punjabi to Hindi. They can also be built in the reverse direction. In fact, it is useful to group the *anusaarakas* for the different languages. (a) South Indian languages (Tamil, Telugu, Kannada, Malayalam, etc.) to Hindi, and vice-versa. (b) Eastern languages (Bengali, Assamese, Oriya, etc.). (c) Western languages (Konkani, Marathi, Gujarati, etc.). (d) Northern languages (Punjabi, Kashmiri, Urdu, etc.). There will be many similarities among the *anusaarakas* within the same group. Effort also needs to be made to build such systems among languages within the same group, for example, from Telugu to Kannada. This task is easier.

Finally, we address the issue of connecting to English. The task of building an *anusaaraka* system between English and Indian languages is harder, because English has a very different structure and vocabulary. It will take some time (probably around five years) for such a system to be built with sufficient power for it to be used effectively. Even then the system might require a longer training to master than the system between Indian languages. However, even if one such system is built, it should proceed by making material from English initially available in one Indian language. The material can then become available in all other Indian languages through the other *anusaarakas*.

The *anusaaraka* output requires some effort and training to understand. For narrow subject areas, specialised modules can be built to produce good quality grammatical output. However, it should be remembered that such modules will work only in narrow areas and will sometimes go wrong. In such a situation, the basic *anusaaraka* output will still remain useful.

Conclusion: Implications for National Cooperation

If *anusaaraka* begins to be commonly used, it has major implications for national integration. The users of *anusaaraka*, through both training as well as exposure to the raw output, will learn the features of the source languages they read. Thus, a reader of *anusaaraka* Hindi will learn features of south Indian languages if he uses a Telugu to Hindi *anusaaraka*. Many new constructions will also enter into the language. For example, Hindi readers will become used to the constructions of Kannada, Bengali, Marathi, etc., if they use *anusaarakas*. This will serve to broaden the target language. Thus, on the one hand while it will encourage people to work in their own languages, and strengthen the various Indian languages, on the other hand, it will further contribute to the mixing of languages, through a natural process of use (which is like viewing the images of various languages through the lens of *anusaaraka*).

Anusaaraka has implications for the three-language formula too. If it is taught in schools and training is provided for it, including a study of important differences among Indian languages, children will learn to access written text in not just one additional language but in all Indian languages. Thus, written material, including literature, magazines, newspapers and official documents, will become accessible to individuals, children as well as adults. Indeed, it is expected that in the near future, within just a few years, computer networks will spread and many such texts will become available online. Libraries will also go online in a big way. At that time, such a training as *anusaaraka* provides, enabling a person to access documents in any Indian language, will prove a big asset.

When a person moves from one language region to another, he might have to learn the spoken form of the language as well. But acquiring the spoken form will be much easier because he will already be familiar with the constructions of the language.

For this vision to become a reality, however, everybody must chip in to construct dictionaries and prepare other languages data so that *anusaarakas* connecting all Indian languages can be built. The government can support this activity, but what is needed is for volunteers to come forward for the task. This should happen for the love of our languages. The right model to be followed for building the systems is the 'free software' model, in which everybody contributes to the effort and the results are open and available for everyone to use. People who contribute to building the system are acknowledged for their work, but nothing is hidden and nobody owns the software. This way one can begin where others have left off, and build on each other's work, in a cooperative activity. *Anusaaraka* can very well become a national people's cooperative project which can be emulated in other fields as well.

Notes

1. In this and all subsequent examples, the labels 'H' and 'E' specify the language of the sentence as Hindi or English. '!E' stands for the gloss in English and '@' denotes an unacceptable construction.

References

Bharati, Akshar, Vineet Chaitanya and **Rajeev Sangal**, 1995. *Natural Languages Processing: A Paninian Perspective*. Delhi: Prentice-Hall of India.

Narayana, V.N., 1994. 'Anusaaraka: A Device to Overcome the Language Barrier'. Ph.D. thesis. Department of Computer Science and Engineering, I.I.T, Kanpur.

http://www.iiit.net/ltrc/index.htm.

5. Philosophical Foundations

Fifteen

Theory East and West: Translation in its Different Contexts

RAMAN PRASAD SINHA

'...the origin of philosophy is translation or the thesis of translatability'.

— Jacques Derrida (MacDonald 1985: 120)

The history of human communication is hidden in the origin and evolution of the civilisations, and human communication presupposes translation or the concept of translation.

India has been a multilingual country since the very beginning. In fact, the India of two thousand years ago quite resembles contemporary India in terms of polyglottism. On the basis of 'Translation-compound' prevalent in Sanskrit and Prakrit, Suniti Kumar Chatterjee underlined the fact that in ancient India the traces of severe language conflicts, and concordances between non-Aryan languages (Dravidian, Austric, etc.) and foreign languages (Greek, Persian and several Iranian languages) with Indian Aryan languages are widespread (Chatterjee 1969: 303). The role of translation in these conflicts and concordances, it can be argued, might not have been confined to a mere translation of words. It is also a fact that translation was the basis of literary exchange from

6th century B.C. to 3rd century A.D. between *laukik* Sanskrit, so-called Buddhist Sanskrit and middle Indo-Aryan languages. Translations were done from different languages into Sanskrit before the emergence of Sanskrit as a pan-Indian language. Linguists even argue that the Mahabharata and the Puranas are merely a translation of various literary texts of middle Indo-Aryan languages into Sanskrit (Sen 1960: 5). The commentaries or *bhasya tika*, that were written on vedic literature, were also a kind of translation—'intra-lingual translation', to use a term from Roman Jakobson (Jakobson 1971: 261).

Sanskrit Poetics and Translation

One major problem that translators generally had to face in the process of translating from vedic to classical Sanskrit was that so many vedic words were not in use and their context was also unknown. One possible solution to this problem could have been to use a methodology in which words were first analysed *etymologically* and then their meaning determined according to their context. This must have been the background of the emergence of *Nirukta* and *Vaiyakarnas* in Sanskrit because in Panini's *Astadhyayi* (and Patanjali's *Mahabhasya* on *Astadhyayi* and Katyayana's treatise too) the main thrust is heavily on the etymological meaning of the word. Yaska's *Nirukta*, quite contrary to the definition of Western etymology, is also not merely a history of Word (Chakravarty 1976: 12–13).

Later, Bhartrhari emphasised the shortcomings of linguistic theories based on word units and their lexical meaning, and strongly objected to the possibility that the meaning of words could be ascertained either by their roots or by the eight formal processes (*aaptavakya, kosa*, etc.) as propounded by the Mimanska school. For Bhartrhari the word carries no meaning on its own; meaning reveals itself not through the word but through the order of words and their relation in a particular context (Kapoor 1991: 65).

It is true that in Sanskrit there has been no engagement reported on the theory of translation as such, but in Sanskrit poetics we find great discourses on the complex relationship between word and meaning, or/and language and world, and this may be significant for conceiving a theory of translation. The concept of universal language that has been propounded by Sanskrit *vaiyakaranas*, especially by Bhartrhari, may also be important in theorising translation.

For Bhartrhari the word is the Brahma and its expression is the cosmos. Word-Brahma expresses itself in three stages—*pashyanti*, *madhyama* and *vaikhari* (Bhartrhari 1984: 59). Later grammarians have included another stage before *pashyanti*, but in Bhartrhari, *pashyanti* is the first stage of expression (Raja 1963: 149). At the first stage, speech and thought are not differentiated and cosmic reality is perceived as a shining flow of consciousness; the *madhyama* stage is also a pre-language stage where all the linguistically relevant contents are present in a latent form like a seed in which all 'tree-content' is present; *vakhhari* is the last stage, where the Word-Brahma takes the shape of a language in which the peculiarities of a particular language emerge, and in which human communication is possible.

Bhartrhari considers the internal structures of languages to be universal. What we discover to be difference is nothing but the difference of the outer structures. In this context translation means going beyond the outer structure and concentrating on the internal similarities, i.e., eliminating the peculiarities of the source language and finding the universal language of the *madhyama-pashyanti* stage, from where one may transform the linguistic details to the target language. Bhartrhari's notion of a language universal is close to the concept of Warren Weaver and Noam Chomsky of the modern West.

Language Universals and Translation

Weaver is the author of the famous 'memorandum' which led American scientists to start research on machine translation on a practical, organised basis. He says in this memorandum:

> All languages were invented and developed by men. And all men, whether Bantu or Greek, Icelandic or Peruvian, have essentially the same equipment to bring to bear on this problem. They have vocal organs capable of producing about the same set of

> sounds. Their brains are of some general order of potential complexity. The elementary demands of language must have emerged in closely similar ways in different places and perhaps at different times.
>
> Think by analogy of individuals living in a series of tall closed towers all erected over a common foundation. When they try to communicate with one another they shout back and forth, each from his own closed tower. It is difficult to make the sound penetrate even the nearest towers, and communication proceeds very poorly indeed. But when an individual goes down his tower, he finds himself in a great open basement, common to all the towers. Here he establishes easy and useful communication with persons who have also descended from their towers.
>
> Thus may it be true that the way to translate from Chinese to Arabic or from Russian to Portugese is not to attempt the direct route shouting from tower to tower. Perhaps the way is to descend from each language down to the common base of human communication, the real but as yet undiscovered universal language and then to re-merge by whatever particular route is convenient (quoted in Chakravarty 1976: 35).

Chomsky also believes that languages differ because of their surface structures, and these structures are only outer casualties whereas the shaping of language occurs in its deep structures. Chomsky considers the deep structure an innate constituent of the human brain and concludes that human language has a common architecture (Steiner, G. 1975: 100–101). He argues that every human being has internalised a grammar that generates not only his language but all languages of the world. His 'generative' grammar contains a syntactic component, a semantic component and a phonological component. The latter two are purely interpretative; they play no part in the recessive generation of sentence structures. The syntactic component consists of a base and a transformational component. The base, in turn, consists of a categorical sub-component and a lexicon. The base generates deep structures. A deep structure enters the semantic component and receives a semantic interpretation; it is mapped by the transformational rules into a surface structure, which is then given a phonetic interpretation by the rules of the phonological component. Thus the grammar assigns semantic interpretations to signals, this association being mediated by the recursive rules of the syntactic component.

The categorical sub-component of the base consists of a sequence of context-free 'rewriting rules'. The function of these rules is, in essence, to define a certain system of grammatical relations that determine semantic interpretation, and to specify an abstract underlying order of elements that makes possible the functioning of the transformational rules. To a large extent, the rules of the base may be universal and not, strictly speaking, part of any particular grammar (Chomsky 1975: 8). There is a double movement inherent in Chomsky's model—from base to deep structure and again from deep to surface structure.

The whole process can be understood by the following diagram:

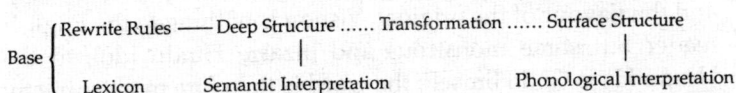

Base	Rewrite Rules ——	Deep Structure	Transformation	Surface Structure
		|		|
	Lexicon	Semantic Interpretation		Phonological Interpretation

The possibility of finding a practical guideline for translation was implicit in the Chomskyan concept of universal base component, and this fact was revealed by Nida, the famous American translator of the Bible. For Nida, Chomsky's concept of language as a generating agent is significant for translation, as it provides a technique for decoding the source language, besides providing an insight into the process of proper generation of its equivalent expression in the target language (Nida 1964: 60).

Chomsky's theory involves three levels of conceptualisation—base component, deep structure and surface structure. Nida simplifies it and adopts only the latter two parts of this model. He summarises his translation methodology as follows: (a) to reduce the source text to its structurally simplest and most semantically evident kernels, (b) to transfer the meaning from the source language to the receptor language on a structurally simple level and (c) to generate the stylistically and semantically equivalent expression in the receptor language (ibid.: 68).

Nida's methodology is to first go from the surface of the source text to its deep structure, and to transfer that deep structure to the deep structure of the target language, so that the surface structure of the target language can be generated. For Nida, the deep structure of one language can be transferred to the deep structure of another language by an 'empathy of spirit'. Nida believes that words are essentially *labels*. If, for example, the word lamb is not to be found in the target language, it can be substituted by seal or pig or, for that matter, by any other form or label in order to achieve what Nida calls 'dynamic equivalence' (Nida 1960). In Nida's translation theory this dynamic equivalence is preferable to 'formal equivalence'. This is because while the former emphasises an equivalence of sympathy, the latter stresses more on the equivalence of words. Sri Aurobindo, the translator of Kalidasa, arrives at the same conclusion when he says,

> ...the business of poetical translation is to reproduce not the exact words but the exact image, associations and poetical beauty, and the flavour of the original. Visnou is nothing to the English reader but some monstrous and bizarre Hindu idol; to the Hindu He is God Himself; the word is therefore more correctly represented in English by 'highest God' than by Visnou... (Sri Aurobindo 1972: 98).

The same idea had been expressed in R. Raghunath Rao's *The Art of Translation*, probably India's first book on translation theory (Rao 1910).

As the need for a perfect scientific theory of translation was felt in the West during the fifth and sixth decades of the last century, all translation theorists of that period based their theories on the concept of equivalence. Nida in America tried to achieve this equivalence with the help of Chomsky's generative grammar, and so in England did Catford with the help of the systemic grammar of M.A.K. Haliday (Catford 1969). In the absence of a translation institute, the impact of Nida's and Catford's theories does not seem to have been so influential, in England and America respectively, in comparison to Germany where translation was being considered a science—*Ubersetzungswissenschaft*.

Equivalence Theory and Translation

The main centre of German *Ubersetzungswissenschaft* is the Leipzig school started in the mid-1960s when Otto Kade, Gert Jager and

Albrecht Neubert theorised the concept of *Aquivalenz*. The main theorist of this school, Otto Kade, tried to explain his concept of equivalence by proposing four types of correspondence. These are (a) one-to-one (*totale Aquivalenz*), i.e., found with completely identical terms as in standard terminology; (b) one-to-many (*fakultative Aquivalenz*) is exemplified in German spannung as against English suspense, stress, pressure, tension, etc.; (c) one-to-part-of-one correspondence (approximate *Aquivalenz*) can be shown in the German 'Himmel' as against the English 'heaven', sky; (d) one-to-none correspondence (*null Aquivalenz*) is testified in the case of culture-bound words.

Kade proposes this methodology: first divide the source text into several units, select the 'optimal equivalent' of these units available in the target language and then hold together these units to create an integrated whole (Gentzter 1993: 69). Kade's system of equivalence-type is limited to the level of individual words and it is clearly a reflection of atomistic linguistics, which was dominant at that time. As modern linguistics developed, the focus shifted from individual lexical equivalence to structural equivalence. The term 'structural equivalence' was coined by Filipec, another theorist of the Leipzig school, who suggested that greater emphasis be placed on equivalence of the entire text than on searching for individual lexical equivalents (Snell-Hornby 1998: 20–21).

The second important centre of German *Ubersetzungswissenschaft* is Saarland University, Saarbruken, where Wolfrom Wilss' book *The Science of Translation: Problems and Methods*, is considered to be the major text of German translation theory (Wilss 1982). Wilss conceives of the science of translation not as a sealed 'nomological' science but as a 'cognitive hermeneutic/associative' one. He believes that intuition is the opposite of prototypical concepts and hence, whereas the translator should be aware of the concept on the one hand, he must also try to keep himself away from accepted norms and methods on the other. Though this method involves risk, it can be exemplified in any good translation.

Wilss's theory is based on the concept of universal language, according to which, the transfer of deep structure is possible via a hermeneutic process. This concept also holds that there is a generative component which translates intralingually from the base to the surface of a given language. In fact, Wilss's translation theory is a mixture of Chomsky's concept of deep structure and Nida's practical experiences of translating the Bible. In one place, quoting Nida, Wilss argues that interlingual communication is always possible because it is based upon two fundamental factors: (a) that semantic similarities in languages are due to the common core of human experience and (b) that fundamental similarities exist in the syntactic structure of languages, especially at the so-called kernel or core level (Gentzter 1993: 64–67).

The science of translation that has been developed by Nida, Catford, Kade and Wilss was primarily based on such a preconceived notion about the nature of language that it is not possible to test it empirically. The concept of deep/surface structure was intrinsically source-oriented and it tends to believe that all information regarding transformation into target language is stored in the deep structure of the original text, to which the translator should be faithful. These ideas, far from being scientific, are utopian in the sense that they conceive of translation as a reproduction of the original text. The biggest problem with the 'science of translation' was that it was evaluative and prescriptive, related with the training of translators. The shortcomings of this normative approach were revealed in the most radical way by some scholars in Belgium, the Netherlands and Israel. Instead of speculating about ideal translation these scholars focused their attention on the process of reception in the target language, and the context in which translation acquires meaning and significance.

The Manipulation School: The Politics of Translation

In the introduction to *The Manipulation of Literature: Studies in Literary Translation* (1985), editor Theo Hermans writes: 'From the point of view of the target literature, all translation implies a degree of manipulation of the source text for a certain purpose' (Hermans 1985). Making the point more obviously, Andre Lefevere, another important thinker of this school, argues that translation is basically some sort of rewriting and whatever its objective, rewriting definitely manifests an ideology and poetics (Lefevere 1992). The mood and temperament of the age manipulates translation as it manipulates history-writing, criticism, editing, etc. The nature of implicit manipulation can be easily understood if one takes into consideration the poetic and the ideological base of a rewriting.

Edward Fitzgerald, the famous translator of *Rubaiyyat-e-Omar Khayyam* writes to his friend E.B. Cowell: 'It is an amusement for me to take what liberties I take with these Persians who (as I think) are not poets enough to frighten one from such excursions, and who really do want a little art to shape them' (ibid.: 1). It is obvious from this letter that Fitzgerald considers Omar Khayyam aesthetically inferior to contemporary English poets. Imperial or Victorian aesthetics has given him courage of an order impossible in the case of poets such as Homer or Virgil.

Scholars who have worked on Tagore's reception in the West have underscored the fact that Tagore's reputation and immense popularity in the west during the first three decades of the 20th century were based not so much on an intellectual appreciation of his works as the notion that the east was an enigma where saints and prophets brought deliverance to ordinary people. In other words, Tagore was supplying another basis for the already existing superstructure of orientalism; he became a representative of the alluring 'other' to the Western world (Dev Sen 1963; see also Mukherjee 1963).

It is not surprising that Tagore chose to translate his poems into English himself, for which he later got the Nobel Prize; not only the selection of these poems but their style, imagery, tone and diction try deliberately to match Edwardian poetics (Sengupta 1990: 57–58).

Andre Lefevere considers the translated text as a refraction and not a reflection of the source text (Bassnett-McGuire 1994: xvii). The linguistics-based science of translation envisages translation as a reflection; 'reflection' refers to a mirror image of the original text, while the term 'refraction' implies a change in perception. This has been exemplified not only in the written tradition but in the oral as well. Narrating her experience of translating the story of Hamlet to a group of illiterate tribals in West Africa, Lara Bohannan, in her article 'Shakespeare in the Bush', writes that the audience advanced various interpretations in their efforts to understand the story. At times they resisted the translation and transfer concepts (ghosts), values (the chastity of Ophelia), customs (the European period of mourning), motivations (Hamlet's madness), material culture and plot sequence, as well as rhetorical and linguistic structures. Bohannan reports that after one such interpretation, 'there was a murmur of applause. *Hamlet* was again a good story to them; but it no longer seemed quite the same story to me' (Tymoczko 1990: 47–48).

In fact the translated text is a processed text. When the literary system of any target language receives a source text, it manipulates it in the very process of its reception. The whole process and nature of this manipulation has been thoroughly analysed by the concept of 'literary polysystem' as articulated by Itmar Even-Zohar and Gideon Toury of the Tel Aviv school in the 1970s. Working on a project called 'The History of Literary translation into Hebrew' at Tel Aviv University, Even-Zohar developed a methodology that could provide an insight into the complete process and dynamics of a translated text in a particular culture at a particular point of time.

The Theory of Culture and Translation

Itmar Even-Zohar is basically a theorist of culture, not of translation. He based his polysystem theory on Russian Formalism, specifically on Tynjanov's concept of the 'hierarchical literary system'. The Russian Formalists believed that culture is a complex system of systems, including the system of literature, the system of science, the system of technology, and so on. Many subsystems are at work under these systems. For example, within the literary system there exist the systems of literary tradition and literary genre; the literary text is itself a unique system. In the same way, the social and economic systems have their own subsystems. These systems and subsystems are interrelated and influence each other.

The kind and nature of 'influence' is determined by the 'cultural practices' of which these systems are also a part (Steiner, P. 1984). Cultural practice is determined by two factors. In the context of literature, one factor is active inside literary systems and the other operates outside it. Patronage is the most important factor outside the realm of the literary system. The norm of patronage could be ideological, economic or status-related. The factor operating within the literary system is constituted of professional critics, teachers and translators, and they are the people who regulate it by the parameters imposed by the other factor, i.e., patronage (Lefevere 1992: 14–16). Giving the example of the different translations, in different languages, of *The Diary of Anne Frank*, Andre Lefevere in his famous article, 'On the Construction of Different Anne Franks' demonstrated how the different literary systems of different languages by their different cultural practices had sculptured altogether different images of Anne Frank (Lefevere 1992: 59–72).

Tynjanov suggests that the 'literariness' of a text depends not solely on its intrinsic properties, but also on its value and function, on the relationship it establishes with other texts in different 'literary systems'. 'Since a system is not an equal interaction of all elements', Tynjanov wrote, 'but places a group of elements in the foreground—the dominant—and this involves the deformation of the remaining elements, a work enters into literature and takes on its own literary function through this dominant.' The 'deformation' caused by the changing position of hierarchical subsystems is the basic reason for any literary evolution; and defamiliarisation is the process by which it works (Benett 1979: 66–67).

Taking a cue from Tynjanov, Even-Zohar regarded translation as an important subsystem of any literary system, and focused his concentration on the analysis of the hierarchical cultural system as a whole. Even-Zohar coined the term 'polysystem' to refer to the entire network of correlated systems—literary and extra-literary—in society, and developed an approach to explain the function of all kinds of writing within a given culture—from the central canonical text to the most marginal non-canonical texts. He argues that the role of any translated text in a particular language depends upon the age, strength and stability of the particular literary polysystem. For instance, the polysystem of an old culture such as the Anglo-American or the French is different from that of Israel or, for that matter, of any new country. A strong system such as the Anglo-American or the French, with well-developed literary traditions and with many different kinds of writing, relegates translations to a marginal position; whereas translation occupies a central position in a country such as Israel or any African country.

In his essay, 'The Position of Translated Literature within the Literary Polysystem', Even-Zohar suggested that the relationship between the translated work and the literary polysystem cannot be categorised as either primary or secondary, but is variable depending upon the specific circumstance operating within the literay system. The position of the translated work in a particular literary system is not fixed but varies depending not on the intrinsic qualities of the text, but on the particular historical circumstance under which the concerned literary polysystem operates (Even-Zohar 1978).

Elaborating further on this, his Tel Aviv colleague Gideon Toury wrote that translations themselves have no 'fixed' identity because they are always subject to different socioliterary contextual factors; so translation has to be viewed as having multiple identities, dependent upon the forces that govern the decision process at a particular time (Toury 1980). It is a preamble of shifting approach to the theory of translation, since from here onwards it would be difficult to posit a single conception of translation equivalence. Translation theory based on traditional linguistics had been attacked from one more quarter that was more radical in nature—Derrida's deconstruction.

Deconstruction and Translation: Translation as Dis-shem-ination

Derrida's theory of deconstruction is a logical outcome of Saussure's idea of language. Saussure conceptualised language as a sign system (de Saussure 1974: 67–70). Each sign is made up of a 'signifier' (a sound image or its graphic equivalent) and a 'signified' (the concept of meaning). The three black marks 'c-a-t' form a signifier which evokes the signified 'cat' in an English mind. The relation between the signifier and the signified is an arbitrary one; there is no inherent reason why these three marks should mean cat, other than cultural and historical convention.

The relation between the whole sign and what it refers to (what Saussure calls the 'referent'—the real furry four-legged creature) is therefore also arbitrary. Each sign in the system has meaning only by virtue of its difference from the others. 'Cat' has no meaning in itself, but only because it is not 'cap' or 'cad' or 'bat'. In the linguistic system, says Saussure, 'there are only differences'; meaning is not mysteriously immanent in a sign but is functional, the result of its difference from other signs. Extending Saussure's idea, Derrida argued that 'cat' is 'cat' because it is not 'cap' or 'bat', but how far is one to press the process of difference? If 'cat' is also what it is because it is not 'cad' or 'mat', and 'mat' is what it is because it is not 'map' or 'hat', where is one supposed to stop? It would seem that this process of difference in language can be traced along infinitely. If every sign is what it is because it is not all the other signs, every sign would seem to be made up of a potentially infinite tissue of differences. Such an analysis raises questions about Saussure's view of the sign as a neat symmetrical unity between the signifier and the signified. The signifier does not directly yield up a signified as a mirror yields up an image; there is no harmonious one-to-one set of correspondences between the level of the signifiers and the level of the signifieds in language.

To complicate matters even further, there is no fixed distinction between signifiers and signifieds either. If you want to know the meaning (or the signified) of a signifier, you can look it up in the dictionary but all you will find will be yet more signifiers whose signifieds you can in turn look up, and so on. The process is not only in theory infinite but somehow circular; signifiers keep transforming into signifieds, and vice versa, and you will never arrive at a final signified which is not a signifier in itself. That means meaning is not immediately present in a sign.

Since the meaning of a sign is a matter of what the sign is *not*, its meaning is always in some sense absent from it too. Meaning is scattered or dispersed along whole chains of signifiers, it cannot be easily nailed down. It is never fully present in any one sign alone, but is rather a kind of constant flickering of presence and absence together (Eagleton 1988: 127–28). This is one of the reasons why Derrida's *differance* implies not only 'to differ' or 'differentiate', but also 'to defer', 'to postpone or withhold' (Cuddon 1991: 246).

Deconstruction is more visible in the process of translation. Derrida believes that translation deconstructs texts and returns to a point before a thing has been named, thereby making visible a path by which meaning has been rerouted or diverted. For Derrida, God is seen as a deconstructionist for He interrupts the construction of the Tower of Babel. In this punning act, God interrupts Himself and thereby produces 'dis-shem-ination'. Addressing the tribe of Shem, Derrida argues that according to God, 'you will not impose your meaning or your tongue, and I, God, therefore oblige you to submit to the plurality of languages which you will never get out of' (McDonald 1988: 103).

Derrida thinks that it is quite impossible to transport pure signifieds from one language into another and within the same language, since the base of meaning is unstable and no such thing as 'deep structure' or 'kernel' is to be found anywhere. Hence, instead of talking about translation we need to envisage the concept of transformation; a regulated transformation—from one language to another and from one text to another text (Derrida 1981: 20).

Since Derrida questions the very definition of translation, a definition in which translation is believed to be the reproducer, transporter and communicator of the 'meaning' of the original text, he suggests that translation may be viewed as an instance where language can be seen as always in the process of *modifying the original text*. Derrida elaborates on this idea with the help of Walter Benjamin's concept of *Uberleben* (afterlife).

Benjamin considers translation as neither source-oriented nor target-oriented, but as a single mode of its own. He argues that since translation gives the original a second life, in some way it is the afterlife of a text—and this does not imply a postmortem so much as a continuation of life. In one place he remarks, 'just as the manifestations of life are intimately connected with the phenomenon of life without being of importance to it, a translation issues from the original—not so much from its life as from its after-life' (Benjamin 1992: 72). Benjamin believes that in translation the original becomes larger; Derrida adds that translation behaves like a 'child' which is not just a product subject to the law of reproduction but has, in addition, the power to speak on its own in a new and different fashion, supplementing language and sounding the 'Babelian note' which causes language to grow (Derrida 1985: 191).

In a series of lectures delivered in 1991, Susan Bassnett-McGuire indicated that a slight opening in cultural hegemony conducive to such language growth was about to occur. She argued that the poet-translators Haraldo and Augusto de Campos from Brazil, for example, use Derrida to develop something like a postmodern and non-Eurocentric approach to translation. In their approach to literary translation, the de Campos brothers refuse any sort of preordained original, but instead view translation as a form of transgression. They do not use terms that are part of the European approach or science, but come up with their own terms, one of which is translation as 'cannibalism'. This is not to be understood as another form of possessing the original, but as a liberating form where one eats, digests and frees oneself from the original. Cannibalism is not to be understood in the Western sense, i.e., capturing, dismembering, mutilating and devouring, but in a sense which shows respect, i.e., as a symbolic act of taking back out of love, of absorbing the virtues of a body through a transfusion of blood. Translation is seen as an empowering and nourishing act of affirmative play which is very close to the Benjamin/Derrida position of seeing translation as a life force ensuring the survival of a literary text (Gentzter 1993: 192).

The area and scope of translation studies in the West has widely increased. Comparative literature is being considered as a subcategory of translation studies instead of vice versa. As an independent discipline, translation studies has established itself not only in the major countries of the West but also in small countries such as Israel, Belgium, the Netherlands and Bulgaria. In India, however, it is yet to establish itself even as an independent subject. Is this not a serious matter, considering the multilingual situation of India?

References

Bassnett-McGuire, Susan, 1994. *Translation Studies*. London: Routledge.

Benett, Tony, 1979. *Formalism and Marxism*. New York: Methuen and Co. Ltd.

Benjamin, Walter, 1992. *The Task of the Translator in Illuminations*. London: Fontana.

Bhartrhari, 1984. *Vakyapadiyam*. Ahmedabad: Lalbhai Dalpatbhai Bharatiya Sanskriti Vidyamandir.

Catford, J.C., 1969. *A Linguistic Theory of Translation*. London: Oxford University Press.

Chakravarty, Asit, 1976. *Translational Linguistics of Ancient India*. New Delhi: Kanakdhara.

Chatterjee, Suniti Kumar, 1969. *Indo Aryan and Hindi*. Kolkata: Firma K.L. Mukhopadhyay.

Chomsky, Noam, 1975. *Aspects of the Theory of Syntex*. Cambridge: The MIT Press.

Cuddon, J.A., 1991. *Dictionary of Literary Terms and Literary Theory*. London: Penguin Books. Third Edition.

de Saussure, Ferdinand, 1974. *Course in General Linguistics*. London: Peter Owen.

Derrida, Jacques, 1981. *Positions*. Chicago: University of Chicago Press, Chicago, 1981, p. 20.

Derrida, Jacques, 1985. 'Des Tours de Babel'. In Joseph F. Graham (ed.), *Difference and Translation*. Ithaca: Cornell University Press.

Dev Sen, Nabaneeta, 1963. *The Reception of Tagore in England, France & Germany and United States*. Indiana University.

Eagleton, Terry, 1988. *Literary Theory*. Oxford: Basil Blackwell.

Even-Zohar, Itmamar, 1978. 'The Position of Translated Literature within the Literary Polysystem'. In James S. Holmes, Jose Lambert and Raymond van den Broek (eds) *Literature and Translation: New Perspective in Literary Studies with a Basic Bibliography of Books on Translation Studies*. Belgium: Leuven.

Gentzler, E., 1993. *Contemporary Translation Theories*. London and New York: Routledge.

Hermans, Theo (ed.), 1985. *The Manipulation of Literature: Studies in Literary Translation*. New York: St. Martin Press.

Jakobson, Roman, 1971. 'On Linguistic Aspects of Translations' in *Selected Writings Volume II*. The Hague: Mouton.

Kapoor, Kapil, 1991. 'Bhartrhari on Lexicon Meaning'. In V. Prakasham and S.V. Parasher (eds) *Linguistics at Large*. Hyderabad: Booklinks Corporation.

Lefevere, Andre, 1992. *Translations, Rewriting and the Manipulation of Literary Fame*. London and New York: Routledge.

McDonald, Christie, (eds), 1985. *The Ear of the Other: Text and Discussions with Jacques Derrida*. Lincoln and London: University of Nebraska Press.

Mukerjee, Sujit Kumar, 1963. *Passage to America: The Reception of Tagore in the US (1912–41)*. Pennsylvania: University of Pennsylvania Press.

Nida, Eugene A., 1960. *Message and Mission*. New York: Harper and Brothers.

———, 1964. *Toward a Science of Translating*. The Netherlands: LEIDEN.

Raja, K. Kunjunni, 1963. *Indian Theories of Meaning*. Chennai: The Adyar Library and Research Centre.

Rao, R. Raghunath, 1910. *The Art of Translation*. New Delhi: Bhartiya Anuvad Parishad.

Sen, Sukumar, 1960. *A Comparative Grammar of Middle Indo-Aryan*. Linguistic Society of India, Pune: Deccan College Poona.

Sengupta, Mahasweta, 1990. 'Translation, Colonialism and Poetics: Ravindra Nath Tagore in Two Worlds'. In Susan Bassnett-McGuire and Andre Lefevere (eds), *Translation History and Culture*. London: Pinter Publishers Ltd.

Snell-Hornby, Mary, 1988. *Translation Studies: An Integral Approach*. Amsterdam and Philadelphia: John Benjamins Publishing Company.

Sri Aurobindo, 1972. *On Translating Kalidasa*. Sri Aurobindo Birth Centenary Library. Popular Edition, vol. 27. Pondicherry: Aurobindo Ashram.

Steiner, George, 1975. *After Babel*. New York and London: Oxford University Press.

Steiner, Peter, 1984. *Russian Formalism*. Ithaca and London: Cornell University Press.

Toury, Gideon, 1980. *In Search of a Theory of Translation*. Tel Aviv: The Porter Institute of Poetics and Semiotics.

Tymoczko, Maria, 1990. 'Translation in Oral Tradition as a Touchstone for Translation Theory and Practice'. In Susan Bassnett-McGuire and Andre Lefevere (eds) *Translation History and Culture*, London: Pinter Publishers Ltd.

Wilss, Wolfram, 1982. *The Science of Translation: Problems and Methods*. Tübingen: Gunter Narr.

Sixteen

Freudian Slips: The Psychopathology of Translation

SHIVA KUMAR SRINIVASAN

Of all the metaphors that Freud used, probably none had more far-reaching consequences than the metaphor of mental illness, and—derived from it—the metaphor of psychoanalysis as the treatment and cure of mental illness. Freud evoked the image of illness and its treatment to enable us to comprehend how certain disturbances influence the psyche, what causes them, and how they may be dealt with. If this metaphor is not recognised as such but, rather, taken as referring to objective facts, we forfeit a real understanding of the unconscious and its workings.

— Bruno Bettelheim (1982: 39)

Introduction

What is psychoanalysis? What are its conditions of possibility? If, as the late Bruno Bettelheim argued, psychoanalysis is not an objective science, but a discourse like literature that must work with forms of figuration (i.e., metaphor), what is its relevance to the problem of translation? And, again, given the prominence that the term 'translation' has acquired of late in the philosophy of psychoanalysis, we cannot underestimate its importance as a tool in the clinical encounter between the doctor and the patient.[1] Hence, the metaphorical 'vehicle' of translation is not a violation of the 'tenor' of the Freudian doctrine.[2]

Whereas critics working on translation theory would wish to maintain that translation is a form of interpretation, psychoanalysts would want to argue that the very possibility of interpretation in psychoanalysis must presuppose the availability of a theory of translation. This, of course, does not mean that the psychoanalyst has a formal theory of translation at his disposal. In other words, at the very beginning of his endeavours the psychoanalyst incurs a debt to the idea of translation.

What is this theoretical debt? And how does the psychoanalyst discharge this debt? I will argue that understanding the way in which psychoanalysis discharges its debt to translation will make both the theorist and practitioner of translation studies better at his or her work. It will make it possible to translate with a greater appreciation of the symptomatic pitfalls that surround the very act of translation. Thus we can annotate the classic adage that students of comparative literature are introduced to in the very beginning: *Traditore, traduttore*. Translators are traitors. All translators may be traitors but each betrays the author in his own way. Psychoanalysis will help to establish the idiosyncratic paths that characterise each such betrayal. Therein lies the translator's *symptom*. It will help us to answer a very simple question: what does the translator desire of his text? Wherein lies the libidinal compulsion to choose a particular text as the object of translation? Unless the translator is willing to address these questions, he cannot even begin to appreciate the difference between the structural and historical compulsions to mistranslate.

The structural compulsion arises from the fact that language by definition is a slippery medium and does not lend itself to the act of translation. It is this that prompts the wags to declare that literature is what gets left out in the act of translation. Historical compulsions pertain to both the political contexts that attend to the act of translation and the libidinal compulsions that the translator must struggle with. While the political compulsions are ones that the translator is aware of, libidinal compulsions often remain unconscious. A good example of historical compulsions where both the political and libidinal aspects of translation are brought into the picture directly is James Strachey's translation of Freud's work from its original edition in German.[3] What better site can we choose to examine the relationship between psychoanalysis and translation than one where even those with psychoanalytic training must struggle with the desire to mistranslate?

Later on in this essay, I will use Bruno Bettelheim's critique of James Strachey's translation of Freud to exemplify these problems. This will demonstrate that the mistranslations of Freud that Bettelheim brings out in his book were not merely a result of bad philology but an enactment of the translator's desire to make psychoanalysis acceptable to the medical community, which wanted a monopoly on psychoanalysis in the United States. The lure of psychoanalysis for the medical community itself arises from a literalisation of Freud's medical metaphors. If, as Bettelheim points out in the epigraph of this essay, the metaphor of the body stands for the soul, then the very logic of the metaphorical vehicle of the body (which, after all, is the natural province of medicine) makes it susceptible to a takeover bid from the doctors (Bettelheim 1982: 39–40):

> In this metaphor, the body stands for the soul. If the metaphor is interpreted literally, as it has been in the United States, our psyche, or soul,—for Freud the terms were interchangeable—seems to become something tangible. It acquires something akin to a physical existence, like a bodily organ; hence its treatment becomes part of medical science.... It is expected that anyone undergoing psychoanalysis will achieve tangible results—the kind of results the physician achieves for the body—rather than a deeper understanding of himself and greater control of his life.

But before looking into how psychoanalysis can discharge its debt to the availability of translation as a tool of interpretation in the analytic situation, let us schematise the problem by looking into its constituent parts: Who translates? And, what is translated? In other words, let us unearth the ethic of the unconscious that is presupposed in translation. But, firstly, what is psychoanalysis?

What is Psychoanalysis?

Whether it sees itself as an instrument of healing, of formation, or of exploration in depth, psychoanalysis has only a single intermediary: the patient's Word. That this is self-evident is no excuse for our neglecting it. And every Word calls for a reply.

— Jacques Lacan[4]

Let us begin with the fundamentals. First, psychoanalysis is a theory of the human subject. Second, it is the most influential form of psychotherapy that has come down to us from the history of European science. The term 'science' should be understood to encompass the Germanic notions of both *Naturwissenschaften* and *Geisteswissenchaften*. In other words, psychoanalysis demands an interdisciplinary matrix that lies in between medicine and literature. The history of psychoanalysis represents the tensions inherent in this parentage. The ideal analyst for Freud was someone who was well versed in both these traditions. Besides, the problem of differential diagnosis in the clinical situation demanded such an extraordinary range of skills. Otherwise a patient with physiological symptoms would be subject to unnecessary analysis. And the hysteric would be tormented with wrong medication.

What were Freud and his mentor, Dr Josef Breuer, confronted with in their early work? The answer, very simply put, is the hysterical symptom. They were trying to cure patients who were suffering from functional disorders such as frigidity, hydrophobia, insomnia, paralyses, tics, and other such 'nervous' afflictions. Psychoanalysis can therefore be understood as a systematic attempt to come to terms with the structure of hysteria. A contemporary Lacanian psychoanalyst goes so far as to say that 'psychoanalysis began with hysteria, and psychoanalytic knowledge will always be worth only what our knowledge of this structure is worth' (Safouan 1980: 55).

Hysterics were saddled with symptoms that lacked an organic basis. A medical examination of these patients would reveal no structural basis to these disorders of either an anatomical or physiological origin. These symptoms, to be fair to the medical profession of the time, lacked an independent ontology. They were not objectively there. They only existed in so far as the patients believed in them. This lead to the accusation that these patients were feigning illness in order to escape the responsibilities of life. In other words, these patients were presenting hysterical symptoms that the medical establishment was unable to cure. While it was true that the 'flight into illness' served them with the sympathetic attention that is generally bestowed on the sick in polite society, their symptoms were not imaginary. Though these symptoms lacked *reality*, they were nevertheless *real* to the hysterics themselves. While the term 'reality' generally refers to that which is external or objective, the term 'real' seeks to go beyond the simplistic opposition between the internal and the external. As Dylan Evans points out:

> *Such a 'naïve' view of the real is subverted by the fact that the real also includes such things as hallucinations and traumatic dreams. The real is thus both inside and outside.... This ambiguity reflects the ambiguity inherent in Freud's own use of the two German terms for reality* (Wirklichkeit and Realität) *and the distinction Freud draws between* material *reality and* psychical *reality.*[5]

In their pioneering book, *Studies on Hysteria* (1895), Breuer and Freud reported a number of such cases where the patients' suffering was alleviated and a path to a cure opened up by asking the patient to speak freely on whatever was bothering her. Fräulein Anna O, the first of these patients, described psychoanalysis as the 'talking cure'.[6] Anna O is the most celebrated patient in the history of psychoanalysis and though the question of whether she was actually cured by Breuer remains shrouded in scholarly controversy (Borch-Jacobsen 1996), the very fact that a mainstream medical practitioner such as Breuer should have even tried his hand at a form of psychotherapy was radical at a time when patients were not recognised as a human resource by the medical establishment. The subject seeking help was often lost behind her symptoms. As Sándor Ferenczi points out, psychoanalysis brought back the Hippocratic spirit to medicine. It returned the doctors, who had been lost in the investigation of specialised pathologies, to the patient rather than to the disease. 'To medicine which has been segmented into all the specialities, psychoanalysis has been a benefactor, for it reminds one, in every form of the disease, to treat the patient as well as the disease' (Ferenczi: 27). Conversely, unlike conventional medicine, which merely used the patient as a point of departure, psychoanalysis began to insist that the patient must do the real work of understanding the significance of her symptoms. It was the patient's interpretation of her symptoms that was to provide a clue to the diagnosis. The patient had to take ethical responsibility for both presenting herself for analysis and for ending the treatment.

It was because the patient could intuitively understand that her symptoms were laden with meaning that she chose to go into analysis instead of seeking conventional medication. In other words, from the very beginning, the psychoanalytic notion of the symptom was dialectical. The symptom was not a rigid formation that would stay in place throughout the analysis. Acts of interpretation by the psychoanalyst would result in changes in the structure of the symptom. The symptom's meaning was not inherent to specific forms of pathology. Its meaning could only be worked out in relation to larger structures of subjectivity such as hysteria, obsessionality, phobia, paranoia, etc. For Freud, each of these forms of subjectivity had an existential dimension. The subject was posing certain fundamental questions about the 'human condition' by presenting an idiosyncratic set of symptoms. The task of the analysis was to work out the unconscious logic of the subject that held these symptoms in place.

Psychoanalysis began to interest the non-medical community of artists, writers, philosophers, critics, etc., when they realised that what it offered them through a dialectical notion of the symptom was a new vision of Man. The symptom, as *Studies on Hysteria* revealed, was an interlocutor who could 'join in the conversation':

> While we are working at one of these symptoms we come across the interesting...phenomenon of 'joining in the conversation'. The problematic symptom reappears or appears in greater intensity as soon as we reach the region of the pathogenic organisation which contains the symptoms' aetiology and thenceforward accompanies the work in characteristic oscillations which are instructive to the physician. The intensity of the symptom (let us take for instance the desire to vomit) increases the deeper we penetrate into one of the relevant pathological

> memories. It reaches its climax shortly before the patient gives utterance to the memory; and when he has finished doing so it suddenly diminishes or even vanishes completely for a time.[7]

Since the formation of the symptom is related to the repressed contents of the unconscious as a substitute formation, I argue that Freudian interpretation presupposes a certain notion of translation. This follows from the fact that the logic of the unconscious is not the same as that of consciousness. They represent two different systems of mental functioning which Freud termed the primary and the secondary process.[8] In other words, they are like *two different languages*. Languages cut up reality in different ways and an examination of the psychoanalytic symptom reveals that it is a product of a dialectical tension between two different orders of cognition; of making sense of the traumas that are visited upon the human subject.

Is it surprising then that the French psychoanalyst Jacques Lacan should go on to compare the structure of the unconscious with that of a language? Though the Lacanian thesis may seem incomprehensible at first sight, Lacan provides a simple explanation. 'What have I taught you about the unconscious? The unconscious is constituted by the effects of speech on the subject, it is the dimension in which the subject is determined in the development of the effects of speech, consequently the unconscious is structured like a language'.[9] Of course, speech (*parole*) is not the same as language (*langue*). And there is a difference between saying that the unconscious is structured like speech and saying that it is structured like a language. Nevertheless, the Lacanian point is that the dialectical structure of the symptom is repressed when the psychoanalyst forgets that the patient's words are all that he has to work on. Though a detailed examination of Lacan's thesis on the relationship between language and the unconscious is beyond the scope of this essay, it is important to remember that the importance of language in the constitution of the human subject has been brought out independently by others with a European sensibility or training in the United States. The most notable for the purposes of this essay, of course, is Bruno Bettelheim who, like Freud, was a product of the Viennese educational system. Others who have worked on this problem were Anglo-American literary critics informed by psychoanalysis.[10]

Who Translates in Psychoanalysis?

> Every science is based on observation and experience arrived at through the medium of the psychical apparatus. But since our science has as its subject that apparatus itself, the analogy ends here. We make our observations through the medium of the same perceptual apparatus, precisely with the help of breaks in the sequence of 'psychical events'; we fill in what is omitted by making plausible inferences and *translating* it into conscious material. *(My emphasis.)*
>
> — Sigmund Freud[11]

There are two parties who collaborate in any act of translation: the author, or the text, and the translator. In psychoanalysis these actors correspond to the patient and the analyst respectively. The patient is the one who, like an author, produces a discursive text. The process whereby this production is facilitated is called free association. In the act of free association, the patient follows the fundamental dictum of the psychoanalytic session which states that the patient must say whatever comes to his or her mind without fear, shame or hesitation. If this dictum or ethic is not strictly followed, the analysis suffers.

It is important to understand this problem correctly since the popular perception of this ethic is based on a misunderstanding. The layperson is tempted to believe that the patient must recount every single incident of import in his or her life to the analyst. But this is not recommended anywhere in Freud. Free association only means that the patient must speak out whatever appears in consciousness during analysis—not everything however will come to his or her mind. Or even be pertinent to the neurosis. If there had to be a one-to-one correspondence between the patient's life and its narration, both psychoanalysis and translation would be impossible by definition. There simply won't be enough time. The act of translation then demands collaboration between the patient and the analyst. The patient spontaneously produces a discourse whose meaning is anything but obvious to him. In this he or she is not unlike the poet that Socrates mocked in the Platonic dialogue. The poet, says Socrates, produces his text in a moment of inspiration but is no more an authority on its meaning than an intelligent critic.[12]

What is Translated in Psychoanalysis?

> Take up the work of Freud again at the *Traumdeutung*.... The important part begins with the *translation* of the text, the important part which Freud tells us is given in the [verbal] elaboration of the dream—in other words, in its rhetoric... (*My emphasis.*)
>
> —Jacques Lacan[13]

The aim of psychoanalysis is to translate the symptomatic contents of the repressed portions of the psyche, which have hitherto remained unconscious. The expression of the repressed is mediated by forms of figuration, which help to distort its meaning. The translation of these contents then demands an understanding of metaphor. A whole array of rhetorical devices are deployed in the formations of the unconscious that emerge from primal repression. These devices can be subsumed under two fundamental categories—metaphor and metonymy.

Repression, however, is not just characteristic of neurotics. The neurotic predicament lies in the fact that when repression is *excessive*, it produces symptoms that function as a *substitute for the repressed ideas*. The task of the analysis is to undo the severity of infantile repression that makes it difficult for the subject to get on with the tasks of everyday life and to replace it with a retroactive condemnatory judgement. The difficulties arise from the fact that symptoms constitute interruptions. The problem in dealing with repression lies in the fact that whenever the analysis touches upon the signifiers that belong to the repressed core of the unconscious, the patient puts up a stiff resistance to the analysis. Resistance then is directly proportional to the underlying repression.

Since the concept of repression is another one of those psychoanalytic ideas that is often misunderstood by the layperson, it may be a good idea to cite a few lines by Freud himself in this context. Speaking at Clark University in the United States, where he had been invited to introduce the fundamental ideas of psychoanalysis to a distinguished audience in September 1909, Freud tried to capture the nature of repression with an analogy. If, in the course of his lecture, he argued, there be a continual disturbance from some quarter of the audience, it might become necessary to ask a particular member to leave the room. That member of the audience has been 'repressed'. It is quite likely that the repressed member will seek readmittance to the lecture hall, hence it might be advisable to post a few chairs against the doors to prevent the said individual from entering once again with the intention of disturbing the proceedings. The space inside the lecture hall in this analogy may be described as consciousness and that outside the room where the troublesome individual has been repressed is the unconscious. As the logic of the analogy would imply, all that is repressed is unconscious, but not vice versa. The repressed is the prototype of the unconscious but is not superordinate to it.

And then comes the interesting twist that seeks to situate the role of psychoanalytic therapy in this drama of consciousness, the repressed and the unconscious. If this troublesome individual were to knock on the door and seek admittance in a highly persistent manner, it might become necessary to arrive at a compromise of some sort. One way out of the situation might be to admit the repressed individual provided somebody, such as, say, the president of the proceedings, is willing to guarantee his good behaviour:

> It may well be that the individual who has been expelled, and who has now become embittered and reckless, will cause further trouble. It is true that he is no longer among us; we are free from his presence, from his insulting laughter and his *sotto voce* comments. But in some respects, nevertheless, the repression has been unsuccessful; for now he is making an intolerable exhibition of himself outside the room, and his shouting and banging on the door with his fists interfere with my lecture even more than his bad behaviour did before. In these circumstances we could not fail to be delighted if our respected president, Dr Stanley Hall, should be willing to assume the role of mediator and peacemaker. He would have a talk with the unruly person outside and then come to us with a request that he should be re-admitted after all: he himself would guarantee that the person would behave better. On Dr Hall's authority we decide to lift the repression, and peace and quiet are restored. This presents what is really no bad picture of the physician's task in the psychoanalytic treatment of the neuroses.[14]

What is the Psychopathology of Translation?

At this point I must note that in order to handle any Freudian concept, reading Freud cannot be considered superfluous, even if it be only for those concepts which are homonyms of current notions.

— Jacques Lacan[15]

Why do we use the term translation rather than interpretation? The use of the term 'translation' can be justified by the fact that the expression of the repressed portion of the unconscious suffers from distortions, which, far from being arbitrary, follow a few well-defined rules that Freud formalised in his book, *The Interpretation of Dreams* (1900). These forms of distortion are condensation, displacement, conditions of representability and secondary revision.

Condensation is the process whereby mental or dream images are constructed with features that are borrowed from other images. The subject, for example, may dream of the condensed image of an elephant with the tiny ears of a giraffe. Since elephants do not have ears resembling those of a giraffe, it is the process of condensation that has rendered such an image available to the dreamer. In displacement the effect generated by the idea of an elephant may be displaced on to a giraffe. So while the subject is under the impression that he is bothered by the image of a giraffe, it is actually the elephant that is bothering him.

Conditions of representability are the minimal rules of narrative construction that the dream work must employ to seek expression. In so far as the dream work follows the rules of narrative construction, it appears that it is not just consciousness that is characterised by narrative logic. The primary difference between the two systems of mental functioning would lie in the fluidity of cathexes that attend to the logistics of these distributions. Secondary revisions are changes to the dream text that the dreamer makes while narrating it in the analysis. For example, the incongruity of an image that fuses the body parts of an elephant and a giraffe might present itself forcefully to the dreamer. This might prompt him to wonder whether it was the size of the elephant's ears that misled him into thinking that it belonged to a giraffe or whether it was a flaw in his recollection. Flaws in recollection are as important as the actual dream text since they are a clue to the functioning of repression.[16]

The point of the discussion here is not to displace the term interpretation by the term translation but rather to demonstrate that the notion of translation is superordinate to interpretation. The term translation brings out the relationship between the two systems of mental functioning. Interpretation, on the other hand, is a way of connecting local details to a larger whole. It is not merely an analogy to say that the two systems of mental functioning are like languages. The primary process, for example, is characterised by a sliding of the signifier that is in excess of the demands of meaning. This overcrowding of the primary process is powered by the fluidity of libidinal cathexes. This makes it possible for the traffic of desire to speed along through the psychic mechanisms of displacement and condensation. Since these mechanisms are in the service of 'censorship', they distort the meaning of the subject's desire, holding him or her thereby in the grip of linguistic mechanisms that mimic a foreign language. In other words, the force of the pathological compulsion in the hysterical subject arises from *a failure of translation*.

There is of course no short cut to translation in the clinical encounter. Freud, unlike some of his overenthusiastic disciples, distanced himself from the temptation of developing a dictionary of symbols. He was more interested in elaborating the syntactic transformations of the dream work. The semantics of the dream (i.e., its interpretation) was less important than the structures that it gave rise to. Here, Freud proceeds in a manner that is analogous to a linguist comparing different languages to work out if they belong to a common family rather than as a literary critic trying to figure out the meaning of a particular phrase or an image in a dream or some other instantiation of the unconscious as an end in itself. It was in the translation of these structures into other formations of the unconscious, such as the Freudian slip, which would include a whole gamut of linguistic errors comprising those of speech, writing, reading and, by extension, as I want to argue here, those of translation. These and other analogous errors that Freud termed the 'psychopathology of everyday life' are the ones that can be most readily picked up in the problem of mistranslation.[17] Mistranslations can either be unconscious slips that are local or a more systematic attempt to hijack the source text as an enactment of the translator's unconscious desire, of his libidinal investments.

The perpetuation of the mistranslation in which the Freudian texts were caught up was only possible because of a turning away from the act of reading Freud's psychoanalytic texts. This task has not been sufficiently appreciated by Anglo-American psychoanalysis since they were content to believe that psychoanalysis was merely an extension of psychiatry.[18] Lacan, however, in his project for a 'return to Freud' attempted to foreground the ethical necessity of attending to the '*poetics of the Freudian corpus*':

> This notion must be approached through what I shall call the poetics of the Freudian corpus, the first way of access towards the penetration of its sense, and the essential dimensions, from the origins of the work to the apogee marked in it by this notion, for an understanding of its dialectical repercussions.[19]

The task of the psychoanalyst is not merely to learn the psychoanalytic formulations of Freud as an external operation, but to understand them in their moment of metaphoric construction. The figurative intricacies of the Freudian text are as necessary to its doctrine as the particularities of a patient's formulations on the meaning of his symptom. The 'vehicle' of Freud's tropology is constitutive of his meaning, of his 'tenor'. According to Lacan, any attempt to pose these questions is impossible without a recognition of the role of language in the constitution of the subject. However, Lacan did not reduce the subject to only a play of signifiers, as the postmodernists would have us believe. In the Lacanian model, the unconscious is both like and unlike a language. In other words only certain aspects of the unconscious can be translated (Miller 1988a). Suffice it to note at this juncture that the philosophical question of *translation* is at the heart of the Lacanian contribution to psychoanalysis.

What the Lacanian critique represents has to some measure been anticipated by Bettelheim. Since Lacan's comments on mistranslations in the Freudian doctrine are scattered in over thirty volumes of seminars—many of which have not been edited even in French, let alone be available in translation—I think it will be more economical to restrict our examination to the specific points raised in Bettelheim. Another advantage that Bettelheim offers us is that he was both an insider and an outsider to the Anglo-American psychoanalytic establishment. The tensions inherent in such a subjective position were not unlike the demand made of both European psychoanalysts and patients in the United States to adjust to the American way of life. The essence of the American way of life is the pursuit of happiness.[20] Freud, however, vehemently resisted the idea that psychoanalysis could effectuate either a complete cure that was objectively verifiable or that it would lead to happiness.[21] The strain in the Freudian argument that both Lacan and Bettelheim take up *ad nauseam* is the necessity of developing an ethic of the tragic. It is precisely this ethic of the tragic that is represented in the lifelong struggle of the neurotic subject against the constraints of the Oedipus complex that was lost in the English translation of Freud.

What did Freud mean by the tragic? Tragedy, for Freud, is an acute awareness of the subject's limitations in the face of the Other, which is alternatively represented by the figure of Oedipus, the suffering inherent in the human condition, our confused enactments of primordial plots which lack resolution, and the certainty of death. No set of narrative arrangements will lead to a situation that promises the subject a life that can be lived 'happily ever after'. In other words, whatever be the set of phantasies we project on to the locus of the Other, a lack always emerges in the life of the subject that cannot but mock these optimistic arrangements. The trajectory of psychoanalysis, as the Europeans understood it, was to facilitate precisely this insight in terms of the unique set of symptoms that the patient suffered from. The end of analysis must be fought for on this terrain of existential limitations.

The Americans however appear to do the opposite. In their reading of Freud's later work, most notably, *Civilization and Its Discontents*, they fail to understand that for Freud a certain measure of discontent is the price to be paid for civilisation. There cannot be a civilisation without discontent. Discontent is inherent to civilisation. To pretend otherwise is to mistake the narcissistic or sexual phantasies of childhood for reality. As Lacan puts it:

> It does not escape Freud's attention that happiness as far as we are concerned is what must be offered as the goal of our striving, however ethical it might be. But what stands out clearly—in spite of the fact that it is not given sufficient importance on

> the grounds that we cease to listen to a man as soon as he steps outside his sphere of expertise—is that I prefer to read in *Civilization and Its Discontents* the idea Freud expresses there concerning happiness, namely, that absolutely nothing is prepared for it, either in the macrocosm or the microcosm. (Lacan 1992: 13).

The Americanisation of this text has led to the simplistic idea that the discontents of civilisation result only from sexual repressions, and that a change in the sexual mores of a society will eliminate this discontent. But for Freud the trauma of sexuality does not arise from the lack of sexual freedom in a culture. In other words repression of the Oedipal signifier is not reducible to the political repressions of a conservative or orthodox society. Primary repression, which is a structural notion, is what constitutes the infant as a subject of the symbolic order. It emerges almost as a rite of passage that gives a subject the symbolic sanction to function as a civilised being by denying him the pleasures of incest in return for the sexual or matrimonial possibilities of adulthood.[22] Again, the trauma of sexuality is linked to its diphasic advent in the subject. It emerges first as infantile sexuality in the child's earliest years and is revived once again during puberty when the subject becomes capable of sexual reproduction. Sexuality often emerges too soon or too late in the life of the subject.[23]

By not even recognising the fact that Freud pitched his arguments around the fortunes of the 'soul', American ego psychologists have opted for a technology of the self that is insured against any possible advent of trauma. If, and when, trauma intervenes it is compensated for by the medico-legal practices of torts, damages, malpractice suits, etc. What gets forgotten is that the very aim of psychoanalysis is to help the patient (one must write analye and at this point to minimise the damage of my own use of medical terminology) understand the real lessons of trauma. What psychoanalysis brings out most radically is precisely the immediacy of trauma. Traumas are not external to the subject, only events are. The trauma arises precisely from the fact that the subject is overwhelmed by stimuli that the soul cannot come to terms with. Therein lies its individuality. This however will remain a lost lesson if psychoanalysis is content to merely replicate the tropological cast of the 'body is a soul' metaphor that functions as the epigraph to this essay. That is why Bettelheim commences his critique of mistranslations is psychoanalysis by discussing this image.

If one of the primary difficulties in translation is the problem of metaphor, let us briefly examine why misunderstanding the metaphorical texture of the Freudian text can alienate the reader from psychoanalysis. Freud repeatedly insisted that he had not discovered the unconscious. All that there was to be known about the unconscious could be found in the works of creative writers such as Sophocles, Shakespeare, Goethe, Dostoevsky, Nietzsche and Schnitzler—to name just a few of the writers that Freud admired. His accomplishment had been no more than a laborious rediscovery of their insights through clinical work and readings in the history of literature.

Why does Freud make this claim if his training as a medical practitioner could offer him more powerful tools to investigate the contents of the unconscious? Is he merely being rhetorical? Or did literary insights offer his discourse such overwhelming prestige that he was willing to put the scientific status of his discourse into question in order to produce another metaphysical theory of Man? Furthermore, given the materialism of his medical training, and the logical positivism that dominated discussions on the philosophy of science in turn-of-the-century Vienna, would it not have been suicidal for Freud to make these claims? Bettelheim, who was a product of the same educational establishment as Freud, argues that the latter's intuitive fascination for literature lies in the fact that the discourse of the unconscious deploys metaphorical formations which Freud was used to finding in his reading of the poets. Freud did not believe that psychoanalysis could become a hard science and that the unconscious could only be explained through analogies, metaphors and comparisons:

> The metaphors that Freud used were intended to bridge the rift that exists between the hard facts to which psychoanalysis refers and the imaginative manner in which it explains them. A second reason is even more closely related to the nature of psychoanalysis. Because of repression, or the influence of censorship, the unconscious reveals itself in symbols or metaphors, and psychoanalysis, in its concern with the unconscious, tries to speak about it in its own metaphoric language. Finally, metaphors are more likely than a purely intellectual statement to

> touch a human chord and arouse our emotions, and thus give us a feeling for what is meant. A true comprehension of psychoanalysis requires not only an intellectual realisation but a simultaneous emotional response; neither alone will do. A well-chosen metaphor will permit both (Bettelheim 1982: 37–38).

If the unconscious can be rendered at least partly as a text because of its discursive structure, the analyst must be someone who is trained in the practices of reading, writing and translation. He or she must be aware of the ways in which the signifier carries the burden of unconscious desire. The unconscious reveals itself mainly through symptomatic errors of a textual cast. In *The Psychopathology of Everyday Life*, Freud discusses numerous examples that pertain to the different uses of language. These errors, or Freudian slips, provide us a clue to the libidinal tensions to which the translator can fall prey in the course of doing his work. Though Freud does not discuss examples that can be directly classified as mistranslations, since this was a pioneering text and Freud was anxious to first of all establish the psychopathology of everyday life, his examples of misreading will provide us the rationale to extend these notions to translations as well. Here then are three examples:

> A philologist whose, most recent and excellent, works had brought him into conflict with his professional colleagues, read '*Sprachstrategie* [language strategy]' in mistake for '*Schachsstrategie* [chess strategy]' (Freud 1991c: 161).

> In Lichtenberg's *Witzige und satirisiche Einfälle* ['Witty and Satirical Thoughts', 1853] a remark occurs which is no doubt derived from a piece of observation and which comprises virtually the whole theory of misreading: 'He had read so much Homer that he always read '*Agamemnon*' instead of '*angenommen* [supposed]' (Freud 1991c: 160).

> One day I picked up a mid-day or evening paper and saw in large print: '*Der Friede von Görz* [The Peace of Gorizia].' But no, all it said was: '*Die Feinde vor Görz* [The Enemy before Gorizia]'. It is easy for someone who has two sons fighting at this very time in that theatre of operations to make such a mistake in reading (ibid.: 161).

In all these examples the interference of an unconscious desire makes it difficult to complete a linguistic act. Though these examples are deceptively simple, it is not difficult to understand the logic behind Freudian slips. If the reader is psychologically prepared to read something into a text, then even the barest resemblance between the word that the reader was seeking and the one actually present in the text is enough to generate a misreading (ibid.: 161). How does the tendency to misread lead to the psychopathology of mistranslation?

Let us begin with the mistranslation of the very title of the book that popularised these ideas, *The Psychopathology of Everyday Life*. According to Bettelheim, a better rendition of the title would be *On the Psychopathology of Everyday Life*. Similarly, the subtitle should begin with the word 'about'. The translation however drops both the German words '*zur*' (on) in the title and '*über*' (about) in the subtitle: *Zur Psychopathologie des Alltagslebens: Über Vergessen, Versprechen, Vergreifen, Aberglaube und Irrutum*. Both these words introduce an element of tentativeness implying that it is difficult to be certain on matters pertaining to the unconscious:

> Freud could have used *über* (about) rather than *zur* (on) in the main title. By choosing instead to use both words, he was apparently trying to make doubly sure that the reader would recognise that the book was only *about* all these topics, and by no means an apodictic treatise on the subject (Bettelheim 1982: 83).

But the title in the English translation gives the impression that Freud meant the book to be a definitive treatment on the theme. This clearly was not his intention. Besides, as Bettelheim's caveat points out, the translator of a text on Freudian slips must be a lot more sensitive to the problem of mistranslation. A great deal of the text is a play on words that renders it untranslatable. Freud's American translator, A.A. Brill, went to the extent of replacing Freud's examples with his own in the hope that they would get the ideas across even more forcefully. But James Strachey did not have recourse to this option since his translations in the *Standard Edition* were meant for the serious student of psychoanalysis.[24] In any case, as Bettelheim puts it, 'the very topic of the book...ought to have alerted them to their own propensity to mistranslate out of subconscious motives' (Bettelheim 1982: 83).

Such problems are not specific to only this text. Another title that could do with some reworking is *The Interpretation of Dreams*. Bettelheim suggested alternatives such as *A Search for the Meaning of Dreams* or *An Inquiry into the Meaning of Dreams*. Both these titles carry connotations of astrology. The German term for astrology, *Sterndeutung*, is very similar to Freud's German title *Traumdeutung*. The difference though is that astrologers believe that dreams are an indication of things to come while Freud believed that they were a clue to the subject's past. In any case, Freud did not give the impression that he was writing a definitive treatise:

> The English title gives the impression that Freud presented a definitive treatise on dreams; by failing to summon associations to astrology, it does not suggest the parallel between the discovery of the true nature of the universe and the discovery of the true inner world of the soul (Bettelheim 1982: 70).

This true inner world of the soul was also lost because the word 'soul' was one that Freud's translators fought shy of. Their scientism made it difficult for them to formulate the problem correctly. Freud's German term '*Seele*' is often substituted with the English 'mind' which clearly has other connotations. For Freud, the mind was just one of the components of the soul. By rendering these terms as synonyms, the impression created is that psychoanalysis is a psychology. In fact, even the differences between the English and German terms for psychoanalysis can be misleading. In English the emphasis is always on the 'analysis'. In German, however, the stress falls on the first part of the term *Psychanalyse*, i.e., the psyche (ibid.: 12).

The parts of the soul—the id, the ego and the superego—also confuse the issue for English readers. The replacement of the term 'I' with ego, 'it' with id, and 'Above I' with Super Ego depersonalise the most intimate parts of the soul. The deployment of such a terminology promotes bad habits of thought in the reader. The unconscious and its workings are seen as problems affecting other people. The reader will find it difficult to internalise the workings of the unconscious if he or she is forced to think in terms of an ego instead of the pronominal 'I' that comes naturally, or a Super Ego instead of the conscience that everyone has to wrestle with.

The propensity of the subject to lie to himself is forgotten in the alienating drama of an ego and its defences. All that Freud meant by the term '*Abwehr*' is to fend off an idea that the subject finds displeasing. The term 'defence' however gives the impression that the subject is fighting against a problem presented by external *reality*. But what the subject is actually engaged in is a defence against the *real* of the unconscious, which is strictly speaking neither inside nor outside. It is *extimate* to the subject—the real is precisely that which calls this opposition between the inside and the outside into question.[25]

Conclusion

Though the psychopathology of translation is mediated by local linguistic miscarriages, it is not reducible to it. There is, in other words, a structural discontent in the act of translation that propels it towards failure. The translator cannot be completely *intimate* with the text. All that he or she can do is to work out, and correct, in retrospect, the symptomatic trajectory of a particular failure. It is by working out the modalities through which the unconscious demands expression that psychoanalysis attempts to discharge its debt to its original faith in the possibility of translation. As Lacan points out, 'the psychoanalytic experience does nothing other than establish that the unconscious leaves none of our actions outside its field'.[26]

Notes

1. See 'Psychoanalysis and Translation', in Benjamin 1989: 109–49.
2. For the difference between the 'tenor' and 'vehicle' of a metaphor, see 'Metaphor' in Richards 1965: 89–112.
3. James Strachey's translations can be found in both the authoritative Standard Edition of the *Complete Works of Sigmund Freud* (London: The Hogarth Press in association with the Institute of Psychoanalysis, 1963) and the *Penguin Freud Library* (London: Penguin Books, 1991). Since this is an expository essay, I have used the more easily available Penguin edition.

4. See 'The Empty Word and the Full Word', in Lacan 1968: 9.
5. See the entry on the 'Real' in Evans 1996: 160–61.
6. See 'Fräulein Anna O', in Breuer and Freud 1991: 83.
7. See 'Psychpathology of Hysteria', in Breuer and Freud 1991: 383.
8. See 'Formulations on the Two Principles of Mental Functioning', in Freud 1991b: 29–44.
9. See 'Sexuality in the Defiles of the Signifier', in Lacan 1977: 149.
10. The earliest of these critics includes I.A. Richards in England and Kenneth Burke in the United States. See 'The Command of Metaphor', in Richards 1965: 115–38; and 'Freud and the Analysis of Poetry', in Burke 1967: 258–92.
11. See 'Psychoanalysis and Translation', Sigmund Freud quoted in Benjamin 1989: 127.
12. For Socrates's comment, see 'Ion', in Plato 1952: 144.
13. See 'Symbol and Language', in Lacan 1968: 31.
14. See 'Second Lecture', in Freud 1991c: 52.
15. See 'The Function of Language in Psychoanalysis' in Lacan 1968: 6.
16. See 'The Dream-Work', in Freud 1991a: 381–655.
17. See especially the chapter 'Misreadings and Slips of the Pen', in Freud 1991d: 153–83.
18. The American psychoanalyst A.A. Brill tried to 'sell' psychoanalysis in psychiatric circles in his lectures on psychoanalysis. See Brill 1944.
19. See 'Interpretation and Temporality', in Lacan 1968: 82.
20. On the American obsession with happiness, see 'The Technique of Happiness', in Jones 1966: 131–65.
21. For Lacan's comment on the problem of happiness, see 'The Demand for Happiness and the Promise of Analysis', in Lacan 1992: 291–301.
22. See Claude Levi-Strauss's treatment of the incest taboo as the essence of the Oedipus complex in Levi-Strauss 1969. Jacques Lacan's notion of the symbolic order as the site of exchange is borrowed from Levi-Strauss' work on the incest taboo.
23. See 'Three Essays on the Theory of Sexuality' (1905) in Freud 1991e: 45–169.
24. See James Strachey's 'Editor's Introduction' in Freud 1991d: 33.
25. For an introduction to the Lacanian concept of extimacy, see Miller 1988b.
26. See Jacques Lacan's 'The Agency of the Letter in the Unconscious or Reason Since Freud', in Lacan 1977b: 163.

References

Benjamin, Andrew, 1989. *Translation and the Nature of Philosophy*. London and New York: Routledge.

Bettelheim, Bruno, 1982. *Freud and Man's Soul*. London: Penguin Books.

Borch-Jacobsen, Mikkel, 1996. *Remembering Anna O: A Century of Mystification*, translated by Kirby Olson in collaboration with Xavier Callahan and the author. New York and London: Routledge.

Breuer, Josef and **Sigmund Freud**, 1991. *Studies on Hysteria* (1895), translated by James Strachey and Alix Strachey. London: Penguin Books.

Brill, A.A., 1944. *Freud's Contribution to Psychiatry*. New York: W.W. Norton & Co. Inc.

Burke, Kenneth, 1967. *The Philosophy of Literary Form: Studies in Symbolic Action*. Baton Rouge: Louisiana State University Press.

Evans, Dylan, 1996. *An Introductory Dictionary of Lacanian Psychoanalysis*. London and New York: Routledge.

Ferenczi, Sándor, 1973. 'Freud's Influence on Medicine'. In Hendrik M. Ruitenbeek (ed.), *The First Freudians*. New York: Jason Aron Inc.

Freud, Sigmund, 1991a. *The Interpretation of Dreams* (1900), translated by James Strachey, edited by Angela Richards. London: Penguin Books.

———, 1991b. *On Metapsychology: The Theory of Psychoanalysis* (1911). London: Penguin Books.

———, 1991c. *Two Short Accounts of Psychoanalysis*. London: Penguin Books.

———, 1991d. *The Psychopathology of Everyday Life* (1901). London: Penguin Books.

———, 1991e. *On Sexuality*. London: Penguin Books.

Jones, Howard Mumford, 1966. *The Pursuit of Happiness*. Ithaca, New York: Cornell University Press.

Lacan, Jacques, 1968. *The Language of the Self: The Function of Language in Psychoanalysis*, translated and edited by Anthony Wilden. Baltimore and London: The Johns Hopkins University Press.

———, 1977a. *The Four Fundamental Concepts of Psychoanalysis*, translated by Alan Sheridan, edited by Jacques-Alain Miller. London: Penguin Books.

———, 1977b. *Écrits: A Selection* (1966), translated by Alan Sheridan, edited by Jacques-Alain Miller. London: Tavistock/Routledge.

———, 1992. *The Ethics of Psychoanalysis 1959–60: The Seminar of Jacques Lacan, Book VII*, translated by Dennis Porter, edited by Jacques-Alain Miller. London: Tavistock/Routledge.

Levi-Strauss, Claude, 1969. *The Elementary Structures of Kinship* (1947), passim, translated by James H. Bell, John Richard von Strummer and Rodney Needham. Boston: Beacon Press.

———, 1988a. 'Another Lacan'. *Hystoria*, vol. 6, no. 7, p. 27.

———, 1988b. 'Extimacy'. *Prose Studies*, vol. 11, no. 3, pp. 121–131.

Plato, 1952. *The Dialogues of Plato*, translated by Benjamin Jowett. Chicago: Encyclopaedia Britannica, Inc.

Richards, I.A., 1965. *The Philosophy of Rhetoric*. New York: Oxford University Press.

Safouan, Moustapha, 1980. 'In Praise of Hysteria' in *Returning to Freud: Clinical Psychoanalysis in the School of Lacan*, translated and edited by Stuart Schneiderman. New Haven and London: Yale University Press.

Seventeen

Just Words: Multiculturalism and the Ethics of Translation

SARANINDRANATH TAGORE

Much is being written today on the issue of multiculturalism. Thinkers are attempting to theorise multiculturalism as a conceptual identity of both political and discursive import. At the political level, nations such as Canada have declared themselves multicultural societies. Concern for multiculturalism, at least in the west, is operative both at the theoretical level of academe and the praxial level of politics. The topic of multiculturalism is also particularly salient for the Indian experience because India is arguably the nation with the longest historical encounter with the dynamics of cultural plurality. Moreover, with the advent of political forces that seem to undermine the multicultural constitution of India's history, the topic needs to be thought through anew.

In the following remarks, the multicultural will be theorised as a philosophical problem of history, defining a space between the modern and the postmodern. These remarks also concern the foundations of translation. Turning on the pivot of the problem of marginalisation, translation will emerge in this essay as a *moral category* in a philosophy of history that is constitutively multicultural.

Multiculturalism and the Philosophy of History

Hegel's system is a plausible place to begin when engaged in the task of situating the topic of multiculturalism within the frames of a philosophy of history. Such a move will have a twofold significance. First, the discussion will be anchored in the tradition; and second, given the postmodern critique of Hegel and Hegelian master narratives, these remarks can be more deeply linked with contemporary European thought.

Hegel offered a foundational account of history. He argued that the flow of historical time and the identities of Nature are constituted by the deep structural movement of Spirit that is pure mind. Phenomena, historical or natural, are fractured moments of Spirit's dialectical movement. In other words, Spirit moves by othering itself from itself in a series of Negations which are reabsorbed by Spirit so that it can move again into another instance of Negativity. The movement of Spirit is teleologically conditioned. In the space of this telos-governed logos, each moment of negation is a progression over the previous because, for Hegel, the movement of Spirit is a journey of self-realisation headed towards Absolute Knowledge, a state where Spirit knows itself as itself. The serial determinations of all the moments of Negation constitute the plane of phenomenal history. Upon the achievement of Absolute Knowledge, Spirit rests—for it does not need to other anymore. For Hegel, ontology begins and phenomenology ends at this juncture. The death of phenomenology thus heralds the death of history.[1]

This sketch of Hegel's phenomenological account of historical constitution must suffice for the present purposes. Only one ramification of Hegel's system concerns the task at hand. This is the teleological orientation of Hegel's philosophy of historical progression. For Hegel, the teleological determinants of Spirit are best profiled in a given culture within a scheme of alternative cultures at a given historical moment. Historical structures as phenomenal determinations of Spirit are conglomerations of cultural frameworks. Within such a phenomenological and foundational context, one can understand Hegel's contention that the apogee of culture is to be found in the Germanic ethos, and his claim that the Greeks evolved a higher form of culture than the Indians or the Chinese (Hegel 1956).

If Hegel's account of historical constitution is used as a hermeneutic pivot, the notion of multiculturalism emerges as a component in a philosophy of history. The Enlightenment conception of autonomy that finds its most brilliant configuration in Kant's notion of pure practical reason inspires an account of history that has perhaps the ironic effect of erasing the tenets of multiculturalism. The effect is ironic because the autonomy of individuals that is enshrined in Kant's account of the moral experience ought to translate into an autonomy of cultures.

Hegel's historicisation of the essentials of Kant's transcendental account of experience precisely denies such a translation. Multiculturalism, then, inhabits a plane space and not a hierarchical space. A plane space accommodates a system of cultures where each cultural complex is autonomous. It is in theorising this plane space of cultural autonomy that post-modern thought launches its attack on Hegelian conceptions of history.

Multiculturalism and Postmodern Pluralism

Jean-François Lyotard, a significant postmodern voice, uses the term 'modern' to designate any science that legitimates itself with reference to a metadiscourse by making an explicit appeal to a 'grand narrative' such as, for example, the dialectics of Spirit, the hermeneutics of meaning or the creation of wealth (Lyotard 1993: 3).

For Lyotard, the Enlightenment narrative, in which the 'hero of knowledge' aspires towards a 'good ethico-political end-universal peace' is just such a narrative (ibid.: 4). The Enlightenment enterprise, consolidated by Hegel for the postmodern in general and by Lyotard in particular is the quintessential posture of modernity. In contrast, Lyotard simply defines the postmodern as incredulity towards metanarratives (ibid.).

This incredulity towards metanarratives engineers the plane space of cultural autonomy. Lyotard displaces the discourse of metanarratives and, inspired by the later Wittgenstein's notion of language games, argues for a cultural space that is populated by 'little narratives'. These narratives, *pace* metanarratives, are governed by their own constituting rules, and are not dependent on extra-narrational, foundational rules for their articulation. Moreover such discursive forms of life are not arranged in a hierarchical order; and thus they are allowed to flourish alongside each other on a plane space of cultural autonomy.

Another postmodern thinker who renders a plane space is Gilles Deleuze. In a seminal postmodern text, *A Thousand Plateaus*, Deleuze and his collaborator, Felix Guattari theorise a crucial distinction between the 'arborescent' and the 'rhizomatic' Deleuze and Guattari 1988). They image the great texts of the Western tradition and the cultural systems in the figure of a tree. The arborescent calls into presence the image of a root that grounds the textual (and cultural) complexes in a foundational matrix in order to uphold a unified, centred and hierarchical system. For example, Plato's account of the Forms, or Hegel's postulate of Spirit serve as root systems that make possible textual and cultural platforms. Within the general context of postmodern thought, the Deleuzian/Guattarian tree has a great theoretical resemblance to Lyotard's conception of metanarratives. Just as the Lyotard theorises little narratives as a pivotal theme of postmodernism, Deleuze and Guattari develop the account of the rhizome as a postmodernist counterpoint to the foundational narratives of modernity.

The root-tree system engenders lines of growth that are regulated and brought to a unified structure by the nature of the root. The rhizome, on the other hand, signifies the decentred and uprooted lines that constitute multiplicities. Rhizomatic analysis posits three kinds of lines. First, the 'rigid segmentary line' generates social identities in the context of normal social institutions. Second, the 'supple segmentary line' shifts away from a normalised, institutional form of life. At this point, cracks open up in the textures of normalcy. Finally, the 'lines of flight' completely break away from all unities and shatter all identities into multiplicities. The rhizome, rejecting all metaphysics of substance and investing its capital in the primacy of the ever-becoming logic of desire, celebrates the multiple both in the self-constitution of individuals and in the creation of the cultural spheres.

Lyotard and Deleuze/Guattari provide two examples of postmodern theory that attempt to critique the foundational narratives of modernity. These critiques are germane to the issue of multiculturalism and, in particular, the ethics of multiculturalism.

I have defined the multicultural in terms of plane space where individual cultures exist as autonomous entities.

At this juncture, the use of 'autonomy' needs to be further clarified. It is perhaps beyond argument that in the western tradition the master discourse on autonomy was developed by Kant. His concern, in his critique of both theoretical and practical reason, is not with collective autonomy but with individual autonomy as is made clear from his theoretical account of transcendental apperception and his practical understanding of the will. The reason why Kant's account of individual autonomy in his critical account of practical reason fails to translate into collective autonomy is instructive for the purposes at hand. The practical analysis of autonomy for Kant is linked to his conception of moral experience. Kantian autonomy is an arborescent notion because it is nomologically grounded in the absolute foundation of the moral law. In other words, the will is autonomous because it renders it possible for individuals to loosen their causal chains of historical, biological and cultural determinants in order to exercise moral freedom by allowing actions respectful of the moral law. In the Deleuzian/Guattarian account, it is just such arborescent thinking that drafts the rigid lines of normalised institutions which rhizomatic multiplicities ought to shatter.

The rhizome implicitly argues for a non-arborescent figure for autonomy. The rhizomatic cultural zones for Deleuze are not rooted in a universalised conception of moral law but are continually forming and unforming in the vortex of libidinal investments. Similarly, for Lyotard, cultural formations articulated as discursive structures of little narratives imply a radicalised autonomy where the logic of marginalisation is cleaved at the roots. It is the opposition of the Kantian and at least these two postmodern views will now allow for the framing of my present thesis concerning multiculturalism and the ethics of translation.

Multiculturalism: Between Modernity and Postmodernity

The hierarchical space of modernity effaces the multicultural ethos, whereas the plane space of postmodernity secures the plurality of cultures. The former endorses a variety of foundationalisms, whereas the latter rejects foundational accounts wholesale. At this point, the confrontational themes between the arborescent and the rhizomatic may be rendered explicit. According to postmodern analysis, Kant, with his moral philosophy, and Hegel, in his largely Kantian philosophy of history, criteriologically substantiate the modern enterprise of rooting cultural discourses in a ground of legitimation. The legitimising discourse of these foundational narratives are then causally linked to the process of cultural marginalisation. The postmodern challenge to the enterprises of modernity cuts across crucial philosophical trajectories, ranging from issues concerning the nature of subjectivity to sustained criticisms of rationality.

In its concern over the discursive function of legitimisation, the postmodern critique of modernity emerges with political resonance. Let us invoke an example to illustrate this point. A theocracy arboreously constructs a political and moral system that is rooted in the tenets of a particular religion. These tenets provide the criteria that allow for the nourishment of particular cultural discourses and marginalise other voices, and in extreme but historically real cases translate into attempts at extermination.

According to the postmodern formulation, hegemonic states operate on a field of philosophical foundationalism by privileging certain cultural frameworks. Postmodern notions such as the rhizome or little narratives appear as politically charged concepts when they are viewed as critical of the culturally totalising movements of root structures and metanarratives.

Postmodern anti-foundationalism opens up the space of multiculturalism. Pluralism in general enfolds the more particular concern with multiculturalism. Calvin Schrag articulates the postmodern pluralist ethos well when he writes that the 'vocabulary of pluralism has become standard fare in the postmodern literature ... and veritably, plurality appears to have become a global phenomenon of postmodern life' (Schrag 1992: 30). And it ought to be noted here that Schrag, though he is not thematising the notion of translation in his book, is interested, just as the present paper is, in the project of disclosing a space between the modern and the postmodern.

Deleuze's rhizomatic constructions and Lyotard's little narrational posture that markedly stamp postmodern pluralism also reopen anew the question of ethics and, as its obvious extension, the problems of politics. For the sake of expository convenience, it is best to briefly focus here on Lyotard. The localised topoi of the plural narrational spaces generate lines of discourses or 'phrase regimens' in the idiolect of Lyotard, which link the paradigms of Kuhn, and are incommensurate and heterogeneous. The radical autonomy of phrase regimens is secured by an explicitly moral appeal proffered through the concept of the *differend*. Lyotard's (1988: xi) definition of this concept needs to be inscribed in its entirety:

> As distinguished from a litigation, a differend would be a case of conflict, between (at least) two parties, that cannot be equitably resolved for lack of a rule of judgement applicable to both arguments. One side's legitimacy does not imply the other's lack of legitimacy. However, applying a single rule of judgement to both in order to settle their differend as though it were merely a litigation would wrong (at least) one of them (and both of them if neither side admits this rule).

Collapsing the distinction between a litigation and a *differend* in order to settle a dispute between conflicting phrase regimens would wrong at least one of the contending parties. A *differend*, then, by virtue of its unresolvable nature, flags the moral space that Lyotard wishes to keep secure for dissensus. The notion of the *differend* articulates a *moral* space because a 'litigiously' arrived at consensus would be a hegemonising event disruptive of the radically autonomous nature of phrase regimes. Nurturing the *differend* and keeping it separated from litigation would, for Lyotard, disallow the formation of a master narrative and thus would block the cultural process of marginalisation.

It is not clearly the case, however, that the cause of servicing the moral imperative of demarginalisation is furthered by the radical heterogeneity and autonomy of localised discourses implied by the cultural constructions of little narratives. Is this not the proverbial situation of throwing the baby of moral evaluation out with the bath water of foundations? While it is urgent that one is sensitive to the caution towards foundational thought that postmodernism so brilliantly invokes, at the same time one has to grant that if the issue at stake is demarginalisation, criteria of moral evaluation are necessary. Even if it is granted that strongly foundational (modern) accounts of morality, secular or religious, operating according to the norms of litigation, 'wrong' at least one contending party, one will still need criteria of judgement that will scaffold the logic of demarginalisation. Postmodern theory flounders when it comes to the task of supplying the ethics that is required of a politics of demarginalisation.[2]

It has been mentioned earlier that multiculturalism is situated on a plane space of cultural autonomy. This proposal should be positioned between the grammars of modernity and postmodernity. The configurations of culture seen from the perspective of a Hegelian account of history rule out the possibility of multiculturalism. For such a project arranges cultures in a hierarchical fashion where the content and the order of the hierarchy is determined by the teleologically anchored criteria of history. Postmodern thought is justifiably suspicious of such conceptions of history because they lead to what Lyotard in a slightly different context has termed 'terror'. The 20th century, Lyotard warns us, saw the face of this terror too many times.

> ...it must be clear that it is our business not to supply reality but to invent allusions to the conceivable which cannot be presented. And it is not to be expected that this task will effect the last reconciliation between language games (which, under the name of faculties, Kant knew to be separated by a chasm), and that only the transcendental illusion (that of Hegel) can hope to totalize them into a real unity. But Kant also knew that the price to pay for such an illusion is terror. The nineteenth and twentieth centuries have given us as much terror as we can take (Lyotard 1993: 81).

Postmodern thought, however, especially as it congeals around the concept of little narratives, by emphasising the radical incommensurability and heterogeneity of phrase regimens, generates a view of cultural autonomy that undercuts the task of demarginalisation so impressively profiled in the postmodern critique of modernity. In order to position the multicultural between the modern and the postmodern, cultural autonomy needs to be reconfigured in a way that keeps in place the postmodern cautionary note concerning the intrinsic hegemony of foundations. Such a positioning should also address the issue of providing an ethics to the politics of demarginalisation.

In Conclusion: Multiculturalism and the Ethics of Translation

The ethics of translation is to be theorised precisely in the interstitial terrain between the modern and the postmodern. Yet, suspicion towards the endorsement of non-founded world views is motivated in large measure by a fear of moral uncertainty. Thinking that resonates from a foundation after all allows for algorithmic solutions to moral problems. Foundations are seen as fencing the world off from the possibilities of moral anarchy. It is equally true, however, that too much of certainty can lead to hegemony and terror. A particular feature of the phenomenology of uncertainty can help the profiling of the present discussion. This transparent texture of uncertainty, in contrast to the opacity of certainty, is germane to the task of reconfiguring cultural autonomy in order to position the multicultural between the modern and the postmodern.

If Lyotardian little narratives are taken to be critical of the totalising discourses of modernity, they are textured by the transparency of uncertainty. In other words, the gesture of incredulity towards the closures of totality ought to translate into the ever-opening horizon of receptivity. The criticism of totalisation otherwise would ring hollow. Does the theorisation of narratives as anchored in a logic of receptivity translate into a foundational claim? The response to this question is clearly negative because the notion is being used purely in a formal manner, and it cannot be used to generate a criteriological ground that can justify one narrative at the expense of another.

The openness of narratives opens up to the openness of other narratives. The openness of cultures opens up to the openness of other cultures. Between cultures is not a mute chasm but an opening in which, to echo Heidegger, truth presences itself. The nature of this claim must be evaluated. In the Lyotardian discourse, the category of truth is paradigm dependent, that is, the epistemological evaluation of a phrase regimen is driven by the rules of the little narrative. Thus, in postmodern thought in general and Lyotard in particular, one reads an underdetermination of communicative rationality leading to contestations between incommensurate cultural matrices.

Articulating truth as a presence in the opening between cultures affirms a hermeneutical view of communicative rationality that better addresses the problem of marginalisation than the Lyotardian strategy can. It was noted earlier that the postmodern critique of foundational enterprises fails to secure a politics and an ethics of demarginalisation. Configuring truth in the clearing between cultures, in the tissues of communicative articulations, allows the conversation of humankind to resonate in a temper that avoids the forced consonance of litigation and the utter dissonance of the *differend*.

Communication, moored between its two poles of speaking and listening, sediments and invents truths. Such a view does not offer up truth as an ultimate ground of justification that is marginalising in its litigious comportments, but seeks the intensification of conversation across the spectrum of cultures which alone can generate an ethics of demarginalisation and as a consequence can fabricate the plane space of cultural autonomy in which to situate the multicultural. Truth emerges from the vortex of heterogeneous discourses not to justify and privilege, but as a framework of new ways of seeing, interpreting and articulating the world.

Now the discussion may be focused on the specific issue of translation. It ought to be noted, however, that what needs to be said about translation is already implicit in the earlier remarks. The task is to profile the ideas explicitly. Translation serves the function of rendering commensurate the apparently incommensurable. Translation, in other words, encodes in language the clearing between cultures where discourses come together. Put more forcefully, translation as a category is a constituting figure of the clearing between cultures that makes the plane space of the multicultural possible.

The ethical view of translation that is being defined here is to be kept separate from what may be called, following Said, the orientalist account (Said 1978). The orientalist conception, extending Said's argument concerning the intrinsically hegemonic nature of orientalism, takes the object (a text, a culture) to be a slave of the master language into which it is being translated. Such a model seeks a criteriological ground in order to structure the master–slave relation. This ground is provided in the structural design of the master-narrative that is universalised across all cultural expressions.

At this juncture, one may recall the Hegelian *Aufhebung* of the Germanic ethos that is used as a sceptre to cast judgements on preceding histories and pagan cultures. Hegel's project, philosophically cast, is the supreme example of the orientalist vision. The possibility of an ethics of translation, however, jettisons the mystery of any one narrative/culture and gains nourishment from the space that *plainly* connects the relevant discursive poles. In other words, the ethical view of translation, in contrast to the orientalist conception, does not violate the condition of cultural autonomy which as noted earlier is the requisite feature of the multicultural.

Walter Benjamin, in his brilliant meditation on the task of the translator, anticipates some of the present concerns of theorising an ethics of translation in the opening between cultural grids when he observes that:

> translation...ultimately serves the purpose of expressing the central reciprocal relationship between languages. It cannot possibly reveal or establish this hidden relationship itself; but it can represent it by realizing it in embryonic or intensive form.[3]

Given the present purposes, we are not commenting on Benjamin's more provocative claim that translation retrieves a pure language of truth that can mediate across all possible discourses. Rather, extending the essentials of Benjamin's remarks, languages emerge not as isolated systems defined by the rules of their own cultural game, but as markers for the interpenetration of cultural forms. This interpenetration occurs in the clearing between cultures, thus ruling out the possibility of hegemenonising acts of translation. Translation calls for the *showing* of the clearing into which cultures open up. As Ludwig Wittgenstein (1978: 26) put it: 'Propositions *show* the logical form of reality. They display it'.

The multicultural that is scaffolded by the ethics of translation markedly differs from what Aziz Al-Azmeh has called 'ideological processes that oversee the constitution of specific identities under specific conditions of socio-economic confinement, buttressed by what is known, in the "host" society, as multiculturalism',

(Al-Azmeh 1996: 5). This view of the multicultural, privileging the figure of identity, effects a strange—and impossible—task: the accepting of the Orientalist/Hegelian differentialist strategy of constructing artificial identities out of polymorphous entities in order to name cultures, and the attempt to render smooth this hierarchical space of Hegel to combat the exclusivistic and marginalising comportments of modernity. It has already been noted that the singular move of rendering plane the curvature of hierarchy cannot eschew marginalisation.

The multicultural that incorporates the ethical primacy of translation does not view a culture as a closed identity, but claims that, in the textures of its uncertainty, a culture is always transparent in virtue of what has been called earlier the logic of reception. The task of translation is to illuminate this transparency, and the possibility of this task hinges upon the view that a culture is neither a free-floating closed identity nor is it an entry in a normatively ordered continuum of cultural configurations. In other words, the ethics of translation positions the multicultural between the polarities of modernity and postmodernity. Translation as a mediating movement between cultural edifices, inscribing the openness of the opening between the heteroglossic frames of cultures, does not found a transhistorical ground of criteria, and is yet able to deliver a source for ethics, and by extension, a politics.

Dismantling the architecture of analytic philosophy with his pointed attacks on foundational thought, Richard Rorty in no uncertain language registers the importance of an ethics of conversation. Rorty's claims concerning such an ethics, in spite of being marked by a vague swaying between the 'conversation of mankind', invoke the powerful idea nonetheless that in the wake of the demise of foundations, ethics has to be reconfigured in terms of the multivalent implications of language (Rorty 1979: 389–94):

> The only point on which I would insist is that philosophers' moral concern should be with continuing the conversation of the West, rather than with insisting upon a place for the traditional problems of modern philosophy within that conversation.

Translation viewed as delivering the ethical source for the multicultural invests heavily in this intuition.

A distinction may be drawn here between two sorts of marginalisations—the marginalisation of a culture that makes possible the constitution of a master culture and the marginalisation of the voice of a culture. The ethics of translation places its accents on the latter, but has clear ramifications for the former. The relation between the two types of marginalisations is not a logical connection, that is, it is possible that allowing all cultural voices to speak can still define a world in which there is one dominating culture. It may be submitted, however, that the allowing of all voices to speak and to be heard practically (not theoretically) diminishes the chances of totalisation that so worries the postmodern critic.

The present formulation of the multicultural, however, minimises the possibility of the relativity-driven dissensus valorised by Lyotard because the ontology of translation spreading over the opening between cultures plots out points of unities across fields of difference. These unities are not to be confused with the totalising unity of modernity because the translating process as an ethical figure is non-reductionistic, that is, it does not conceive of an original unity, formal (Kant) or content-filled (Hegel), or of all unities, but seeks to disclose the play of unities as they form, shatter and re-form in the making of history. The continuous deployment of the force of translation will resist the structures of dominations and marginalisations that neither modernity nor postmodernity can effect. It is in this sense that the making of a translation is both an ethical and a political event.

Finally, the issue of history needs to be revisited. At the outset of this essay, the following claim was made: translation will emerge as a moral category in a philosophy of history that is constitutively multicultural. History is a vortex out of which unities emerge and into which they dissolve. These movements in the present account do not follow the rigour of dialectical necessity but are contingent happenings in the field of difference. The appearance of these unities, temporally ephemeral though they may be, gives being to the clearing, the shared awning, between voices and cultures. The continuous profiling of the changing contours of this clearing is important to service the cause of demarginalisation. Given, however, that the unities that inhabit the clearing are not temporally fixed but historically mutating, translation, in disclosing the plays of these unities, becomes a moral category in a philosophy of history that attempts to secure the multicultural between the modern and the postmodern. The ethics of translation resonates with the meaning of Friedrich Schlegel's contention: 'Just as there is a geography and a description of the universe, there should also be a translation of it'.

Notes

1. See Hegel (1977: 480–93) for an account of the termination of Spirit's movement.
2. Habermas in his debates with postmodern theorists has been arguing this point for some time. See Habermas 1983; also see Habermas 1981. For remarks on the Habermas-Lyotard debate, see Rorty 1984.
3. See 'The Task of the Translator' in Benjamin 1968: 72.

References

Al-Azmeh, Aziz, 1996. *Islams and Modernities*. London.
Benjamin, Walter, 1968. *Illuminations*. New York.
Deleuze, Gilles, and **Guattari, Felix,** 1988. *A Thousand Plateaus*. Minneapolis.
Habermas, J., 1981. 'Modernity Versus Postmodernity'. *New German Critique*, vol. 22, pp. 3–14.
———, 1983. 'Modernity—An incomplete Project'. *The Anti Aesthetic*, pp. 3–15.
Hegel, G.W.F., 1956. *The Philosophy of History*. New York.
———, 1977. *Phenomenology of Spirit*. Oxford.
Lyotard, J.F., 1988. *The Differend*. Minneapolis.
———, 1993. *The Postmodern Condition*. Minneapolis.
Rorty, Richard, 1979. *Philosophy and the Mirror of Nature*. Princeton.
———, 1984. 'Habermas and Lyotard on Post-Modernity'. *Praxis International*, vol. 4, pp. 32–44.
Said, Edward, 1978. *Orientalism*. New York.
Schrag, Calvin, 1992. *The Resources of Rationality*. Bloomington.
Wittgenstein, Ludwig, 1978. *Tractus Logico-Philosophicus*. London.

Eighteen

Speech Acts: The Philosophy of Language and Translation[1]

RUKMINI BHAYA NAIR

Translation, I suggest, means trouble, in the sense of meaning$_{nn}$ or 'non-natural' meaning which, according to the philosopher Paul Grice, is implicated in sentences of the sort 'those clouds mean rain' or 'or those spots mean measles' (Grice 1989). No one, that is, would want to insist that the word 'clouds' *literally* means 'rain' or that the phrase 'those spots' is equivalent in meaning to 'measles'. Grice's point, rather, is that all speakers and hearers proceed on the assumption that ordinary language allows a bountiful degree of latitude in interpretation. Aphoristically, to learn to mean is to learn not to *be* mean.

In most language transactions, including monolingual ones, conversationalists do not insist on a strict, 'literal' semantics. They are quite prepared to accept, in the interests of easier, more efficient and, often, more exciting communication, that the 'mean' in utterances like 'translations mean trouble' may be substituted by 'imply' or 'suggest'. *Implied meaning*, or meaning$_{nn}$ as Grice prefers to call it, rather than formal meaning is, on this account, what conversationalists naturally deal in; it is what they are good at ferreting out. Interpretation, or the capacity to fathom implied meanings, thus lies at the heart of human communication.

My own contribution to what might be called the 'theory of translation' is to extend Grice's universalistic assumptions about human communication into the arena of translation, and more particularly into the troubled zone of (post) colonial translations where meanings are always embattled because political ideologies are rather obviously at stake. In this essay, I will discuss the basic notion of the speech act and its import within the philosophy of language. I will ask: how does the concept of the speech act help to clarify some of the problems of meaning$_{nn}$ or interpretation that arise when speakers and hearers communicate with each other through the special speech act of translation? The essay will also propose, for the first time in the literature, a set of formal speech-act 'felicity conditions' on translation.

Speech Acts

If we deal in natural language, we deal in ambiguity. Ambiguity, in turn, calls for interpretation—for an appeal to the notion of implied meaning or meaning$_{nn}$. Indeed, the phrase that heads this section is itself an illustration. 'Speech acts' is both a sentence that expresses the proposition that speaking constitutes a species of action, and a noun phrase which refers to some sort of linguistic object. Any competent speaker of English would recognise this ambiguity.

But which interpretation to choose? Why? When would one exercise one's linguistic right to opt out of the process of deciding on ambiguous meanings? Now, the standard answer to such questions about interpretative choices is: well, that depends on the context. Yet context is *prima facie* a confusing notion to invoke. Context, after all, refers to everything from the linguistic environment of an utterance, to the background information shared by speakers and hearers in a communicative situation, to the intentions and beliefs held by these speakers and hearers. How is it possible to formalise such a chaotic notion?

It is the distinction of speech act theory that it does attempt to show that there exists a grammar of context. Context *can* be formalised. In his classic *How To Do Things With Words* (1962), J.L. Austin first presented the seemingly simple idea that any natural language enabled its speakers to *perform actions through words*. Philosophers, said Austin, had over the years become obsessed with the problem of how one decided on the truth or falsity of a sentence. Yet, most sentences were neither true nor false. They were not designed as philosophical propositions at all. Rather they were meant to *do* things, to achieve a particular set of goals. For example, consider five sentences:

(a) Have you read *Gora*?
(b) I promise to give you my copy of *Gora* tomorrow.
(c) What a wonderful book *Gora* is!
(d) Please lend me your copy of *Gora*.
(e) *Gora* was written by Rabindranath Tagore.

Of these five sentences, only the last has a truth value. If (e) said, '*Gora* was written by Leo Tolstoy', it would be a false statement; as stated here, it is true. Sentences (a) to (d) however have nothing to do with truth or falsity. It would be absurd to categorise 'Have you read *Gora*?', for example, as 'true' or 'false' for this is just not the relevant parameter of communication. Instead, a user of English would see right away that (a) actually performs a question. Similarly, (a) performs a promise, (c) performs an exclamation and (d) performs a request. These speech acts constitute the basic building blocks of communication. With them, we can build bridges of any size or complexity between speakers and hearers.

The rather novel solution that Austin offered to the problem of analysing 'context', was that this diffuse notion could be pinned down and explained *linguistically*. That impossible question—what is 'context'?—could be answered very simply by laying down conditions for the performance of different classes of speech act. Later, systematising and extending Austin's work on speech acts, J.R. Searle (1969) laid down the contextual rules or 'felicity conditions' for the performance of five basic kinds of speech acts, across the spectrum of cultures.[3] These are:

(a) directives (including commands, requests and questions);
(b) commissives (including promises);

(c) exclamatives (including greetings, expressions of delight, surprise, anger, etc.);
(d) declaratives (including assertions of belief on the part of the speaker); and
(e) representatives (including the class of statements about the world).

How does a speaker-hearer distinguish between the classes of speech act (a)–(e) Searle's set of 'felicitity conditions' for the acts (a), (3) and (4) are reproduced as illustrations:

Types of Rule (Collectively known as 'Felicity Conditions')	*Types of Speech Act*		
	Request (Class: Directive)	Assert (Class: Declarative)	Thank (Class: Exclamative)
	Sample Sentence: Please read *Gora*.	Sample Sentence: I think you should read *Gora*.	Sample Sentence: Thanks for lending me *Gora*.
Propositional Content Condition	Future act A of Hearer H.	Any proposition P.	Past act A done by H.
Preparatory Condition	i. H is able to do A. Speaker S believes that H is able to do A.	i. S has evidence (reasons) for the truth of P.	i. A benefits S and S believes A benefits S.
	ii. It is not obvious to both S and H that H will do A in the normal course of events of his own accord.	ii. It is not obvious to both S and H that H knows (does not need to be reminded of etc.) P.	
Sincerity Condition	S wants H to do A.	S believes P.	S feels grateful or appreciative of A.
Essential Condition	Counts as an attempt to get H to do A.	Counts as an undertaking to the effect that P represents an actual state of affairs.	Counts as an expression of gratitude or appreciation.

Comments	The speech acts 'order' and 'command' have the additional preparatory rule that S must be in a position of authority over H. 'Command', however, probably does not have the pragmatic condition requiring non-obviousness. Furthermore, in both, the authority relationship infects the essential condition because the utterance counts as an attempt to get H to do A *in virtue of the authority of S over H.*	Unlike 'argue', the speech act 'assert' does not seem to be essentially tied to the attempt to convince. Thus, 'I am simply stating that P and not attempting to convince you' is acceptable but 'I am arguing that P but not attempting to convince you' sounds inconsistent.	Sincerity and essential rules overlap. Thanking is just an expression of gratitude in a way that, for example, promising is not just expressing an intention.

(Searle: 1969, pp. 66–67)

While this is not the forum for a detailed exposition of speech act theory, it should be obvious that the sort of theory advanced by Austin and Searle focuses on rules that systematically differentiate between the *beliefs, intentions* and *desires* appropriate for various classes of speech act. It is these rules, rather than the esoteric ability to specify truth conditions for sentences, that yield what one might call *an elementary grammar of context*. Bernard Harrison (1979) put the matter like this:

> It is widely accepted that the most plausible—perhaps the only possible—alternative to a truth-conditional theory of meaning is a theory couched in terms of the beliefs and intentions of speakers and hearers in specific, concrete contexts of communication…Theories of this kind fall into two main classes. On the one hand there are those, such as Austin's and Searle's which locate the distinguishing features of language as a species of intentional action in the fact that it is *rule-governed* and proceed

> to try and elucidate the rules in question. On the other hand, there are theories such as those of H.P. Grice, Jonathan Bennett or David Lewis, which endeavour to avoid any reference to an unanalysed notion of rule at a fundamental level by analysing such notions as rule and convention in terms of speakers' and hearers' *intentions* and *beliefs* (Harrison 1979: 165).

In this essay, I combine both approaches to pragmatic or contextual meaning mentioned by Harrison—the Austinian/Searlean and the Gricean—in order to try and illuminate certain dark areas within translation theory. One of the murkiest of these zones, as I've already mentioned, might be identified as 'context'. It is in order to disambiguate the notion of context in relation to translation that I am prompted to ask the questions: what are the felicity conditions that technically define 'context' in the speech act of translation? How does one recognize a felicitous translation? I begin my exploration of these questions by proposing a set of felicity conditions for translation.

Rules or Felicity Conditions	*Speech Act: Translation*
Propositional Content Condition	Any text (T) from language A reproduced in language B as an equivalent text (T1).
Preparatory Conditions	(1) The speaker (S) knows both languages A and B. (2) T actually exists as a text in language A prior to its restatement as an equivalent text T1 in language B. (3) It is not obvious to either S or the hearer (H) that T1 is already available in language B in the equivalent version that B is presenting it.
Sincerity Condition	S wants to present text T from language A as text T1 in language B and believes himself capable of rendering the equivalent version of T in A as T1 in B.

Essential Condition	Counts as an undertaking that T1 has been rendered as an equivalent version of T by S.
Comments	T is here understood as any fragment of a given natural language, written or spoken—a word, a sentence, a story, etc. Likewise, when I say 'S knows languages A and B' it is assumed that he knows these languages *adequately* for the purpose at hand—which in this case is translation. I've also kept to the terminology of speech act theory in referring to the person who performs the speech act of translation as the speaker S, and to his/her audience as a hearer H, although it is conceded that much translation involves written texts. Furthermore, in order to keep things as simple as possible, I restrict myself to a consideration of standard natural languages (such as Bengali or English) and do not take account of either artificial languages or of dialectal paraphrase. However, I should imagine that the conditions outlined here should hold, with minor changes for translations in these areas as well. Finally, it should be noted that translation resembles in many respects the allied speech acts of quotation and paraphrase and a more extended treatment would certainly consider these similarities.

Learning how to communicate is learning to master and internalise felicity conditions for the performance of speech acts such as translation. In keeping with the general spirit of Austinian and Gricean theories of communication, the rules I've suggested here for the speech act of translation are also meant to be universal—that is, they should apply *across* cultures. Any further and more complex interpretative moves will depend on first having access to these basic rules.

It goes without saying, however, that anyone who goes about setting up 'universalistic' rules of this kind is quite likely to have one's whole enterprise challenged and, maybe, shot down. What earthly use, an interlocutor might well demand, are these rather technical speech act rules to practical translators? And why do you call them universal? What about the cultural specificity of context? Is this not likely to get lost in the sort of schematic analysis you suggest?

To my mind, objections of this kind are legitimate. In the rest of this essay, I shall therefore do my best to demonstrate the relevance of the speech act rules that I have framed to the practical dilemmas faced by translators (including myself!). I shall also attempt to show that the ideological positions adopted by individual translators such as Sujit Mukherjee and Tejaswini Niranjana actually derive from their intuitive knowledge of speech act rules on translation and to their apprehensions about the consequences that would result if these rules were in fact broken or 'violated'. Before that, however, in the very next section, I discuss the standard 'mimetic' model that most translators operate with and its relation to 'violations' of the speech act conditions that I've just mentioned.

Mimesis and the Marksman

For a very long time, translation studies have relied on an engagingly simple model of translation which looks a bit like this:

SOURCE LANGUAGE	→	TARGET LANGUAGE
(original text)	(translator as marksman)	(transmitted text)

What this metaphor tells us, in effect, is that the translator 'shoots' from a territorial base in the source language—his bullet or arrow being the text—while the impact of his shot is felt in the zone of another language. Translation thus exemplifies the wound, the mark, left on the surfaces or even the innards of another language by the translator as marksman, who can subsequently be evaluated in terms of how accurately he manages to hit his 'target'. However, such a description leaves the notion of the 'target' and the criterion by which a 'good' marksman is to be judged relatively unanalysed. How might a translator score a bullseye?

It is precisely in order to answer this large question that the notion of speech act rules or 'felicity conditions' has been invoked in this essay. These rules are supposed to specify the circumstances under which a speech act is felicitously or acceptably performed. So what happens if these rules are broken? As an illustration, I will briefly consider the preparatory conditions on the speech act of translation.

Preparatory Condition (1) simply states: 'S knows both languages A and B'. There are four logical possibilities here: S knows both languages (adequately); S knows A but not B; S knows B but not A; S knows neither language. Apart from the first possibility, notice that some of the bitterest accusations against a translator (S) can stem from the perception or judgement among audiences or hearers (H) that S does not know one or the other or, in extreme cases, both the languages in question. This is the charge of *linguistic ignorance* and it derives directly form the charge that Preparatory Condition (1) has been violated.

Nor are violations of Preparatory Condition (1) as rare as one might imagine, especially in India where 'language quacks' proliferate—for example, godmen claiming an extensive knowledge of Sanskrit and producing cartloads of false etymologies and translations. Since Sanskrit is no longer a 'living' language, and yet continues to possess great cultural caché, there is great scope for 'translation abuse' or deliberate violence by the translator as marksman here. References to similar 'howlers' produced through an inadequate knowledge of the languages in question are widely documented in the 'secular' arena as well. Here, for example, is Jawaharlal Nehru in a letter to Indira Gandhi on the Hindi translation of his *Glimpses of World History*:

> I am inclined to agree with the U.P. boys about the Hindi translation of the *Glimpses*. There are some very obvious howlers in

> it...I hesitate to interfere as I am no scholar of Hindi. (Letter from Almora Jail, 4 April, 1935.)

Unlike Nehru who hesitates to interfere because he is 'no scholar of Hindi', it is important for any present-day guild or community of translators to discuss instances of violations of Preparatory Condition (1). I will return to a discussion of this condition in a later section, but move on now to a brief commentary on violations of the other two preparatory conditions.

Preparatory Condition (2) says that: T actually exists as a text in language A prior to its restatement as an equivalent text T in language B. Suppose, however, that I just make up a text in English (T1) corresponding to an alleged prior text in Hindi (T), this would not count as a translation, however 'creative' my production is. Many debates in translation theory centre on the question of how much latitude a translator can have and how much s/he can 'transcreate'. Yet all these debates assume that there *is* an original text T that has to mimed or recreated. Thus creativity in translation is typically indexed as *departure from an original*. That is, to return to our model metaphor, it is measured in terms of the distance travelled by the translator's arrow between a source text and a target text. What Preparatory Condition (2) makes clear is that if there is no evidence of an original text T, then we cannot have a felicitous translation, no matter how exquisite the object T1 created by the 'translator'.

Violation of Preparatory Condition (2) would result in a charge of *textual forgery* being levelled against the translator. An example from India's colonial history will illustrate. William Jones was, as is well known, interested in the ancient texts of India, and especially in the Ashokan Brahmi inscriptions which had not yet been deciphered. A copy of these inscriptions was accordingly sent to a Lieutenant Francis Wilford, based in Varanasi (then, Benares) who subsequently announced in 1793 that:

> ...after many fruitless attempts on our part, we were so fortunate as to find at last an ancient sage who gave us the key and produced a book in Sanskrit, containing a great many ancient alphabets formerly in use in different parts of India. This was really a fortunate discovery...

John Keay (1981), who reports on this incident and analyses it at length, remarks:

> According to the ancient sage, most of Wilford's inscriptions related to the wanderings of the five heroic Pandava brothers from the *Mahabharata*... The sage just happened to have the code-book; obligingly he transcribed them into Devanagari Sanskrit and then translated them...Poor Wilford was the laughing stock of the Benares Brahmins for a whole decade. They had already fobbed him off with Sanskrit texts later proved spurious on the source of the Nile and the origin of Mecca. After the code book, there was a geographical treatise on the Sacred Isle of the West which included early Hindu references to the British isles. The Brahmins, to whom Sanskrit has so long remained a sacred prerogative, were getting their own back. One wonders how much Wilford paid his ancient sage. (Keay 1981)

Despite the fact that the manuscripts proffered by Wilford's 'ancient sage' did exist as prior texts T written perhaps by the sage himself, who also undoubtedly displayed a rather radical 'creativity' in translating them, they was still not *texts T in language A*, as required by Preparatory Condition ii) and therefore could not have mimetic equivalents T1 in language B which was in this case, 'Devanagari' Sankrit.

If we return to the notion of 'context' for a moment here, it now becomes clear that this apparently a-historic preparatory condition suggested by me logically requires the *historical embedding* of a text T within the context of a pre-existing language A. Indeed, as Keay points out, 'selling' forged 'translations' was in this case to be understood a mode of subversion against colonial appropriation by the 18th century Brahmins of Varanasi. It is my contention that such resistance was achieved precisely through a violation of Preparatory Condition ii). As with Preparatory Condition i), I shall therefore return to Preparatory Condition ii) for a second round of analysis, but, for now, the third and last preparatory condition claims our attention.

According to Preparatory Condition iii), it is not obvious to either S or H that T1 is already available in language B in the equivalent version that H is presenting it. As far as this preparatory condition is concerned, we should begin by attending to the qualification 'already available'. It will be recalled that people often object to a 'new' translation of, say, a classic like *Gora*, by pointing out that a perfectly adequate translation is already at hand. Why, then, produce a fresh translation, for would that not be a waste of time and energy? Sometimes a translator may in fact be discouraged from producing a new translation, but he may also choose to argue that his translation is different enough from existing translations to warrant consideration as another 'equivalent' version. Now this leads us to a piquant contradiction.

On the one hand, the notion of equivalence, which *ceteris paribus* we are bound to treat as 'perfect' equivalence, seems to assume that text T1 in language B will mimic as perfectly or exactly as possible the properties of text T in language A; on the other hand, the idea that there can be several 'equivalent' versions in language B is predicated on the acceptance of difference. That is, if we subscribe to the idea of (perfect) equivalence, this would dictate that all the texts T1 $\ldots_n$ in language B should *converge* towards one perfect, or most exact, version. Yet, translators of 'new' versions of texts usually defend their versions of texts on the basis of *divergence*. In other words, they claim their versions can compete with existing versions because they are significantly different. What Preparatory Condition iii) brings out is that there is *a logic to this inherently contradictory position adopted by translators*. For, consider the consequences for the translator if this condition were to be violated.

If a translator S ignores the condition that there is already available a text T1 in the equivalent version that S is presenting it, what s/he would in effect be doing is producing a *copy* of an existent text T1 in language B. Such a move would then surely subject S to the charge of *translation plagiarism*. That is, in translation making a copy from an 'original' is encouraged, but making a Platonic 'copy of a copy' is, so to speak, considered an act of bad faith. The controversy which erupted not too long ago when a well-known Western scholar simply lifted or copied A.K. Ramanujan's (1973) distinctive translations of Tamil Bhakti poetry in *Speaking of Siva* offers an apt example from the ongoing history of translation in our own context, which demonstrates that translation plagiarism is a common enough violation of Preparatory Condition iii).

Thus, I hope I have shown in this section that violations of the three preparatory conditions that I have suggested on the speech act of translation each results in major charges against translators, namely, linguistic ignorance, textual forgery and translation plagiarism.

Moreover, these three charges seem to me typical of the way in which speech act theory in general functions. Because this sort of theory deals with *speakers' intentions* and *hearers' interpretations*, it has perforce to treat the translator as a 'morally' responsible agent. The charges, for instance, do not merely point out flaws in a translated text as any purely textual theory might do. Rather, even as they emanate from a formal model of 'contextuality', they ultimately lay the onus on the translator for any violations of his speech act. Speech act violations, that is, are simultaneous indicators of 'trouble' both with the text *and* for the translator. That is the strength of speech act theory.

In the sections that follow, I consider some actual instances of translation and develop further the theme of the 'responsibility/responsiveness' of the translator in relation to three fundamental aspects of speech act theory that I have already mentioned. These comprise (a) meaning$_{nn}$ and context, (b) intentionality and ideology and (c) theoretical positioning.

Meaning$_{NN}$ and Context

It was my initial argument that a subscript of Gricean non-natural meaning always attaches to the speech act of translation since it invariably signals the disruption of the patterns in one language through the intervention of another. I also suggested that this process of 'trouble-making' becomes even more painfully obvious in historical situations that involve a post-colonial re-reading of colonial texts. Translation as a speech act, I held, signals that a speaker-hearer is straightaway confronted with problems of ambiguity or interpretation. The violations of speech act conditions on translation that I examined in the last section then elaborated on this theme of interpretive 'trouble'.

Grice however would probably disagree with me on any special status for translation. He would insist that there is nothing particularly mystical, or even political, about the process of translation.

It is simply part of a *continuum of interpretative strategies* to which all users of language are acclimatised whenever they engage in conversation. In communicative situations, those clouds *always* mean rain. The skies are never absolutely clear when it comes to discerning meanings. This is so because every conversation takes place under conditions of what one might call 'radical uncertainty', but only in the very mundane sense that other minds are to us irredeemably opaque.

For, it is apparent that mental opacity is just an arbitrary physical constraint. Biology could have decreed otherwise. It is quite easy to imagine ourselves, in a sort of Swiftian fashion, as having been constructed so as to carry transparent panels on our chests or foreheads which recorded our thoughts; in which case, there would neither be the need to communicate nor to translate. Under such conditions, neither might the capacity to tell lies and to use language to deliberately mislead—that finely honed and uniquely human activity—have developed in us. Naturally, our intellectual worlds would have looked very different in this counterfactual universe. As it happens, though, humans seem to belong a species of being who can never know *for certain*, although they can make extremely skilled suppositions about, whether the words and sentences of another speaker match up precisely with the meanings and/or intentions attributed to them.

Translation does no more than simply foreground this general human *engagement with crisis* in everyday life. We inhabit relativistic universes in a material, physical way, just as Noam Chomsky's innate 'language organ' belongs within the human mind in a material, physical way. Exactly from such materiality spring our epistemic difficulties.

Biology, history, culture—all thesc 'realities' together form the complex imaginative worlds that we mentally inhabit; they make up the 'web of belief' from which the human intellect can never, in effect, free itself. This, indeed, is the principle reason why 'the indeterminacy of translation' continues to be a problem which returns to haunt philosophers and linguists such as Wittgenstein, Quine, Sapir, Whorf and Davidson even in this pragmatic century.

Ergo, taking an ostrich-like attitude to what philosophers, with a simplicity both deceptive and disarming, refer to as 'the translation problem' will not yield results. Indeed, to drastically change my metaphor at this point, the discerning reader will notice that a translation 'toggle switch' unavoidably operates, so to speak, between the two 'languages' of philosophy and literature in this very essay, monolingual as it purports to be. As I move on now to some of the more literary segments of the essay, there is quite apparently an abrupt change of tone. It is as if the imaginary readership I am addressing has subtly changed. The word 'context' itself is perhaps understood by this literary readership in a very different manner from the way in which philosophers might interpret it in terms of speech acts or other such formal categories. My translations of a dozen 'real' little linguistic universes in English cast up in as bubbles from an originary moment when an anonymous anti-colonial quatrain was composed in Bengal during World War II, should serve as illustration.

Bengali original:	**Grammatico-literal version:**
sa re ga ma pa dha ni bomb pheleche japani bomber modde keute shap british bole—bap re bap!	do re mi fa so la ti bomb—have thrown—Japanese bomb (+ possessive case)— inside—snake British say—exclamation!
English versions:	**Comment:**
1. Do re mi fa so la ti Bomb dropped by Japanese Inside bomb a keute snake British say—father oh father!	'Bad' literal translation. Parodic 'Indian English', e.g., articles dropped. 'keute' left untranslated.
2. Do re mi fa so la ti A bomb dropped the Japanese In this bomb a *keute* snake The British go—pop, oh, pop!	Still horribly literal. 'keute' remains opaque. Articles put in, but 'pop, oh, pop!' sounds unidiomatic, awful.
3. Do re mi fa so la ti A bomb thrown by the Japanese The bomb contains a deadly krait Oh my God! the British said.	Move away from literalism. Verbs changed. 'keute' translated as 'krait'. Attempt at rhyme.
4. Do re mi fa so la ti A bomb hurled by the Japanese In that bomb a deadly cobra Help! Help! the British blubber.	Rhyme maintained, but what if an 'exact' translation equivalent in semantic terms is just unavailable if the rhyme is to be maintained?

5. Do re mi fa—di do dum! The Japanese have dropped a bomb! Inside that bomb a snake so vicious Yell the Britishers: Goodness gracious!	Change of tune to Latin parsing mid-sentence. Plenty of cultural knowledge needed. Cross-culturally impermissible move?
6. Do re mi fa so la ti Bombs dropped by Japanese Within the bombs, some snakes are hid Oh! we've been bit! exclaim the Brits.	Grammar: is Bengali 'bomb' singular or plural? Can the form be legtimately pluralised? And how much can one play around with the exclamative 'bap re bap'?
7. Do re mi fa so la ti! A bombing by the Japanese! Their bombs release a deadly venom Holy snakes! the Brits have gone 'ome.	What about the use of the gerund form 'bombing' instead of the nominal 'bomb'? Maintenance of rhyme now taking precedence over 'sense-making'?
8. Do re mi fa so la ti Japanese bombs have hit the city! Deadly snakes within these bombs Good grief! how the British jump	Too much licence? E.g., *bap re bap* has been eliminated and replaced by other exclamatives and the agency shifts from the people to the bombs.
9. Do re mi fa so la ti The Jap, he is a Bombardee In his bombs, snakes there be The Brit is brought down to his knee.	Does the use of the singular male gender for the collective Bangla noun 'Japani' introduce ideological changes? What about the wonky intertextual shades of Gibert and Sullivan here?
10. Do re mi fa so la ti A bomb dropped by the Japanese Inside the bomb, a cobra snake! The British do a double-take!	Quote marks removed. The British thereby 'robbed of voice'? Can hegemonic forces be so robbed? Is 'double-take' too 'foreignising' a translation?
11. do re mi fa so la ti the jap chaps hurl a bomb—he! he! a krait inside the bomb—oh god! the brits are praying—save me, lord!	Shortening of Japanese to Japs, reminiscent of 'chaps'. The opposite case of 10—of too domesticating a translation? The orthography, miming Bengali, is presented here without capitals.

12. SA RE GA MA PA DHA NI A BOMB thrown by the JAPANI Inside the BOMB a COBRA SNAKE OMIGOD!—the BRITISH quake.	Retention of 'original' jingle. Extensive use of capitals. Back to the question—how much to leave opaque in a translation?

Here's translation at work. So how would one go about evaluating these multi-verses of language thrown up by processes of translation? The answer, I perversely suggest, is to appeal to the first felicity condition on translation, namely, the Propositional Content Condition, but some historical detail, so important in literature and the social sciences, if not in philosophy, needs to be filled in first.

The four lines of early 20th-century doggerel in Bengali that constitute the subject of discussion here embody as well as encapsulate the property of boundedness that every human idiolect is subject to, as it continually nudges and bumps against others within the robotic space of culture. Literary and non-literary, written and oral, canonical and marginal, humorous and serious, authored and anonymous, coloniser and colonised—various cultural typologies confront each other within the concentrated space of this verse, which is why this quatrain seem to me almost a metaphor for the intermediate, and intermediating, position of translation itself.

Basic questions about what gets translated, and why, arise when one grapples with this sort of 'throwaway' poetry, because like much casual talk, like ordinary conversation, it can be thought of as *both* ephemera, not to be preserved, *and* as a fundamental structure which exhibits the human ability to circumvent and survive the basic crises of communication inherent in all acts of linguistic performance. In short, literature and language come together here in a way that could be of intrinsic interest to philosophers.

In these translations is preserved the flotsam and jetsam, that casual but pervasive and persistent litter that is a vital mark of cultural activity. As surely as any fragment of high literature from Rabindranath Tagore or Bankimchandra Chatterji, here are the shreds of history, preserving memories of trauma and of war. The unholy glee these verses express at the discomfiture of the British sums up a whole episode in the history of anti-colonial resistance.

Unsurprisingly, that history is somewhat specific to Bengal and to the contribution made by Subhash Chandra Bose to a peculiarly Bengali consciousness. These verses record a time when Bose's Indian National Army chose to ally with the Germans and Japanese against the express wishes of Gandhi and the Congress party who had extended their 'support' to the British to counter Hitler's forces during World War II. Bose's political position obviously stood in sharp opposition to the ideology of pacifist resistance developed by Gandhi and signalled one of the grand rifts in the vocabulary of struggle against colonial power. However, the purpose of this essay is not to decode that well-documented inner conflict within anti-colonial thought in India, but simply to assert that it is against this background of grand national narrative that the tenuous yet hardy weed-like capacity of doggerel to survive in memory should be evaluated. Herein may lie the value of recovering in the net of translation such still circulating cultural 'junk'.

It is at this point that we may call to mind once again my Propositional Content Condition, which defines the speech act of translation as: Any text T from Language A reproduced in language B as an equivalent text T1. If this deadpan definition is to help us to choose between the various versions of doggerel we have, I believe, to concentrate on the phrases 'any text T' and 'equivalent text'.

Discussions of synonymy or linguistic equivalence, across languages, as we know, continue to distract all translators even though studies in historical linguistics and language acquisition, not to mention numerous arguments concerning the indeterminacy of translations presented by philosophers, have made it painfully clear that perfect synonymy is impossible.[4] Nevertheless, it remains a kind of translators' holy grail.

Now, one way to cut the Gordian knot and analyse how the notion of a (perfectly) 'equivalent text' functions in context, I suggest, is to begin by theoretically distinguishing between being *bilingual* and being truly *biliterate*. Biliterateness requires a knowledge of the literary resonances in a culture, of which the natural bilingual might be innocent. The biliterate's access to literary memory includes knowledge of a range of genres and repertoires. As this is a specialist and trained memory, it can enable a reassessment of the significance of the some very durable 'flotsam-jetsam' lodged within a culture. For example, compare the similar but far better known example of doggerel verse in the common English children's rhymes:

(1) Ring a ring of roses
A pocket full of posies
Hush a, hush a
All fall down!

(2) Remember, remember.
The Fifth of November
For gunpowder
Treason and plot!

In these instances, a biliterate translator would know what a child or an innocent bilingual may not, namely, that the first of these nursery rhymes commemorates the plague, or Black Death, in medieval England while the second records the incendiary nature of Guy Fawke's assault on the English parliament, just as my verses recall the Japanese bombing of Pearl Harbour. My point is that historically informed or biliterate translators would be in the best position to judge whether such apparently 'trivial' material should at all be translated in the first place. Supposing their task was to translate nursery rhymes from English into Bengali, they might actually *choose* to translate 'Ring a ring of roses' or Guy Fawkes rather than other more innocuous rhymes because they would appreciate that 'equivalence' is not to be understood merely in linguistic terms but in terms also of a significant transfer of *historical context* from one language to another. After all, anybody can translate the actual words and syntax, the 'literal' meaning, of a nursery rhyme. Linguistic difficulty therefore cannot be the key to the speech act chamber of propositional content here. The key is contextual knowledge. Biliterate translators, possessing such knowledge, should be able to *mediate*, as any good Gricean conversationalist would, between the notions 'any text T' and 'an equivalent text T1'. That is, they would be capable of picking out with confidence *some* texts out of a set that includes 'any text' in language A as rich in translational possibilities because they would know that these particular texts carried long-term cultural memories.

Choices about best translation/best meaning require in my view such a thoroughly biliterate awareness, which is sophisticated enough to replace the phrase '*any* text T' in my Propositional Content Condition with '*some* text T' and the requirement of '*an* equivalent text T1' with 'equivalent *texts* T1'. Texts such as these, which would not necessarily be the most obvious ones from 'high' canonical literature, would be the texts most capable of creating *many equivalences*, not just one, in the mind of a reader—a sort of semantic carnival. In the fairground or *mela* that is translation in India, the search should now be not merely for bilingual but for biliterate translators who can create interpretative multivalence for readers/hearers out of strict propositional equivalence.

Intentionality and Ideology

Where are such biliterate magicians to be found? Why are they, by and large, conspicuous by their absence? In this section, I consider the matter of *textual presence/absence* and its relation to *intentionality*. Intentionality is, as I have already explained, a crucial concept in speech act theory because this sort of theory attempts to treat speakers as agents responsible for creating certain mental effects in their hearers and, vice versa, hearers as agents burdened with the constant 'moral' responsibility of interpreting the speakers' meanings, including implied meanings$_{nn}$. Intention is thus a very important element of 'context'.

Translation, however, obviously complicates any simple attribution of intention. As a philosopher like Derrida might agree, the Platonic fascination with the idea of the author as an absentee is complemented by the notion of the conversationalist who is always present, always alive. The translator, as I've contended in this essay, may be cast as that Gricean figure—the ubiquitous conversationalist. The rest, however, is a story of loss, of substantial loss of meanings$_{nn}$. For, in translation, it is not just the author, but the *text*, that is presumed missing. There is no body to do an autopsy on; instead, the reconstituted figure, the translated text gets up and speaks, and it is translator as *conversational mediator* who is dominant as the interpreter of this suddenly vitalised text.

In translation, the lone figure of the marksman is also the one who performs the rites of revival. That is why colonisation seems *prima facie* to offer a paradigmatic case of the violence inherent in translation. Conventionally, a utopian belief triggered by the concept of the animatedly conversational author is that a translated text enriches the resources of the culture to which it is brought. William Jones translating Kalidas' *Shakuntalam*, for example, sees himself as 'discovering' a cultural treasure trove that will, post-translation, prove a source of pleasure and profit for all native speakers of English. But far from being a marker of enrichment, we might ask whether a text translated from the language of the colonised to that of the coloniser in fact marks the site of a double absence? Not only is the author absent because the written form of his text does not conventionally require his presence but also, in the colonial context, the act of translation ensures that the author is a mere meaning$_{nn}$ subscript to the looming figure of the translator. It is the intentionality, the ideology, of the *translator*—a William Jones or a William Carey—that is foregrounded.

It is in this sense that it may be said that every translation, but especially translation in some historical contexts, carries one or more subtexts of loss—loss of verbal form, loss of historical and/or personal sensibility, and so forth. Plato's nightmare of grasping at the shadows of the 'real', for example, comes to life again even in my paltry attempts at translating four lines of colonial verse from Bengali to English because of its unavoidable yet uncapturable connection with family and local inheritance. For instance, the sense of subterranean rejoicing at the bombardment of a colonial power and the connotations of that temporal moment in the memories of my father and grandmother, who had first 'taught' me the verse in question could not be, and were not, felt by me as a translator. My time (the 1980's) was slightly dislocated from their time (the 1940's). Despite the fact that I culturally 'belonged' to the same milieu, emotional engagement with the verses in question proved temporally impossible. I could certainly mime *ad infinitum*—twelve times or twelve thousand—the *literary form* of the text (that which survives) but I could not quite revive the *feelings*, the *intentions*, it had presumably incorporated. Paradoxically, this poem resonated for me not at all because of it literary evocativeness, but because of its *historical allusiveness* (that which does not survive).

The implication of regarding a translation as an allegory of 'loss' therefore seems to me that it encourages us to read a translated 'text', in fact, ultimately, any text, as having once had an 'ideal meaning' and evoked 'real feelings' while at the same time forcing us to accept the brutal fact that the idea of the ideal is itself an artifact of language. Those spots always mean measles, or trouble or

Kuhnian 'communication breakdown'. In the world of conversation, or of translation, there seem to be few historical enclaves that have not been claimed, vandalised or taken before you arrived to do your bit.

Post-colonial sophistication notwithstanding, I am left, then, with Plato's ancient philosophical quandaries as they are brought out once more by the speech act of translation, but when I look around for help I find in fact that his themes have been considered in some detail by contemporary Indian theorists. In the next section, I therefore take the liberty of setting up two such theorists—Sujit Mukerjee (1981) and Tejaswini Niranjana (1992)[8]—as magisterial but opposing authorities on literary translation, occupying stereotypical roles—male, old fashioned and personal, versus female, new fangled and postmodernist. In spite of the unfairness of the move, though, I feel myself justified in 'translating' them here for where I had groped, they may illuminate.

Theoretical Positioning

My purpose in this section is to show that in fashioning their cogent ideological positions on translation, both Mukherjee and Niranjana are intuitively responding to the 'felicity conditions' on the speech act of translation that I have constructed above. Though their answers are often at odds, the important questions they raise are, as we shall see, founded on (1) The Propositional Content Condition, (2) Preparatory Conditions, (3) The Sincerity Condition and (4) The Essential Condition

To begin with, then, here is the Propositional Content Condition repeated. In its revised form it says: Some text T in language A reproduced as equivalent texts T1 …$_n$ in language B. In this formulation, the propositional content implies that:

1p. Every translator, but especially a biliterate one, has to admit the possibility of a multiplicity of other translations, with other ambitions, other forms, other meanings, attaching to the 'same' original text.

1q. The Translator's Question: Under these relativist conditions, can any 'best' translation be justified?

Mukherjee's Solutions in *Translation as Discovery* (1981)	Niranjana's Deconstructions in *Siting Translation* (1992)
1a. No, if we accept the importance of context in textual evaluation, a 'best' translation is very provisional, changeable.	1a. Yes, there are larger political/ethical imperatives that do enable us to make meta-judgements about a 'best' translation.
Message: Multiplicity implies freedom of choice in deciding on a suitable, rather than the 'best', translation.	Message: Multiplicity does not mean duplicity or that moral choice is impossible.

The Propositional Content Condition has already been discussed. Mukherjee's and Niranjana's sharply opposing answers can now be read against that background. I therefore press on to the Preparatory Conditions, which have also already been analysed and related to particular kinds of 'violation'.

From Preparatory Condition 1, 'S knows both languages A and B', for example, it logically follows that

2p. Every translator is, at least, bilingual

and

3p. Every 'literary translator' has to be an informed reader before s/he is a translator. This implies that s/he is likely to recognise certain genres as being more 'worthy' of translation than others.

From which assumptions then arise:

2q. The Translator's Questions: Is being bilingual sufficient qualification for performing the speech act of translation? Or is biliterateness a requirement? If so, is it qualitatively different from bilingualism?

and

3q. The Translator's Questions: Why would anyone ever want to translate sub-literary genres like doggerel? What bearing do issues like these have on the project of 'literary translation'?

Mukherjee	Niranjana
2a. No, bilingualism and biliteralism are not qualitatively different; they're a continuum. The 'true' bilingual *is* biliterate. Translation is 'New Writing' in the 'Other Tongue'.	2a. All post-colonial 'subjects' have been 'inscribed'. So they are *ipso facto* 'biliteralised' *even if* they aren't bilingual. Before post-colonial subjects translate, they need to think about the 'Ethnography of Translation'.
3a. Sub-literary genres such as Nair's may be translated in some cases because of immediate contextual demands (e.g. academic imperatives, publishing interests, etc.)	3a. Sub-literary genres should definitely be translated because the literary and the non-literary are not socially, culturally, politically, separable.
Message: Strict equivalence is unlikely because even if the linguistics of the languages concerned allowed synonymy, contextual demands keep changing radically. The charge of 'linguistic ignorance' proposed by Nair when Preparatory Condition i) is violated is an occupational hazard which all translators face, bilingual or biliterate.	Message: True equivalence is quite impossible, given the transformative effects of history on language. The charge of 'linguistic ignorance' is inevitable, given that the translator is a prisoner of history. However, the biliterate translator, schooled in translation ethnography, is likely to cope better with decisions about 'equivalence'.

It will be observed that, 'in responding' to the literary implications of Preparatory Condition i), Mukherjee and Niranjana both produce arguments *against* strict equivalence. Both come to the conclusion that there are good reasons why literary flotsam should be preserved, although their reasons for saying so are, once again, quite different. Consider now Preparatory Conditions ii) and iii).

Preparatory Condition ii) says that 'T exists in language A prior to its restatement as T1 in language B. In other words, the implication here is:

4p. Every translation T1 in language B has an 'original' or 'source' T in language A

and thus gives us

4q. The Translator's Question: Does it?

Preparatory Condition iii) says that 'It is not obvious to S and H that T1 exists or has been made available in language B in the form that S is now presenting it. Here, the implication is:

5p. Every translator S presenting a text T1 must maintain the fiction of the inaccessibility/opaqueness of its original T in language A.

5q. The Translator's Question: Why? If it does not, is the 'authority' of the translator liable to be undermined?

Mukherjee	Niranjana
4a. No, every translation need not have an original, especially if the author is also the translator (as in, for example Rabindranath Tagore's *Gitanjali*). This involves the notion of 'Translation as Perjury' and relates, as it were, to the 'morals' of a translator.	4a. The question is not directly addressed, but it is implicitly assumed that there *is* an original 'ground' to be 'contested', 'in all subsequent readings, including the translator's'. Translation is here presented, in every case, as an 'Act of Re-reading', which in turn, must be regarded in all cases as a 'political' act.
Message: If you are bad, bold and smart enough you can indeed 'create' a translation without an	Message: Whatever the 'original', it is always strategically changed in a re-reading. It is because

'original'. This privilege in general belongs, in my view, to authors as translators. Other have less 'authority'. The author is the first reader.

5a. No, it isn't necessary that the original is inaccessible. We live in a multilingual post-colonial society. Therefore, translations between the modern Indian languages, including English, can always be 'checked'. In fact, translations should, ideally, lead us *towards* the original, and even encourage the idea of our finally reading it in the 'original' language. This is what motivates my idea of 'Translation As Testimony'.

The 'absent original', so to speak, exists in a simultaneous space.

Message: If you are not as inspired as the author—in fact if you are not the author—then be as humble, self-effacing and faithful as you can. In practical terms, this means that you can leave phrases or passages that you cannot find equivalents for untranslated or in 'rough drafts'. After all, better translators than yourself are quite likely to come along.

translation is an act of reading that no author has 'authority' before s/he is is re-read/translated in a historical context.

5a. The original is virtually inaccessible in a society such as ours. To regain cultural 'control' over colonised texts, the subaltern must learn to read, write, speak, all over again. A translation in a post-colonial site might in fact lead us *away* from the original. We should recognise translation as a place or 'site' where the long-silenced subaltern can at last speak in some form and give her testimony.

The absent original has to be *brought* into existence.

Message: The political 'morality' of the translator should inform her translation. This is an imperative especially in post-colonial societies. You should not fear to leave portions of text untranslated, if your cultural interpretation of these has not yet emerged.

Finally, we come to the Sincerity and Essential Conditions on translation which I have not treated earlier in this essay. These conditions focus on the mental states (wants, desires, beliefs) appropriate to a speaker S who engages in the speech act of translation.

The 'Sincerity Condition', for example, states that 'S *wants* to present text T from language A as text T1 in language B and *believes* himself/herself capable of rendering the equivalent version of T in A as T1 in B. Such a language of intentionality must, however, logically entail that:

6p/a. The translator S may hold false beliefs about his capabilities.

6p/b. The translator S may want to present text T from language A as text T1 in language B, but may fail to satisfy the preparatory and other felicity conditions.

and

6p/c. Even if the translator's beliefs are warranted and his/her desire to translate backed up by the fulfilment of all other felicity conditions, s/he may find herself in an anomalous position. This is because every translator, and especially a literary translator, is, and must regard himself/herself as, both an 'author', i.e., a producer of a 'new' text T1 in the target language B, and a 'critic', i.e., an interpreter of an 'old' text T in the source language B.

The consequences of the Sincerity Condition lead to:

6q/a–c. The Translator's Questions: How damaging to the felicitous performance of the speech act of translation is the holding of false beliefs or unsatisfiable desires by S? What problems of Janus/Ganesa identity, memory, history, politics, intertext, are raised by the mediating, or even schizoid, position that a translator invariably occupies? And how knowledgeable must a translator be to reconcile his/her two roles of critic and author?

	Mukherjee		Niranjana
6a/a–b.	The most important component of a translator's mental make-up is his desire to translate. Even if he holds 'false beliefs' about his capabilities, the practical process of translating is likely to change those initial beliefs and make the translator more self-aware. So, holding false beliefs is not such a problem if a translator sincerely wants to translate a text. Since I believe that there is a continuum between bilingualism and biliterateness, a translator who is initially only bilingual can develop his capabilities and turn into a competent biliterate translator able to deliver satisfactory 'equivalences'.	6a/a–b.	A translator at different historical periods is likely to be burdened with different forms of 'false consciousness'. In a post-colonial society, the politically aware biliterate translator has to take on the task of showing how many colonial translations deliberately induced 'false' beliefs among reader/hearer communities. The meta-theories or political frameworks that we hold enable us to tackle the problem of possible false beliefs. The translator should critically examine not just her own beliefs, desires and motives but those of previous translators in other historical periods. This requires biliterateness in judging equivalences.
6a/c.	A translator should include as much information as possible about the 'original'	6a/c.	A translator should include as much information as possible about the subalternised

context of the of the text T in language A as possible—in notes, essays, commentaries, etc., accompanying the text. Since I hold that 'Translation is Discovery' the translator as reader constantly discovers 'new' things about the 'old' text when s/he translates, This is the point where the roles of the translator as a 'critic' in language A and an 'interpreter' in language B come together.

self, both of author *and* translator. This information should be presented as explicit socio-theoretical analysis rather than as simply biographical detail. Translation, ultimately, is a project in the recovery of a lost (precolonial) discourse. The translator does play a role as a critical interpreter but, as far as the 'authorial voice' is concerned, the translator should ideally seek to reinstate the lost or previously appropriated voice of the 'original' subaltern author.

Common Cause: Translation is a culturally indexed speech act; commentary, therefore, is part of the translator's task. A translation must always go 'beyond' the text T which is its source.

We now consider the Essential Condition which states: 'Counts as an undertaking that T1 in B has been rendered as an equivalent version of text T in A by the speaker S'.

This condition logically encompasses the possibility of even a felicitously performed speech act not 'counting as' that speech act for reasons beyond the control of the translator as S. In the other words, there is always the danger of:

7p. Even the most sincere undertaking or assurance to his/her audience H not helping a translator when s/he faces the challenge of generic/cultural/phrasal untranslatability. From which derive:

7q. The Translator's Questions: How potentially dangerous is the challenge to the translator S of such possible 'untranslatability'? Does not endemic 'untranslatability' logically and severely undermine a translator's 'undertaking' to provide readers/ hearers a satisfactory equivalent translation?

Mukherjee	Niranjana
7a. Untranslatability: Social facts, such as those widely observed on the Indian subcontinent, disprove this thesis. Bilinguals are 'natural' translators. The essence of 'translation' described by the Essential Condition depends on such social receptivity to translation.	7a. Untranslatability defines the subaltern. Translation as a means of recovery and resistance is therefore a political necessity, whether or not it comes 'naturally' to us. The essence of translation as a linguistic and social act is that it can provide readings 'against the grain' that are liberating.

Common Cause: Translation makes sense. It is a primary resource within cultures for the production of interpretive meaning or meaning$_{nn}$. Hence, as a performative speech act it is both socially necessary and desirable.

As is evident, Mukherjee and Niranjana take strong ideological stands in their putative responses to the questions raised by and through my 'felicity conditions', sometimes coming together to make common cause and often seriously disagreeing. And while this is the exactly the way that, in my view, an invigorating debate should proceed, it should also be apparent at this point is that I have all along been 'fictionalising' or interpreting or attributing meaning$_{nn}$ to these theorists here. It is not as if I sent them a questionnaire and they then responded. Rather, I have shamelessly extrapolated from their written work to my own concerns in this essay. But is this legitimate practice? I believe my procedure in setting up Mukherjee and Niranjana as 'conversationalists' in this essay is justifiable precisely in terms of the Gricean model of 'meaning interchange' that I have adopted. As academics who have each written a book on the subject of translation, Mukherjee and Niranjana are after all not so much 'doing' translation as 'talking about' it, expressing, that is, their theories of, and ideological positions on, the speech act of translation.

It is just such an expression of opinion that seems to me to relate philosophically to the matter of 'intentionality'—which, as the reader will recall, was one of the words that headed a previous section of this essay, the other being 'ideology'. Intentionality, in a famous philosophical formulation, *is* 'aboutness'. We don't, that is, simply have intentions; we have intentions *about* things, For example, one intends to write a book, or eat ice-cream at noon or propound the ideology of marxist-leninism. One doesn't just 'intend' in the abstract. In their case, Mukherjee and Niranjana expressly intend to discuss translation and it is just this intention to which I claim I have attended by including them as feisty discussants within the framework of my essay. Yet, the stubborn question remains: what, in the end, have I achieved by the exercise? Well, this is a query to be answered in the main by the readers of the essay, but in the brief concluding section that follows, I offer a summary of my own intentions.

Conclusion

Any theory of meaning is concerned with two primary relationships—the first is the words-to-words relationship and the second the words-to-world relationship. The first sort of relationship is in the domain of linguistic semantics proper; it deals with 'literal' or 'dictionary' meaning. The Austinian speech act theory and the Gricean theory of meaning$_{nn}$, or 'non-literal' meaning detailed in this essay focus, in contrast, on the second kind of relationship. That is why concepts such as 'context' and 'intentions about things in the world' are important aspects of these latter theories.

Constraints of space have prevented me from enlarging on other important notions such as the idea of indirect perlocutionary effects of speech acts on readers of translations or the Gricean ideas of specific maxims of conversation or relevance and preference rules. I remain convinced, however, that this set of ideas, on which I have written elsewhere,[5] can be rigorously developed further in relation to translation practice. To consider just one possible application, when Akshar Bharati, in this volume dwell on the need to train a human 'post-editor' to take over from where their machine translation leaves off, I feel that such a translator post-editor would benefit from exposure to the idea of felicity conditions and how to 'test' for a number of translation violations. This, to my mind, is just one of the practical spin-offs of attempting, as I have done, to formalise the unruly notion of 'context' in terms of step-by-step felticity conditions.

More generally, a persistent question from lovers of literature to philosophers has always been: why formalise at all? And my answer here is, briefly, that formalisation in the guise of speech act conditions, or in other forms, serves to clarify confusions and hence, is eventually likely to be of help even in the conduct of practical intellectual tasks. However, I should emphasise, in closing, that the purpose of this essay was not just to provide an exposition of speech act theory or even to set up original speech act 'felicity conditions' on translation. While I hope I have succeeded in showing how such conditions and their consequences for the cultivation of a 'biliterate awareness' can be worked out in a systematic fashion, this was not all I wanted to accomplish.

In putting forward the idea of cooperative conversation as a measure of 'meaning', Grice, I knew, was philosophically appealing to the idea that all language exchange is full of semantic mysteries, hints and allusions. Language, I heard Grice as saying, would fall apart at the seams if conversationalists did not volunteer each day to knit together again the web of meaning by using context as a sort of warp and weft and intentionality as a shuttle. Likewise, it seemed to me undeniable that professional critics have made it their particular trade to discern meanings within literary texts.

As part of a larger design, I therefore wished to pull together through the Gricean idea of a 'cooperative conversation' two very disparate discourses. Philosophical cogitation is typically 'dry' and does not concern itself overmuch with actual data or 'real' materials; its self-consciously 'a-political' task is to lay bare structure, to identify areas of intellectual 'trouble' and to clarify confusions. Consequently, it deals with attenuated sentences and tiny fragments of the lexicon. Literary criticism, on the contrary, revels in a rich expanse of texts and aligns comfortably with modes of historico-political analysis such as post-colonial theory.

My own meta-intention in this essay was, as I have earlier indicated, to try and bring these two apparently uncongenial modes of talk together, even if the process required a degree of violence. For, what better demonstration could there be of the 'troubles' inherent in the process of translation, or of the dislocation and cultural hooliganism that translation could often provoke? Indeed, it will have been noticed that I quite deliberately used the terminology of speech act 'violations' in discussing translation 'crimes' such as plagiarism or forgery. Not that these offences were unknown elsewhere but because of the classic problem of the Derridean 'double absence' of both the original text and author in translation, I saw this as an area of language transaction where the identification of culprits is significantly more fraught. Translation as an activity was full of linguistic loopholes, of subtle possibilities for foul play that could interest learned magistrates in the courts of both philosophy and literary criticism.

Speech act theory claimed to provide a 'just' set of rules that would arbitrate between felicitously performed and infelicitous translations. These rules sought to present, as it were, a sort of *felicity-ethics* of translation. Literary criticism, however, had traditionally dealt in aesthetics. Therefore, I asked myself whether a Niranjana or a Mukerjee could ever be co-opted into the same framework of conversation as a Grice or an Austin. Or did the disciplinary divisions run too deep? Were the premises, the goals, the discourse, of philosophical analysis and literary criticism inherently incompatible? These were the meta-questions about 'collaboration' between literary theorists and philosophers raised for me in thinking about translation as a speech act.

That is why I thought it useful to mimic and at the same time to defamiliarise the speech act of translation by reflecting briefly on my own role as 'translator' between the disciplinary 'languages' of philosophy and literary criticism. The text of this essay could in this sense be regarded as an illustration of any translator's difficult experience. Furthermore, the choice I made within my text to try my hand at actually translating in multiple post-colonial versions a marginal text that was yet historically resonant, could then perhaps be seen as a 'story within a story' or, rather, a 'translation within a translation'.

Treating translation as a formal speech act predicated on a knowledge of at least two languages and two sets of speakers brought out for me the truly logical nature of its complexity. Always calling up its mimic double, translation came packed with twin layers of both literal meaning and non-literal meanings$_{nn}$, cross-hatched and parti-coloured. It was thus of great potential interest to both philosophers of language and literary critics; and yet it did not appear to be central in the discourse of either. As I have emphasised, I see my own text as well as this book, in the end, as symbolising something of this ironically divided, indeterminate position that translation occupies by its own irrefutable logic—liminal but always a crux, absent yet present, speech as well as action, and a continuing challenge to the literary instincts of philosophers as much as to the philosophical urges of literary theorists.

Notes

1. This chapter has its genesis in the paper entitled 'Translation Troubles: Twelve Versions of One Verse' presented at the All India Symposium on Literary Translation, British Council, March–April, 1993.
2. The subscript 'nn' in Grice's term 'meaning$_{nn}$' stands for 'non-natural' or additional interpretative meanings which are not part of the literal meaning of an utterance.
3. See also Searle, et. al., (1980), Strawson (1964), Sperber and Wilson (1986) and Levinson (1983).
4. See Wittgenstein (1953). Also on linguistic relativism and 'untranslatability', see Quine (1960), Whorf (1956).
5. A significant part of my own work dwells on this alleged 'boundary of translation' between the logical and the emotional or the pragmatic and the sensual. See also Nair (1986, 1988, 1990a, 1990b, 1991a, 1992a, 1992b, 1992c, 1992d, 1992e, 1992f, 1993a, 1993b, 1995a, 1995b, 1995c, 1996a, 1997a, 1998b, 1999c, 2000c).

References

Austin, J.L., 1961 in J.O. Urmson and G.J. Warnock (eds) *Philosophical papers of J.L. Austin* and Austin J.L., 1962. *How to do Things with Words*, Oxford: Oxford University Press.

Davidson, D., 1985. 'On the Very Idea of a Conceptual Scheme' in *Inquiries into Truth and Interpretation*. Oxford: Oxford University Press.

Grice, H.P., 1989. *Studies in the Way of Words*. Cambridge, Mass: Harvard University Press.

Harrison, G.B., 1979. *An Introduction to the Philosophy of Language* London: Macmillan. London.

Keay, John., 1981. *India Discovered*. London: Windward Publications, W.H. Smith and Sons.

Levinson, S.C., 1983. *Pragmatics*. Cambridge: Cambridge University Press.

Mukherjee, S., 1981. *Translation as Discovery & Other Essays On Indian Literature in English Translation*. Delhi: Allied Publishers.

Nair, Rukmini, Bhaya, 1985. 'The Voyeur's View in Midnight's Children and Shame' *Bulletin of the Association of Commonwealth Language and Literature Studies*, Seventh Series, Vol. 1. pp. 57–75.

———, 1986. 'Telling Lies: Some Literary and other Violations of Grice's Maxim of Quality' in *Nottingham Linguistic Circular*, Vol. 14, Special Issue on Pragmatics.

———, 1988. 'Rewarding Risks: Clines of Metaphoricity' (with Ron Carter and Michael J. Toolan), *Journal of Literary Semantics*, pp. 20–40.

———, 1989. 'Text and Pre-text: History as Gossip in Rushdie's Novels' in *Economic and Political Weekly*, pp. 994–1000.

———, 1990a. 'Pre-linguistic Similarity and Post-linguistic Difference: Some Observations on Children's Conceptualization in a Cross-cultural Context', in A. Kwan-Terry (ed.) *Child Language Development in Singapore and Malaysia*. Singapore University Press, Singapore.

———, 1990b. 'Salman Rushdie: The Migrant in the Metropolis' (with Rimli Bhattacharya) in *The Third Text—Special Issue on the Rushdie Affair*. Summer. pp. 16–30.

———, 1991a. 'Expressing Doubt and Certainty: The Tag Question and the "to" particle in Indian Languages', in *Studies in the Language Sciences*, Oxford. December. pp. 207–227.

———, 1991b. 'Dissimilar Twins: Language and Literature', paper at the British Council Seminar on the *Teaching of English Literature*, Delhi, March 1990, published in R. Sundar Rajan (ed.) *The Lie of the Land: English Literary Studies in India*. Oxford University Press: Delhi.

———, 1991c. 'From Freud to Rushdie: Notes on the Interpretation of Dreams' in *Seminar*, Volume 348. pp. 32–36.

———, 1992a. 'Language and Linguistics in India', guest-edited, with an Introductory essay in *Seminar*, March. pp. 12–16.

———, 1992b. 'Monosyllabic English or Disyllabic Hindi: Language Acquisition in a Bilingual Child', in *The Indian Journal of Linguistics*. pp. 57–89.

Nair, Rukmini, Bhaya, 1992c. 'Gender, Genre and Generative Grammar: Deconstructing the Matrimonial Column' in M. Toolan (ed.) *Text and Context: Essays in Contextualised Stylistics*. Routledge: London.

———, 1992d. 'All About Searches', review article on *Theatre and the World: Essays on Performance and the Politics of Culture* by Rustom Bharucha and *Contingency, Irony and Solidarity* by Richard Rorty, in *The Book Review*, Volume 16(3).

———, 1992e. 'Smoke Signals', review of *Interpretation & Overinterpretation* by Umberto Eco with Richard Rorty, Jonathan Culler and Christine Brooke Rose, edited by Stefan Collini, in *The Times of India*, 2 August 1992.

———, 1992f. 'Now you See, Now you Don't', review of *Appearance and Reality: A Philosophical Investigation into Perception and Perceptual Qualities*, by P.M.S. Hacker, in *The Times of India*, 12 February 1992.

———, 1993a. 'What Makes Asia Tick?', review of *Sir William Jones: A Reader*, edited by Satya P. Pachori, in *The Hindu*, 2 May 1993.

———, 1993b. 'The Very Short Story and the Very Tall Tale: Towards an Inferential Model of Narrative Structure' in *Critical Spectrum: Responses to Contemporary Literary Theories*, B. Chandrika (ed.) Papyrus Press.

———, 1994. 'Out of Practice', review of *In Theory* by Aijaz Ahmad and *Indian Responses to Colonialism in the Nineteenth Century*, edited by A. Bhalla and S. Chandra, in *The Book Review*, Volume 18 (2–3). pp. 58–60.

———, 1995a. 'Why Does Rushdie Offend?' in *Seminar* Vol. 437, Annual Issue. pp. 103–109.

———, 1995b. 'The Pedigree of the White Stallion: Postcoloniality and Literary History', in *The Uses of Literary History* (ed. Marshall Brown), Duke University Press.

———, 1995c. 'The Sacred Thread of Theory', review of *Outside in the Teaching Machine* By Gayatri Chakraborty Spivak and *The Location of Culture* by Homi Bhabha, in *The Book Review* Volume 19 (12). pp. 25–26.

———, 1996. 'Heaney's Sense of History at Work and History's Sense of Heaney at Work', in *Literature Alive*, June. pp. 52–62.

———, 1997a. 'Acts of Agency and Acts of God: The Discourse of Disaster' in *Economic and Political Weekly*, March. pp. 535–542.

———, 1997b. 'The Excitement of India!' review of *Granta 57, India! The Golden Jubilee Issue*, edited by Ian Jack, in *The Pioneer*, 17 May 1997.

———, 1997c. 'Postcoloniality: The Literature of the Trace', review of *Contemporary Postcolonial Theory: A Reader*, edited by Padmini Mongia, in *The Book Review*, Volume 21(9), September. pp. 38–40.

———, 1998a. 'The Life and Death of Salman Rushdie', in the *American Review of Books*, July–August. pp. 10–12.

———, 1998b. 'What is like to be a Bot?' review of *Language Behaviour and Evolutionary Biology* by R. Narasimhan in *The Hindu*, October 1998.

———, 1998c. 'The Mystery of the Extra Kharam', review article on *Of Many Heroes: An Indian Essay in Literary Historiography* by G.N. Devy, in *The Book Review*, Volume 22(9), September. pp. 28–29.

———, 1999a. 'History as Gossip in *Midnight's Children*' in *Rushdie's Midnight's Children: A Book of Readings*, edited by Meenakshi Mukherjee, Pencraft International.

Nair, Rukmini, Bhaya, 1999b. 'Postcoloniality and the Matrix of Indifference', Lead Paper in the *India International Centre Quarterly*, May–June. pp. 7–24.

———, 1999c. 'Sense and Insensibility', review of *The Fateful Question of Culture* by Geoffrey Hartman in *The Book Review*, Vol. 123(9), pp. 7–9.

———, 2000a. 'Brainchildren', review article on *Advances in Human Cognition*, in *Biblio*, Volume 5 (11–12). pp. 11–15.

———, 2000b. 'A Question of Answers: An Essay on the Information Age', in *The Express Magazine*, 24 September 2000.

———, 2000c. 'Poetry in a Civil Society', review of *Landscape with Lines* and *The Girls on the Wall* by Diana Bridge, in the *Hindu Literary Review*, 20 August 2000.

———, 2000d. 'Stealing Fire from the Greeks' in *Memories of the Second Sex: Gender and Sexuality in Women's Writing* edited by Dominique S. Verma and T.V. Kunhi Krishnan, Somaiya.

———, 2000e. 'Surrogate Tongues', in the *Telegraph Millennium Magazine: Twenty-one Ideas for the Twenty-first Century*, January. pp. 62–65.

———, 2001a. 'The e-Writing on the Wall' in *Angle*, Inaugural Issue, Spring. pp. 11–13.

———, 2001b. 'Intimations of Immortality', review of *The Perishable Empire* by Meenakshi Mukherjee and *Babu Fictions* by Tabish Khair, in The *Hindu Literary Supplement*, 6 May 2001.

———, 2001c. 'City of Walls, City of Gates' in *City Improbable: An Anthology of Writings on Delhi* edited by Khushwant Singh. Viking Penguin.

———, 2001d. 'Singing a Nation into Being', in *Seminar*, Annual Issue Vol. 497. pp. 95–100.

———, 2001e. 'Is Astrology Different for Feminists?' In *Seminar* Vol. 505, pp. 71–79.

———, 2001f. 'The Testament of the Tenth Muse' in *Indian Poetry: Modernism and After* edited by K. Satchidanandan, Sahitya Akademi.

———, 2001g. 'A Celebration of the Poetic Imaginary', review of *Chandrabhaga: A Magazine of Indian Writing*: New Series: Volumes 1, 2 and 3, in *The Book Review*, Volume 25(8), pp. 33–35.

Niranjana, T., 1992. *Siting Translation: History, Post-Structuralism and the Colonial Context*. Berkeley, Los Angeles & Oxford: University of California Press.

Quine, W.O., 1960. *Word and Object*. Cambridge, Massachusetts: MIT Press.

Ramanujan, A.K., 1973. *Speaking of Shiva*. Harmondsworth: Penguin Books.

Searle, J.R., 1969. *Speech Acts*. Cambridge: Cambridge University Press.

Searle, J.R., Kiefer, F., and **Bierwisch** (eds), 1980. *Speech Act Theory and Pragmatics*. Dodrecht, Holland: Rerdel Publishing Company.

Sperber, D. and **Wilson, D.**, 1986. *Communication and Cognition*. Oxford: Basil Blackwell.

Strawson, P.F., 1964. 'Intention and Convention in Speech Acts' in *Philosophical Review*, Vol. 73, No. 4.

Whorf, B.L., 1956. *Language, Thought and Reality*. Cambridge, Massachusetts: MIT Press.

Wittgenstein, 1953. *Philosophical Investigations*. Oxford: Basil Blackwell.

About the Contributors

Aditya Behl teaches in the Department of South Asian Studies in the University of California at Berkeley, USA.

Akshar Bharati is a team of computer scientists who are working on machine translation in Hyderabad. **Vineet Chaitanya** and **Amba P. Kulkarni** teach at the Language Technologies Research Centre, International Institute of Information, Hyderabad. **Rajeev Sangal** is Director of the same. **G. Umamaheshwar Rao** teaches at the Centre of Applied Linguistics and Translation Studies, University of Hyderabad.

Samantak Das teaches in the Department of English, Visva-Bharati, Shantiniketan.

C.T. Indra is Professor of English in the University of Madras.

Lachman M. Khubchandani is Director of the Centre for Communication Studies, Pune.

Jhumpa Lahiri is a full-time writer based in New York. Her collection of short stories *The Interpreter of Maladies* was awarded the Pulitzer Prize for Fiction in 2000.

Ritu Menon is a publisher and founder-editor of the pioneering Indian feminist press, Kali for Women.

Sujit Mukherjee is an independent scholar based at Hyderabad, who was until recently Consulting Editor with Orient Longman, New Delhi.

Rukmini Bhaya Nair is Professor of Linguistics and English in the Department of Humanities & Social Sciences, IIT Delhi.

R. Narasimhan retired as Professor of Eminence from the Tata Institute of Fundamental Research, Mumbai, and is currently CMC Fellow in Information Technology, Bangalore.

Tejaswini Niranjana is Director and Senior Fellow, Centre for Media and Culture Studies, Bangalore.

K. Ayyappa Paniker is a well-known writer and scholar in Malayalam, who retired as Head of the Department of English, University of Kerala, Trivandrum.

Krishna Rayan is an independent scholar based in Pune who works on Sanskrit poetics.

Udaya Narayana Singh is Director, Central Institute of Indian Languages, Mysore.

Raman Prasad Sinha is a Research Scientist in the School of Languages, Jawaharlal Nehru University.

Shiva Kumar Srinivasan teaches in the Department of Humanities & Social Sciences, IIT, Delhi.

Saranindranath Tagore is Associate Professor at the University of Texas, San Antonio.

Vanamala Viswanatha is Reader, Department of English, University of Bangalore.

Index